EUROPEAN CINEMAS, EUROPEAN SOCIETIES 1939–1990

Through the Second World War and its aftermath, from economic boom to industrial decline, Europeans have faced similar changes in politics and outlook on life, but on the eve of the formation of a single European Community their cultural backgrounds are still very diverse. In *European Cinemas, European Societies 1939–1990*, Pierre Sorlin looks at the way the nations of Europe have expressed their cultural individuality through film. He examines European cinema as a whole, contrasting its productions with those of Hollywood, and provides a comparative study in European film of some of the main themes – including urbanization, immigration, sex and gender – drawing on examples from French, German, Italian and British films such as *Brief Encounter, Umberto D., Pierrot le fou, The Marriage of Maria Braun, My Beautiful Laundrette, Rosa Luxemburg* and *Wish You Were Here*.

Aimed at those studying modern history and film, this book will also make fascinating reading for students of sociology and communication.

Pierre Sorlin is currently Professor of Sociology of the Audiovisual Media at the Université de la Sorbonne Nouvelle, Paris.

STUDIES IN FILM, TELEVISION
AND THE MEDIA

General Editor: Dr Anthony Aldgate
The Open University

EUROPEAN CINEMAS, EUROPEAN SOCIETIES 1939–1990

Pierre Sorlin

First published 1991
by Routledge
11 New Fetter Lane, London EC4P 4EE

Simultaneously published in the USA and Canada
by Routledge
a division of Routledge, Chapman and Hall, Inc.
29 West 35th Street, New York, NY 10001

© 1991 Pierre Sorlin

Printed in Great Britain by TJ Press (Padstow) Ltd, Padstow, Cornwall

British Library Cataloguing in Publication Data
Sorlin, Pierre
European cinemas, European societies 1939–1990.
1. European cinema films, history. Sociological
perspectives
I. Title
302.2343094

Library of Congress Cataloging in Publication Data
Sorlin, Pierre.
European cinemas, European societies 1939–1990/
Pierre Sorlin.
p. cm. – (Studies in film, television, and the media)
Includes bibliographical references.
1. Motion picture – Social aspects – Europe. I. Title.
II. Series.
PN1993.5.E8S67 1991
302.23'43'094 – dc20   90–35003

ISBN 0 415 04787 0
0 415 05671 3 (pbk)

CONTENTS

ACKNOWLEDGEMENTS

Most necessary to research of this kind is permanent access to the films which must be checked up again and again. My gratitude goes to the Cinémathèque Universitaire in Paris, to the Film Archive of the University of California at Los Angeles and more precisely to Claude Beylie, Michel Marie and Sylvie Pliskin in the former, and Steven Ricci and Robert Rosen in the latter. Without their help I would not have found and seen the material I needed.

Books on social science have no 'auteurs'; their writers merely collect and order ideas launched but not fully developed by their friends or colleagues. I am especially grateful to my initial readers. The manuscript was first scrutinized by Sarah Bussy. She was extraordinarily effective not only in tracking my mistakes but more importantly in raising fresh questions and in obliging me to answer them. She is as responsible as I am for the final aspect of the book. Then came Tony Aldgate. His impeccable expertise in films and film literature was an invaluable help and gave me confidence in the achievement of the project. While I was working Luisa Cigognetti looked at and commented upon various parts of the text. I wish to express my gratitude to them all for sharing their perspectives with me.

I am in debt to Giovanna Grignaffini, Martin Loiperdinger, Giuliana Muscio, Lutz Raphaël, Sarah Street and Peter Stead whom I interviewed on specific questions and who provided me with information and useful suggestions.

I also owe a lot to long and often passionate discussions over the past five years with Ina Bertrand, Gianpiero Brunetta, Francesco Casetti, David Ellwood, Marc Ferro, Michèle Lagny,

Daniel Leab, Arthur Marwick, John O'Connor, Peppino Ortoleva, Robert Rosenstone and Christopher Wagstaff, whose influence is perceptible in many pages of the volume.

The author and publishers would like to thank the following for supplying pictures for the book: Avant-Scène du Cinéma for the still from *Cinema Splendor*; Cineteca Comunale, Bologna, for stills from *Westfront 1918* and *Yesterday Girl*; the National Film Archive, London, for stills from *The Knack, Journey's End, It Happened Here, It Always Rains on Sunday* and *A Taste of Honey*.

INTRODUCTION:
IMAGES IN SOCIETIES

We Europeans create and imagine the world through Holly-wood's lenses. American productions overwhelm our screens, amounting to three quarters of the programmes in some countries and never dropping under 40 per cent.

The US preponderance is grounded on two equally strong bases – economic and aesthetic. In the New World movies have been considered as industrial objects almost from the first day of their existence; they have been manufactured rationally in factory-like studios where the division of labour has always given work its maximum efficiency. By direct absorption or thanks to their subsidiaries, distribution and exhibition, the film companies have created an integrated market which makes movies pay and which enables the producers to sell abroad at bargain rates pictures already amortized thanks to the domestic demand. Attempts were made in the Old World to build up big companies, as was the case with the Rank Organization, but the audiences' response was never satisfying and the firms had either to give up or to diversify outside cinema – which Rank eventually did.

The importance of technical considerations must not be overrated; art was as much a factor of success for Hollywood as money. America has created a movie style which has to be labelled as 'classical'. Classicism cannot be easily defined, but everybody knows empirically what a 'classic' is: good, sharp pictures, a sound-track which helps the spectator to follow the plot-line without ever encroaching upon her or his pleasure, audible dialogue, good actors and, more importantly, a well-defined story, with a situation revealed at the outset, developed logically, and unambiguously closed or solved at the

1

end. Classical movies are merely an extension of the style of narrative which has existed in Europe since the eighteenth century; initially they might have developed as successfully on this side of the Atlantic as on the other. Hollywood won at the beginning of our century because it was the first to settle the formula and because it was financially stronger than its European competitors.

The wonder is that in Europe the cinematic institution did not collapse. It has been almost permanently on the verge of disaster; countless reports and papers have complained about American domination and warned that, as audiovisual productions go, Europe is a colonial continent. Yet the European production after the difficult period of the Second World War and subsequent reconstruction nearly equalled the American. In the late 1950s, when the television challenge was not yet critical, at least on the continent, Hollywood offered yearly just over 500 movies and Europe slightly above 450. During the same period European exhibitors, whose patrons had regular habits of consumption but were not fanatical film-buffs, needed about 500 new films every year; the European companies were able to meet the demand. On the other hand, undoubtedly the American classics were of better quality because more money and skill were spent on them. Language was also an obstacle: when they bought US films the British were not obliged to translate the dialogue and in the other countries the distributors would rather dub in only one language – English – than four or five. However, the most important reason for the failure of the European producers to take over the continental market was the parochialism of their various customers. Apart from the classics, which were preponderantly American, the various European nations wanted a depiction of indigenous themes related to their own cultural and historical backgrounds; they longed to find on their screens some of the characteristics which, rightly or not, were assigned to their particular citizens. Even nowadays European cinema illustrates the diversity of Europe: less than 10 per cent of European non-domestic films are shown in most countries and, among those which are projected, a good many have been chosen by the distributors because they are felt to be typical of a 'national personality'.

Of course, the cinema is not an exceptional case: the

European countries are widely different in many respects; they do not work, eat, enjoy their time off, vote or believe in the same way. But a peculiarity of the cinematic industry is that it has been internationalized for a long time. At the very beginning of the art in the late 1890s, the technicians, directors and actors began travelling from one country to another according to the facilities they would find here or there; this flow of mutual exchanges has not been interrupted since. Foreign investments which existed already between the World Wars have increased with the rise of multinational co-productions. Although cinema is more and more a world business the European national studios have not given up their traditions and still work predominantly for a restricted, almost provincial, market.

Economically and even politically Europe is already a reality. Culturally it is a patchwork, a juxtaposition of various conceptions and practices of entertainment, a collection of individual ways of singing, dancing, telling stories, practising sport and having some rest. In this respect a comparison between the European film productions could help to define the contrasts, oppositions, and even, sometimes, convergences between cultural areas. It is, however, necessary to emphasize the fact that this does not imply any idea of 'national personality' or 'national genius'. Habits, tastes, modes of thinking can only be reached and studied in a practical manner, that is to say through actual, material data. We can compare different representations, ways of staging events, actors' performances and expressions, but, even if we find permanencies, long-term consistencies in the national film productions, we may not relate them to a hypothetical, abstract 'soul of the nation'. Most differences are to be related either to the past of the diverse countries or to the specific experiences they were going through when the movies were produced, but those are again factual connections which have nothing in common with a so-called 'spirit'. Nations are taken here as political, administrative, linguistic and cultural entities, and that is all.

European populations are highly conscious of their specific differences. Yet the Old World which was divided during the first decades of the century into irreconcilable, hostile camps has faced since the end of the Second World War events and problems common to all its member countries. It has been reordered according to the interests of the two dominating world powers and, willingly or not, its western part has followed the fate of the Atlantic side. In terms of current events – those events which get the headlines in newspapers – the contrasts seem amazing. The political rituals do not coincide, the taxation systems are opposed, the state does not have the same share in the economy and the various governments are hampered by extremely specific problems. For instance Britain and Holland got rid of their colonies very quickly, whereas the same process paralysed France for twenty years. And Germany and Italy have been threatened by indigenous terrorism which has nothing in common with the long-lasting separatist unrest faced by Spain and Britain. In short, Europeans inherit secular traditions of national pride and isolationism based on language, political institutions and suspicion towards other Europeans. Yet those who are not content with appearances cannot but be impressed by the convergences: ruined by the war, Europe went through a reconstruction period which witnessed a deep involvement in the economy by the various states, attempts to improve social welfare and, in defeated countries, the institution of democracy. In the late 1950s and in the 1960s Europe took part in the economic growth of industrial societies. This 'glorious', prosperous era has often been described and it is not necessary to redefine its consequences here; suffice to remember that a new style of urban life spread all over the continent within less than twenty years. Finally, the economic recession, brought about by financial disorders that Europe is unable to master, has affected in comparable ways the various components of the Old World.

The impact of local problems, of particular situations, can be easily detected in films; excellent works have already proved how much can be learnt about the history of a population by looking at the films it produces. As Arthur Marwick has pointed out,

> one of the most important reasons for studying film is that it directs historians' attention away from the traditional topics of high politics and macro-economics to matters which, affecting the ordinary mass of the people, are also of great significance: life style, moral values and culture in general.[1]

4

Now, instead of looking separately at the various parts of the Old World, why should we not take Europe as a whole, as a historical entity, a cluster of nations which, at least since the middle of the twentieth century, have been involved in a common experience? Europeans have gone through the same social, economic and mental changes but their cultural backgrounds are far from unified, and it is this gap which seems interesting: how were identical transformations inter-preted with respect to the cultural habits of the nations? A parallel implies objects that are comparable, and the films fit in very well because not only their substance (raw material, size, speed, number of frames, reproduction of sound) but also their form (average length, technical crews, casts, narrative rules), moulded according to the dominant (American) standards, permits little variation. 'Likenesses and Contrasts' could be the subtitle of the book: it is not a study of indigenous cinemas, let alone a socio-political survey of Europe, but rather a research into comparative social history which draws its material from a still popular means of entertainment – cinema. The films will not be treated separately but will be examined in association with each other and in close relationship with the evolution of Europe during the past half-century.

Historians have admitted for a long time that films are important pieces of evidence for any study of the twentieth century, and it is no longer necessary to justify an incursion into this field. Yet it still seems hard to decide what is to be done with the objects themselves. Two answers have been given to this question. Some scholars think that movies open a window onto reality. The actors are living people: when they are pictured in actual surroundings (or surroundings made to resemble real places) and have parts in stories related to daily problems (unemployment, industrial rivalries, housing, family crises) is it not legitimate to consider the films as imitations of life? Excellent works have already illustrated this interpretation of the cinema. But audiovisual texts are also artefacts; they depict situations which (given the artificial contraction of times and the framing of the screen) remain fictional even when they have been directly borrowed from actuality. Therefore other historians believe that it is the distance between the social data and their representation which is illuminating: brilliant papers have emphasized the revealing power of films and proved that they are often fictional answers to urgent questions raised by a situation.

In this book I would like to treat the movies merely as images sold on the market. The word 'image' is sometimes misleading and it is likely to confuse us if we do not begin by fixing its precise use in the pages to come. 'Image' is defined here as anything, palpable or not, which enables us to get the world in perspective. We cannot think except in images which are models or derivations of reality. Let us start with a very trite example. When we drive for the first time in an unknown town we feel lost since for us the streets are undifferentiated and we can make no sense of the various things we are confronted with. An arrow with some information, 'market', 'station', will help us; these are (abstract) images of parts of the city. If someone comes to advise us he or she produces another image ('second to the left, then straight'). After a few days we have our own image, a derivative of the town that is functional to our needs. A fact, or a state of affairs, is only thinkable when it can be rendered into an image. The notion of 'image' makes us get over the opposition between actuality and representation. Images are not the reality but they are our only access to reality. Our relationship with events and people is mediated by images; some we produce for ourselves but most are assigned to us by the society we live in and are therefore common to virtually all members of the group.

In any given community many systems of images are at work. They overlap onto each other but there are also noticeable differences between them. Some are freely available, while some have to be paid for. Some require specific technical knowledge or skill, and others do not. Some are purely informative, others mostly entertaining, while still others are both. Interactions prevent us from defining any system precisely: the cinema has much in common with theatre, television and any other sort of performance involving actors or settings, and it also borrows elements from literature, photography and music. Many a system has recourse to spoken or written language, which remains at any rate the vehicle through which all other systems can be transcribed and confronted. Given this centrality of language, some researchers have tried to use the tools elaborated by linguists to describe other systems of images. Fashionable historians (or at least some of them) mock the attempts made by semiologists towards a definition of basic elements and structures in audiovisual productions: they simply show that they have not understood what the semiologists wanted to do. Semiology did not aim at an explanation of individual films; it simply aimed to discover rules which explained how combinations of sounds and pictures can convey a meaning. After two decades of research semiology vanished at the end of the 1970s, but its inheritance is not negligible. Its most important effect is that film-analysts can no longer be content with summarizing the plot or describing the themes developed in the movies but have to consider the way written stories (the scripts) have been transformed into an *audiovisual* product. The negative consequences are also important. The semiologist hoped that it would be possible to find the smallest possible units, the 'cells' of the cinematic works. But images resist precisely that sort of division; no image, be it the least elaborate one, can be reduced to a restricted, unique significance, since it is always linked to previous or successive images and these relationships also produce meanings. It is true that in order to analyse we have to divide; however, the parts, shots or sequences are not isolated; they must be continually referred to the whole and also to other, external images which they evoke.

Images are inserted into various chains of signification: every shot is a part of the filmic chain it belongs to; it is also linked to directly related or distantly akin representations and it can find equivalents in other systems of images used in the same society. Any interpretation has to take into account at least some of these possible interactions. There is, first, in any film (as well as in any item of other systems; but let us be content with movies) an amount of factual information on which most viewers will agree. For instance, we will say that in *The Knack and How to Get It* (1965) there are three male characters and a female one, that at the outset we see two lads who live in the same house and a girl, that they do not know each other and are only connected by the editing-process which intercuts the boys indoors and the girl walking along various streets and so on. What does this hint at? We are now raising the question of 'meaning', which cannot be answered except contextually. A continental spectator will interpret the film as a British fantasy: in white-painted or overlit surroundings a girl wanders

The Knack: A fantasy . . .

through a town while two boys chatter, and they finally meet
after a fantasy sequence in which they drive around on a bed.
A British viewer who has never left her or his countryside will
admit there is much that is fanciful in the picture, but has been
provided with enough clues to identify the town as London. A
Londoner will immediately spot most of the locations – (s)he
will follow the girl from Victoria Coach Station to Knightsbridge
or drive on the bed towards Shepherd's Bush – so that (s)he
will find the film rather realistic. The context is therefore the
amount of previous knowledge which a given public invests
into the images, and it changes considerably according to the
place and period in which the film is presented. Where a
historical approach is concerned it is up to the analyst to define
the context in which (s)he wants to 'read' the material. Most
historians follow half-knowingly this rule when they insert a
picture into the socio-political history of the period it was
made. Instead of unconsciously sticking to a principle we shall
rather define right from the outset the context in which we
shall work.

8

or a realistic vision of London?

We are not interested here either in films as works of art or in cinema as a language; we want to take the movies as images (made of sounds, pictures and words) available in contemporary societies. Films are objects but objects of a certain kind, industrially produced, sold to audiences which buy them for their pleasure, and our 'context' must include all these characteristics. Manufacturing comes first. We shall avoid the word 'film-maker', which is restricted to those working in studios. All those involved in the visual media are indirectly connected with cinema. Money is invested in films not only by bankers but also by industrialists or businessmen who expect profits and want to diversify the range of goods they distribute. Politicians and governments are equally concerned because movies are supposed to influence the viewers and shape their opinions – and also because the extremely unstable film-market is constantly threatened by foreign competition. The origins and birth of any film are a complex process which cannot be reduced to the writing of a script and the finding of the requisite amount of money. If it is only a secondary sector

9

in industry, cinema is also an intersection of various financial and ideological interests. This is quite obvious, even if historians sometimes only reluctantly take into account the combination of so many different influences.

Penetrated by many other social activities, the world of the studios is, however, a restricted circle which tends to ignore anything outside itself; the main reference of cinematographers is cinema as a whole, cinema in all its aspects. Films beget films, films imitate other films. Many moments of *The Knack* (to continue with the same example) are borrowed from American silent comedies (the curtain too small to hide two ladies, so that when one tugs it the other is left uncovered), European slapstick (to show a quick insert of a group of pupils who repeat a sentence only just uttered by one of the characters was a trick used right at the beginning of the sound era on the continent), westerns ('aim between the eyes', a colleague tells Colin, who is used to throwing pieces of chalk at his pupils) and so on. Each film could be considered a small bit in the huge text of all the already-shot movies. Those who study a director, a genre, rightly emphasize their originality. When socially produced images are the target, it is the general context – cinema – which must be considered.

Although living in close contact in the narrow universe of studios film-people struggle hard against one other. Contrary to what happens in most industrial fields, including that of information (papers and magazines, television), the number of movies is not automatically adapted to the prospects of the market. This book does not deal with Hollywood, but the American cinema will be mentioned persistently, and this overwhelming, unavoidable presence is what gives cinema one of its most specific features. Economically, technically, fiction-ally, Hollywood is the context of film-selling. Yet, if America settles the rules of film production and consumption, the audiovisual productions are only a restricted part of entertain-ment; other competitors such as sport, television, music and dance are a threat and must be borne in mind. In order to evaluate the impact of cinematic images we have to know where and how people can enjoy their time off other than in movie-theatres.

The audience is thus the last element of the context. Reception is the blind-spot of film studies. How do spectators react? Apart from a few Gallup polls (which are seldom reliable, since the questions are oversimplified) we cannot answer the question. We often have recourse to the writings of critics, but they are too much involved in film-production (they will earn their living as long as films are projected) to be genuine witnesses of the common opinion. In fact, this inadequacy is not damaging to our enquiry. We are not concerned here with what people thought; we are not trying to assess the impact of movies on taste, outlook or behaviour. We would like to speak of images: suffice to determine how often such and such representations were offered to the viewers. In this respect available statistics are sufficient.

For practical purposes (the everlasting necessity to divide an object into smaller bits) we have distinguished three components of context, which are (1) production, in the broadest sense of the word; (2) competition, with special reference to the USA; and (3) the public. The interactions between all these fields are evident: production is intended to please the viewers and caters for their preferences; film-buffs are informed of the 'general', 'extended' cinematic text and react to the newly offered movies according to their consistency (or lack of it) with older films. Context is like a magnetic field where several opposite or consonant streams interact: the results of the various interwoven forces do constantly shift, and it is one of the historian's duties to delineate the changing configuration of context.

The commonplace that ours is a 'civilization of pictures' is not satisfactory; words have not lost their power and are still the only means which can express the images. But images evolve with societies, and we do not see our surroundings with the conceptual tools people used even half a century ago since pictures are a much more important component part of our supply of images. The combination and interaction of three kinds of images – words, sounds and pictures – related to one another, is characteristic of our universe. In this respect the cinema has no originality: films are some of the countless products that focus our attention by catching our eyes and ears; neither the materials nor the means of transmission allow us to distinguish a movie from an advertisement or a TV quiz. It is rather the context which makes the difference. Unlike many other programmes, movies are produced to make money

11

directly, not through the promotion of goods (adverts), teams and competitions (broadcasting of sporting events) or rock bands (video clips). But there is another feature which distinguishes films. Most audiovisual texts are conceived, both by makers and audiences, as direct transcriptions of events; if nobody, or at least few spectators, would mistake them for the actual facts, they are nevertheless meant merely to reflect reality and to transfer it immediately to far-away locations. Feature films are predominantly fictions – that is to say, images. Movies are images in two different respects. Like all audiovisual productions they are made of visual and verbal images, borrowed from the actual world and artificially reproduced. At the same time they aim at creating new objects independent of the present, concrete circumstances but which are also images.

This duality often puzzles social scientists who begin studying movies. What must they put the emphasis on – the constituents, the 'primary images', such as can be found at any point of the cinematic chain, or the final result, the 'global image', in other words the whole film? Various, contradictory answers have been given and there is probably no good solution. In fact, it is the kind of information expected from the films which must determine how they will be examined.

Images which are our key to the world shape our perception and knowledge: it is inasmuch as we have the word 'London' in mind and have already seen pictures of the Tower or the Horse Guards that, without having even visited the town, we can decide where *The Knack* takes place. Our awareness of what is going on around us is multiplied by images: not only do we become familiar with distant people or countries we would never imagine 'unless by sight in the picture papers', as Virginia Woolf used to say, but we get information on our neighbourhood as well; by selecting aspects of our vicinity, pictures constrain us to look at them instead of absent-mindedly skimming them. Yet images can also conceal the world since permanent recourse to the same words and pictures, a repetition of the same clichés, prevents us from seeing. The same Tower can be an incitement (we know where we are, now let us explore the visual presentation of the town) or a block (we are in London and that is enough). The point is, as far as historians are concerned, that images do not stop moving: words emerge and die, facets of our universe are revealed or forgotten. What does a society take into account regarding itself? What does it know of its basis and functioning?

Interesting, though limited, research has already been completed in this field. Symptomatically, S. Harding has entitled the paper he has written on the topic 'Why has the Sex/Gender system become visible only now?'.[2] Sex and Gender are not the only categories which deserve consideration; it is the visible itself, the range of objects, people, species we can distinguish and label, which is the core of the problem. Human beings have, of course, known for ages that there are two different sexes but, until recently, mankind, as a species, was uniquely represented by male figures; there was a dichotomy between the practical division of domestic, sexual and economic duties and the images which had no gender since they showed only one sex. This is extremely well documented for our century thanks to the visual images. We have enough photographs taken before the First World War to assume that both sexes were equally present in the streets of the largest western cities. Nevertheless, on 'public' pictures – that is to say, on the postcards sold to the tourists, on newspapers and magazines, on posters – the crowd, 'people', were predominantly male. Occasionally women were presented but exclusively when they were assigned to some precise activity – maids going to the market, nurses, secretaries (all labelled, thanks to their clothes) or other girls unmistakably identified by captions. Queen Victoria or a famous actress would be seen on the cover of a magazine, but not anonymous females. A woman could be a personality, a role, but in no case a nameless specimen of humanity. With the war, genders began to timorously differentiate. Yet, in the 1920s the 'flappers', who figured extensively in papers, were described as a peculiar breed of girls; there were more women photographed than in the 1910s but the social duality of genders was not yet accepted.

Attention has been focused here on the first years of the century, a period for which available films are not numerous and permit fewer comparisons than they do snapshots on the variations of the 'visible'.[3] At first, it might be said that what has been explained about Sex/Gender is merely a section of ideology: the common discourse in the early twentieth century implicitly took it for granted that males had to protect and guide females; men assumed it, most women accepted it (remember Virginia Woolf in *Mrs Dalloway*, mocking, at the beginning of the 1920s, the wives who take shelter in 'a common femininity, a common pride in the illustrious qualities of husbands and their sad tendency to overwork'). Those who spoke on the subject of women sought to rationalize an existing state of affairs, and this was possible not only because they stuck to the situation but also because there were no images enabling them to think differently; the physical distinction between the sexes was admitted, but the participation of both genders in social activities could not be figured, let alone expressed. It was the emergence of new images, in close relationship with irreversible changes in the division of jobs, that introduced another discourse on sexes/genders. Images are mere instruments for ideology but, when they are lacking, the ideology does not evolve, it is blocked; the endless repetition of the same worn-out images is then likely to reinforce conformity and submission to the established rules. Once some pictures have become familiar, they tend to be accepted as reality itself. Economic or cultural modifications are not necessarily felt or understood when they occur, so that contemporaries may find accurate and perfectly convenient images which do not permit them to evaluate, or even simply to perceive, what is happening. The consonance or discrepancy between an evolution and its perception by those it affects is therefore of the greatest importance for historians: in this respect film is a rather good look-out post.

Films are also 'global images'. They combine their materials to portray (be it very roughly) situations, actions, individuals or groups; there are images of youth, sex, London, houses, spread throughout *The Knack*, which cannot be assigned to a precise part of the film but which are built up by the interaction of converging or conflicting elements. What are historians to do with these images? A popular reply is given by the 'mirror theory' which has been brilliantly explored by R. Durgnat in his *Mirror for England*.[4] Those who make films live in the same country as most of their future spectators, the problems and hopes of whom they partially share; unless they indulge in pure fantasies they will include some of their concerns in their movies, be it only to catch the public's attention. Films are not reality but they never totally get rid of the actual situation; like mirrors which frame, set limits, sometimes distort, but eventually reflect what is in front of them, films exhibit aspects of the society which produces them. In critical periods the cinematographers, without hiding the problems, stick to the old, reassuring images, but when things seem to be looking up they have recourse to novelties and sometimes even anticipate, thus promoting images ahead of actuality. Is not *The Knack* typical of this kind of expectation? In one sense, it simply magnifies some changes that became obvious in the mid-1960s – the outburst of permissiveness, the emphasis put on youth, the gap between the traditional values championed by those over 40 and the lack of defined references among the youngest. In 1965 no painted bed would drive along the streets, stop the cars, cross the Thames. However, is it forbidden to understand this fable as a premonition of what was not yet called the Consumer Society? In the mid-1960s objects still appealed to people – lads desired motorbikes and girls clothes – but the same young people were ready to despise and debase things.

This 'reading' of the film is perfectly acceptable. Excellent accounts have been written to emphasize the congruency between some films and their historical context or to show how a close study of plots and characters illuminates noteworthy shifts in attitudes, beliefs or values. If I do not want to follow that way it is not because I consider it a dead end but because others have already done the job very well; it could, of course, be taken further, but there is no need to hammer it in. I also confess I am afraid there is some risk of redundancy: we do not lack evidence about what was happening in the mid-1960s and by scrupulously watching the movies made in these years we will not do more than confirm what was previously known. Undoubtedly *The Knack* points out something, but if we concentrate on freedom of behaviour, conflict between genera-tions, disruption of values, we merely emphasize what was expressed in the original play released two years before the completion of the film. The difference does not lie in the plot or characters common to the play and to the movie but in the shooting which entails some specific features of the filmed images.

The play is largely 'immaterial'; its permanent, invariable substance is reduced to words which can be printed in diverse types or recited in many ways. *The Knack* will be restaged next year or in 2062 and every performance will contrast with the others. The texture of the film consists of permanent elements: its words and actions are embodied in actors whose voices and silhouettes are indissoluble from them. Hundreds of actresses will be the girl in Ann Jellicoe's play but, for the film, there is exclusively Rita Tushingham. This does not mean that there is more 'reality' in the film: all images are images; they cannot be classified according to any ascending degrees of actuality. Nevertheless, in the future, the image of a provincial arriving in London, in 1964, will be chiefly that of Tushingham. And here the context, as defined previously, has to be considered. When *The Knack* was made, Tushingham already had four films behind her and she was associated with a bearing or features which delimited her fictional personality. The portrait of actors is shaped by the parts they have taken in antecedent movies, their look (including their voice), the way they have been pictured, and these factors are capital in the building up of an image. In his *Narration in the Fiction Film*[5] David Bordwell has suggested that the classical film (he speaks of the 'classical Hollywood film' but adds that Hollywood has 'crucially influenced most of the national cinemas') is a particular and very simple configuration of extremely limited options: reduced to their basic components, film plots are more or less equivalent. *The Knack* involves three lads and a girl; two lads fight to assert themselves and incidentally possess the girl, while the third is mostly a witness: the same elements are to be found in lots of movies. Even technique is, according to Bordwell, obedient to the transmission of standardized plot-lines. What then makes the difference? The actors. Cinematic images are inseparable from those who *are* the characters, the verb 'to be' being used purposely since fictional characters do not exist except on the screen as they are interpreted and photographed.

The appeal of a movie – its effectiveness – is closely linked to the cast, but the relationship between characters and actors is not easy to define. It is generally accepted that *Saturday Night, Sunday Morning* (1959) introduced a fresh vision of the Nottingham working class in the film-theatres; Arthur Marwick notes that 'working-class visibility is established in the pre-credit sequence when we see Arthur Seaton at his lathe'.[6] It must be recalled that the part of Seaton is played by Albert Finney. Apart from his talent, what made Finney look so convincing, right from the beginning? His ruddy complexion? His bluntness? Or the fact that the spectators were ready to accept at face value any gifted lad – to label him immediately a 'genuine portrayal of a factory worker'? We cannot get rid of the question by speaking of 'verisimilitude'. Is Finney a possible metal-turner? Surely, but he might be a barrister as well or a clergyman. In the early 1960s Tushingham and Finney were in two contrasting but equally significant positions; the former was already typecast as the naïve, slightly inadequate girl whose awkwardness made the other characters disclose their own shortcomings; her reputation preceded her participation in *The Knack* and strengthened the conviction that hers was the 'typical' image of a 1960s girl. Finney, although a bit older, was new to the screen and therefore convenient for any social function, provided the featured character was meant to be short-necked and wide-shouldered. Actors do not just carry out stage work: they interact with the spectators who simultaneously trust them and perceive them as stereotypes. The emergence of cinematic images and their power must be continually referred to the people who haunt the screens as well as to those who enjoy the actors' skill.

In *The Knack* Tushingham is often shot in close-up from a slightly distorted angle which exaggerates some aspects of her face; she is also framed by a window, a door, the bars of the bed. A similar treatment, not as systematic, but quite recurrent, is to be found in the antecedent *Girl with Green Eyes* (1964), in which the same actress was already the star. Cinema has its fashions and vogues; lighting, delimitation and division of the surface, compositional rules and motions of the movie-camera are quite stable at a given time: there are styles, characteristic of periods. It is always possible to refresh a play, to stage it according to today's standards, whereas a film cannot hide its age. It has often been said that languages do not modify very quickly: new terms are introduced or lost daily, but the stock of available words evolves in the long run. Talking of the development of languages, Raymond Williams notes that 'it needs the passage of centuries to show itself actively, by results, at anything like its full weight'.[7] Verbal images enjoy some sort of apparent stability which is not granted to cinematic images or figures of style. When a film is first released, its viewers, used to the accepted signifying figures of the moment, find 'normal' the forms and organizations of the cinematic elements which, twenty years later, will look 'dated'.

The mirror theory detects accurately the changes which occur in story-lines or in the definition of characters; this is necessary, but merely preliminary, work since movies cannot be reduced to their plot. *Four in the Morning* was made and released in the same year as *The Knack*. The difference between the two stories is glaring, but the mirror theory will account for it. If the characters in *Four in the Morning* are rather young, they belong to another, more ancient period; men and women like them were not exceptional in 1960s England and, thanks to the opposition between the films, we can observe the permanence of the past (three tired people who go to work early in the morning or come back home) as well as the premisses of a less coercive, more permissive, society. The trouble is that whereas the situations and plots do not coincide, similarities can be detected between the movies. Bordwell reminds us that in the classical cinema,

> causality is the prime unifying principle . . . [everything] is subordinated to the movement of cause and effect. Causality also motivates temporal principles of organization . . . Dramatic duration [can be defined] as the time it takes to achieve or fail to achieve a goal.[8]

But causality is very loose in *The Knack* or *Four in the Morning* and no goal is achieved; both movies develop according to a very imprecise, flimsy logic of the locations. *Four in the Morning* begins alongside a wharf which is the only (and at the same time very arbitrary) link between three possible stories which do not start, do not end and, consequently, never build up a coherent action. With totally different characters, locations and surroundings, *Four in the Morning* and *The Knack* avoid recourse to the obvious before/after link which is the shibboleth of a clear, organic temporal continuity. Does the consonance between two otherwise opposed movies signal a shift in cinematic modes? Yes and no, because the visual (and even verbal) devices are used in rather opposed ways. *Four in the Morning* is classically framed, lighted and edited, while *The*

Knack has recourse to simple central lighting (with no gradation of shadows and an overexposure of some shots) and does not hesitate to link up, several times, a unique picture of a character or uncoordinated bits of dislocated actions.

Superficial though it is, the parallel enlightens three aspects of film: the story (an initial situation, a setting, some characters), the narration (how the story is told, how its elements are ordered) and the manipulation of images. The mirror theory does wonders with the first but misses the others. Yet very often, it is not the plot but the way it is told or filmed which tells us something about the state of mind of the cinematographers and spectators; the shooting of *Four in the Morning* is as serious as the people it presents us with, while *The Knack* is filmed with the supposed casualness of youth. Two styles of picture, two editing modes call out to the spectators, each of them with an unmistakable reference to a defined sector of society; these films therefore have something to tell us about an imaginary division of Londoners according to their age and condition. Simultaneously the narration emphasizes a convergence: even those who place themselves on the older, more serious side of society accept a shift away from classicism; their vision of the generations may still be clear-cut and unquestionable, but they no longer need established conventions to appreciate a story. The 'primary images' have not changed; they remain what they were expected to be, but the construction of the 'global image' has moved in a way which implies more attention, more mental activity, on the part of the public.

For purely practical reasons we have contrasted two levels of images, the 'primary images' which are the simplest themes, such as can be perceived and analysed in stills, posters, magazines, paintings as well as in films, and the 'global images' running throughout the entirety of the films. The distinction is a perfectly artificial one; it aims only at making us realize that if many elements or images included in films do not belong specifically to the cinema, the film gives them a particular inflection and thus creates cinematic images. The singularity of these images relies on the film language (the superimposition and interaction of three systems of images – words, sounds and pictures), as is almost universally accepted, but also on the necessary mediation of actors and on the constant variation of stylistic norms. Whereas verbal images are more likely to illuminate long-range variations in societies, films have something to tell us about short- or middle-term changes.

Arthur Marwick remarks that films have to be considered 'not simply as evidence of social change but as an actual part of social change'.[9] When seeing images of their daily life, people understand and appreciate it differently. Notions as simple as those of generations, division of work or future expectation become obvious, sometimes even too evident, once they have been represented by well-defined images; it is partially because youth was staged as such in many a movie of the 1960s that the concept of a separated, autonomous, relatively steady (and not transitory) 'youth' could emerge. Images reproduce – 'mirror' – what existed previously in the world but was not acknowledged as worth noticing; by framing some things, images make them visible; they help an audience to identify what was known beforehand and to learn what was not yet identified. In this book, I would like to question a few 'images' promoted by the different European cinemas during the last half-century.

A few more words are necessary to justify the conception of this work.

Ideally it should deal with the fourteen national cinemas of Western Europe. However, the film output of many countries is irregular and, rightly or not, remains almost unknown outside their borders. Denmark, Greece, Portugal and Sweden have made excellent movies which deserve close attention for the part they have played in the evolution of cinematic language; however, these films are isolated works which are not merged in a wider, less artistic, production. Comparisons are therefore impossible, and there is little that the social historian can gain from an analysis of these movies. Spain is the only arguable case for inclusion: she has been producing yearly a reasonable amount of films since the middle of the century; she has also sent some hits abroad and has established a good tradition in some 'genres'. But at least until the middle of the 1970s it is hard to compare the Spanish movies with the other European productions – unless one is content with endlessly noting that 'Spain is different'. For decades the Iberian peninsula lived in isolation, ignoring the transformations and crises the other countries went through; I have found it better to leave it apart, at least in this particular research. Attention will, then, be focused on the four more important (at least statistically) countries – Britain, France, Germany and Italy, the cinematic production of which amounts to three quarters of the European total.

Work on film is carried out in film-archives rather than in libraries. Quite often the papers on cinema written by specialists are very helpful and illuminate many aspects of the films they deal with. Yet I am not convinced that in a book like this the footnotes have to be widely developed. The reader must be entitled to contest my opinion but what is under discussion is the interpretation of films, not the additional information found in books. By reducing the references I have spared more space to speak of movies.

The questions which have been taken into account and which give the chapters their titles are not the only possible ones; I shall try to justify my choices, but some readers could be surprised by the absence of the Second World War: was not this dramatic crisis the end of the Europe of nationalities and the beginning of a new era? In fact, we shall meet the war and its aftermath very often, even if we do not cross it directly. Excellent work has already been completed on the years 1939–45 in films: catalogues are available in all countries and two books, Roger Manvell's *Films and the Second World War*[10] and Anthony Aldgate and Jeffrey Richards's *Britain Can Take It. The British Cinema in the Second World War*,[11] are a sufficient introduction to the theme. I preferred to dig out less well acknowledged images.

I have constantly borne in mind that the general public may not be familiar with foreign movies; so as often as possible I scrutinize films which have been widely diffused. The book never becomes a sample of titles; it covers few films but analyses them in depth. The names of directors are only mentioned when they are famous cinematographers. The country of origin (F. = France, G. = Germany, I. = Italy) is given for all the films except those made in Britain. Unsure what to do with regard to the film-titles, I have decided on a rather inconsistent solution. The titles are in English where there was an English distribution; otherwise they are given in the original language (with a translation in the index). In the first case the films are generally known under their common title, which is part of their history, and the original title would be misleading. I admit that there may be some inconveniences with the uncomfortable meeting of four different languages but such is, after all, the fate of Europe – different words for a common evolution.

1

THE COMING WAR

The first war movies were not produced in response to the outbreak of the first world conflict. War films had appeared almost as early as cinema itself, and during the years which preceded the First World War fighting of various sorts was shot and screened in all countries. From 1914 through 1918 neutrals as well as belligerents filmed the hostilities extensively. But, after the peace treaty, the theme was quickly forgotten, and in this field Hollywood played an important part: all through the 1920s, while the European cinemas were declining and the American movies sold well abroad, the United States exported war films which were popular and, without ever questioning the legitimacy of the American intervention, described life in the trenches, the sufferings of the wounded and the general destruction in a realistic, unyielding manner.

King Vidor's *Big Parade* (1925) was the most famous of some twenty movies which strongly impressed the cinema-goers. However, something totally new occurred in 1930 with Milestone's *All Quiet on the Western Front*. The most striking innovation was the treatment of the sound-track. Today we are used to hearing the cracking of machine-guns and the explosion of bombs that our television sets emit constantly, but at the beginning of the sound era this produced a frightening, overwhelming impression. Milestone cleverly managed the combination of noises; before his characters arrive on the front line, the sound-track is soft and combines harmoniously words, music and shouting. When the young recruits reach the trenches by night the screen erupts, with monstrous flashes of lighting and unbearable explosions. Later silence is re-introduced in the film but, instead of being an absence of

23

sound, it is so different, so opposed to the dominant war-hum, that it is also frightening. At the beginning of an important technological change Milestone inaugurated a cinematic effect which film-analysts have never fully explored because it is hard to describe. It could be called 'echoing' since it produces an emotional reaction by combining echoes and sounds, not by having recourse to words and pictures. But these were, after all, mere tricks which audiences would have coped with quickly, and Milestone would have been less influential had it not been for two other aspects of his work. Without strongly modifying the classical narration, *All Quiet* altered it. There is no hero – just a crew of comrades, one of whom is simply the most important; nor is there a plot, a challenge which has to be overcome. Nothing can evolve; the only issue is death. Thematically, Milestone developed a condemnation of war (any war, not specifically that war) which the movies of the 1920s avoided. *All Quiet* was a great hit in Europe. It is generally hard to get statistics for this period but we are lucky enough to have some figures for Germany:[1] the film was temporarily banned from commercial exploitation and was distributed by the Socialist Party which made reports on its success. We know thus that in Berlin 400,000 people attended the projections in a few weeks, and that about 1,000,000 Germans saw it before it was permitted to be shown.[2]

Milestone has been taken here as an example, but it must be added that shortly afterwards directors as interesting as Frank Borzage or Howard Hawks, not to mention less well-known cinematographers, made pictures on the same period. It is in this context that the Europeans began to film the war again. We cannot speak of imitation: eight movies devoted to the theme were in the making when *All Quiet* arrived in the Old World. However, the American vision of the fighting was highly problematical; it did not fit with the patriotism or prudence of the few movies shot during the 1920s. All those who decided to screen the war knew that they would be obliged to compete with the good, provocative American productions. It is then surprising that the Europeans, instead of deserting the field, held possession of it; in the 1930s, Europe made more films on the years 1914-18 than Hollywood, and some of them – Pabst's *Westfront 1918*[3] in 1930, and

Table 1. War films of the 1930s

UK	France	Germany	Italy
1930			
Journey's End[ac]	La Rebelle	Westfront 1918[ac]	
Two Worlds	Les Deux	Zwei Welten	
Suspense[ac]	Mondes		
French Leave[a]			
The W Plan[a]			
1931			
Tell England[ac]	Les Croix de	Niemandsland[c]	
East Lynne on	bois[ac]	Berge in	
the Western	Les Monts en	Flammen[c]	
Front	flammes[c]	Die Nacht der	
	Un soir au	Entscheidung	
	front[a]	Douaumont[c]	
	Verdun,	1914, Die letzten	
	souvenirs	Tage vor dem	
	d'histoire[c]	Weltbrand	
	Sous le casque		
	de cuir[a]		
1932			
Josser in the		Kreuzer Emden[c]	
Army[a]		Tannenberg[c]	
1933			
I Was a Spy[a]	La Voie sans	Morgenrot[c]	Camicia nera[b]
On Secret	disque[a]		
Service[a]			
1934			
	Cessez le feu[b]	Stosstrupp 1917[c]	
		Ein Mann will	
		nach	
		Deutschland	
		Heldentum und	
		Totenskampf	
		unserer	
		Emden[c]	
1935			
Moscow Nights[b]	Nuits		Milizia
Forever England[a]	moscovites[ab]		territoriale[ab]
	L'Equipage[a]		Passaporto rosso[b]
	Koenigsmark[ab]		Le scarpe al sole[ac]

Table 1. continued

UK	France	Germany	Italy
1936			
Mademoiselle Docteur	Mademoiselle Docteur	Das Schloss in Flandern	Cavalleria[b]
The Secret Agent[a]		Im Trommelfeuer der Westfront[c]	Tredici uomini e un canone
1937			
Dark Journey	Boissière[a]	Patrioten	
The Wind Mill[a]	Grand Illusion	Unternehmen Michael[ac]	
Secret Lives[a]	Ultimatum[a]	Signal in der Nacht[c]	
A Romance in Flanders[ab]	J'accuse	Urlaub auf Ehrenwort	
	Marthe Richard au service de la France[a]		
	Sœurs d'armes		
1938			
Who Goes Next?[a]	Le Héros de la Marne	Pour le mérite	
Thirteen Men and a Gun	Paix sur le Rhin[b]	Dreizehn Mann und eine Kanone	
1939			
The Spy in Black[a]	Le Déserteur	D III 88[c]	Piccolo alpino[a]
	Deuxième bureau contre Kommandantur		
	Les Otages		
	Paradis perdu[b]		

Note: [a] The film is adapted from a literary source (play, novel, memoirs).
[b] The main part of the plot takes place before or after the war.
[c] War-actions have an important place in the film.

Renoir's *Grand Illusion* in 1937 – were even bigger hits than *All Quiet on the Western Front.*

A chronologically arranged table (Table 1) will provide us with a first insight into the differences between the countries. I would never say it is complete, but no important film has been left out.[4]

War films amounted to about 3 per cent of the European production; it is a small sample, all the more limited in that a few directors especially interested in the topic (Victor Saville and Anthony Asquith in Britain, Giovacchino Forzano in Italy, Karl Ritter in Germany, Georg Wilhelm Pabst in Germany and France, Abel Gance in France) made a good many of these movies. And this business was indeed truly European. The synoptic table shows that five films were produced simultaneously or successively in two or three different European countries,[5] but the links between those involved in the making of war movies were even closer than can be inferred from the list. The same actors (Dita Parlo, Eric von Stroheim, Conrad Veidt, Harry Baur, John Loder) continually crossed national boundaries to perform more or less the same parts. The Italian script of *Thirteen Men and a Gun* was shot in Italy by Forzano and in Britain by the Italian Mario Zampi. The three versions of *Two Worlds* were directed by a German cinematographer, E. A. Dupont, whose French assistant E. T. Gréville made *Secret Lives* in Britain as well as the English version of *Mademoiselle Docteur*, while the French one was made by Pabst. Luis Trinker is possibly the most significant example of close co-operation. His first film, *Berge in Flammen*,[6] a German and a French version of which he shot at the same time, pictured a small episode of the war in the Alps. He then made two appealing movies on the German *émigrés* in America. He was invited to Italy where he strongly influenced the few war films dealing either with fighting in the Alps or with the *émigrés* who came back to the peninsula and volunteered for the duration. Ideas, themes, people and money circulated. There were, of course, differences attributable to national traditions, but there was also throughout the whole of Europe a strong concern for the remembrance of and the visual depiction of the Great War.

When speaking of the 1930s we must beware of anachronism. Everywhere, since 1945, films have denounced the errors, sometimes the crimes, of High Command and depicted the futility of some war-actions. A film like *King and Country* (d. J. Losey, 1964) was unthinkable in the 1930s.[7] A few 'pacifist' films showed the horrors of the trenches,[8] and in *Westfront 1918* Germans and Frenchmen, who are obliged to kill each other, suffer as much and die as painfully. Abel Gance went so far as to imagine that fraternity was likely to overcome national traditions and prejudices. But nobody, with one exception, discussed war with reference to its origins, its deepest roots. Jeffrey Richards, who has scrutinized the files of the British

Westfront 1918 (G.): A men's war

Board of Film Censors,[9] proves that officials were concerned to prevent the screening of any story which could develop pacifist feelings and rejected projects involving, as was the case with Gance's *J'accuse*, the return of the dead soldiers to urge the living not to begin another war. However, Gance himself was not very happy with his film which was sharply criticized by the Left as well as by the Right. Patriotism was still strongly rooted in people's minds, and it was difficult to question it. It is true that the Nazi films were more warmongering than most of the European productions, but even in democratic countries movies like *Forever England* said that dying for one's country was glorious and rewarding.[10]

The synoptic table stresses the importance of the war pictures. Why was the theme up to date in the 1930s? Nicholas Pronay, who has compared the cinematic representation of the conflict after 1918 and after 1945, has developed an interesting theory:

The experience of the inter-war period suggests that after a decade there comes a re-surfacing of the worst of the memories in a way which allows people to face them again through the recreative power of art . . . The sudden 'popularity' between 1928–32 of autobiographies, plays, and novels (and films); the simultaneous re-publication of earlier and even wartime literature . . . and even the assembling and exhibition of paintings or photographs of the First World War . . . was a striking phenomenon in Britain, and was paralleled in the other participating countries. [Around 1932 there was an increasing number of people] for whom 'the war' was like any other historical romance.[11]

Nicholas Pronay is right when he pinpoints the close relationship between films and other arts, especially literature: two fifths of our films were based on printed texts. The percentage was particularly important in Britain where, apart from international productions intended for fairly different publics, most of the movies were adaptations of famous plays or novels. A literary origin is not necessarily a shortcoming: Milestone and Pabst drew their inspiration from novels and were able to give the original works a cinematic inflexion. Nevertheless, there is an obvious contrast between Germany, where film-makers such as Karl Ritter devised stories for the screen, and Britain where the directors were keen on merely sticking to the theatrical tastes of the public. Milestone's example of intelligent adaptation to the screen, which was carefully scrutinized in Germany and even in France, was ignored by the British.

There was a 'literary style' of war film which was not limited to England but which was developed there more than anywhere else. I am not concerned with deciding whether these pictures were good or not; I only want to stress the fact that, cinematographically, they were different and constituted a specific category. *Journey's End* and *Tell England*, which intend to describe seriously how war alters people's behaviour, concentrate on a few individuals. We find in the former a central character, Captain Denis Stanhope, and all the actions, debates or problems are filtered through his personal vision; in other words, we are not shown aspects of war but the reflection of war in the mind and demeanour of a man. Cinematic devices are systematically avoided, war noises are reduced to a vague sonorous background and light is only used to illuminate the setting which is almost limited to a series of dug-outs. *Tell England* includes some well-shot sequences of disembarkation beneath the cliffs of Gallipoli, but they are simply intercut with extended sequences of dialogue and look like documentary interludes rather than parts of the plot. We face here an important aspect of narration. Adaptations beget 'classical' films with a central character and a linear plot. Therefore pictures have a secondary function in the telling of the story, which entails a rejection of any purely emotional (that is to say, visual) description of the fighting; feelings are not excluded but are merely conveyed by words. The label 'talkies' sometimes applied to the films of the 1930s is especially appropriate to these works, in which well-coined sentences convey a message; intent on catching the significance of the words, spectators do not concern themselves either with the images or with the sounds. In addition, serialization must be taken into account. There was not only one adaptation since the British cinema appropriated fifteen texts which, from the point of view of the public, have to be considered as a whole.

Journey's End: A gentlemen's war

In the case of adaptations viewers are more interested in the process of transcription than in the story itself: are the films close to the texts? To a large extent, these movies are only derivatives of the plays or novels. As can be inferred from the opinion of the critics, attention focused not on the theme (war in this case) but on the accuracy of the reproduction. The impact of adaptation must always be borne in mind where the British cinema is compared to its continental counterparts.[12]

The most challenging aspect of Nicholas Pronay's assumption is his interpretation of a revived curiosity about war in the 1930s. It is generally considered that it was the international crisis, the sabre-rattling, which induced the producers to make films consonant with the fears and obsessions of their clients. On the contrary, Nicholas Pronay states, people had forgotten sufficiently to be able to accept a partial, inaccurate vision of what had happened in the trenches. This is an exciting starting-point for a discussion of war movies. We shall first compare the representations of the Great War in the four countries and we shall then try to discern how these images were likely to influence the cinema-goers.

WAR AS AN END

War films do not constitute a *genre* in the ordinary meaning of the word; they belong to the various categories of drama, adventure, documentary and comedy. Their specific value is the representation of scenes relating to the conflict and the use of hints which undoubtedly refer these scenes to the 1914-18 period. War films are historical films inasmuch as they imply a minimal knowledge regarding the situation and a capacity to identify the opposed sides. Nowadays we do not fully catch the implications of the plots because we miss some clues which were obvious in the 1930s. For instance, most spy stories play on love affairs between agents of conflicting countries which looked scandalous at the time but, for us, are merely trite love/hate dramas with an ill-defined political background. War films are also narrations; they organize a few actions or events in order to fill the screen for eighty minutes. Narratively, the conflict can be a historical event against which the story is built, or the very centre, the theme of the film.

Paradis perdu ('Lost Paradise'), *Journey's End* – the titles of

31

these films tell spectators that life finished with the conflict. Nevertheless, despite the fact that the latter film was an English production, Britain did not indulge in this theme, which was also rarely – but more interestingly – treated on the continent. *Cavalleria* (I., 1936) is the most melancholic of the 'end-films': the time of romantic love, evening dresses and masked balls is over, cavalrymen lose their horses and die like infantrymen. The same nostalgia is expressed in Gance's *Paradis perdu* (1939): the conflagration has modified everything and happiness will never be again what it used to be. In both movies the war sequences are short but their style is totally different. In the Italian film, war bursts out all of a sudden. Slow motion, underlined by long panning-shots, gives way to quickly edited images photographed by a still camera, with soldiers running about in all directions and filling up space. Shooting and editing are co-ordinated to create an easily understandable feeling – a way of life sunk during the hostilities; although made during the fascist era, the story, which ends with the death of the main character, does not suggest that a better future is at hand. Gance's war is less heroic than that; it is confined to a dug-out where soldiers wait and are killed. There are some likenesses between this passage and the whole of *Journey's End*. Clearly the visualization of war installations is common to all Europeans; but the narrative use of the same setting is extremely diverse. The English film takes advantage of apocalyptic scenery to reach a conclusion that *Cavalleria* will later develop – the end. With Gance, after a long period in the depths, life will start again, hard, less happy but endurable: we shall come back to this contrast later.

Two other films which finish with the war are devoted to the emigrants. The relationship between them is too obvious to be purely casual. *Ein Mann will nach Deutschland* (G., d. Paul Wegener, 1934) and *Passaporto rosso* (I., d. Guido Brignone, 1935) tell the same story: when the time comes emigrants remember their country and overcome every obstacle or difficulty to reach the front line. A comparison is not in this case an intellectual exercise; the films are intended to force it. The main character in the German film is a successful man, well known in South America where he has a good job as a civil engineer. He has gone as far as he can; he has made a lot of money and has nothing more to hope for – his going back to

Germany will not change his fate. The Italian who is much younger is not yet well off; one day he will be an engineer as well, but only when he has followed the prescribed path. At the present he does his utmost to be integrated into Argentine society to such an extent that he asks to be called Juan instead of Giovanni. The Italian film is an intimate family story concerning two generations. The grandfather had arrived from the peninsula with a red passport, the passport given to the long-term emigrants, while the father, an emigrant likewise, continued to live in an Italian environment. His son is at last in a position to become, as he likes to say, 'a true American'. The German has only to overcome the opposition of people and geography; he wants to go back to Germany, and his will and doggedness of purpose are enough to make him succeed. Right from the beginning we guess he will return to his country and are more intent on seeing how he gets over the obstacles than on waiting for a predictable ending. On the other hand, with the young Italian, we are at the centre of what turns out to be a drama for him: he would like to stay in Argentina and could do so inasmuch as, having been born there, he is Argentinian. All through its first part the film aims at involving the spectators in the endeavour and progress of the family as it devotes all its energy to joining the local community. The war is thus a break in the narrative: it is not forecast in the film by indirect clues, as is generally the case for catastrophes which close a story. The style itself changes: instead of a few, well-developed actions illustrating the progress of the Italians we are faced with short, quickly edited sequences. The father decides to enlist; the son understands where his duty lies and agrees to leave. The final scene is particularly striking in its briefness: at the bottom of a dug-out (note what has just been said of the typical scenery) Juan/Giovanni writes to his family/short flash of the family/a helmet falls down while we hear machine-gun fire/flash of the mother who seems to feel a blow/wooden cross with the name of Giovanni (no longer 'Juan'). As in *Cavalleria* it is the same feeling of an unavoidable fate which destroys individual destinies. The mother cries when her only son kisses her goodbye, and he is as desperate as she is. War itself is pictured in the four above-mentioned shots, and the film is intent on telling us that the boy was killed in 1916 (that is to say, immediately after he joined the front line).

Passaporto rosso was produced one year after *Ein Mann will nach Deutschland* and at the same time as Trinker's first work on emigrants. We cannot but emphasize the gap between the two versions of a common situation; the Germans master history by identifying its trend while the Italians hopelessly submit to it. For twenty years fascism repeatedly celebrated war as an exceptional period in which ordinary men become heroes but, 'unwittingly', films disclose another reality, a strong resistance, in a 'popular' art, to Mussolinian bellicosity

WAR AS A STARTING-POINT

Instead of closing the story, war can open it; here, again, Italy presents a contrast with Germany. In 1938 (the year in which Mussolini proudly presented his army to Hitler) there were two films – one Italian, *Luciano Sera pilota* (d. Goffredo Alessandrini), one German, *Pour le mérite* (d. Karl Ritter; the title refers to the most famous German medal, instituted by Frederick II at a time when French was spoken at the Prussian court) – in which pilots, who were war-heroes and are disappointed with peace, try to start life afresh. These works are strikingly different. *Pour le mérite* is a war film which pictures thrilling moments of air raids. *Luciano Sera* begins after the peace treaty and does not entail (even as a flashback) any representation of the fighting.[13] We have noted how allusive the war sequences are in *Cavalleria* and *Passaporto rosso*; the same can be said of another movie, *Camicia nera* (d. Giovacchino Forzano, 1933), which evokes the front line in a quick scene and jumps to peacetime. It is not a question of sensibility or money (war sequences are expensive), since the Ethiopian war with its savage fighting fills up the second part of *Luciano Sera*. In fact, the Italians avoid picturing the First World War whereas, as we shall see, the Germans never hesitate to represent its most unpleasant aspects.

The most intriguing contrast between the two 1938 films concerns the after-war period. Two brave pilots demobilized in 1918 witness the laying up of aircraft. Luciano Sera is unable to cope with the situation; he loses any faith in his country and, despite his wife and son who need him, he emigrates . . . to Latin America. He is still an Italian but he does not imagine any possibility of serving his country except by crossing the

Atlantic or – later – joining the Italian troops in Abyssinia. Prank, the German officer, never despairs. When the German airforce is destroyed by the Allies he decides to reorganize it. He acts side by side with his superiors and fellows since none of them conceives any break between war and peace; what they began when fighting the French pilots has to be carried out against the Weimar Republic. Luciano Sera does not try to understand why the 'armata azzurra' – the Italian 'blue army' – was dispersed, while Prank knows the culprits – politicians, Allies and all those who want to prevent Germany from restoring its strength. It is not by chance that Luciano Sera dies after succeeding in a purely defensive action (he flies to pick up his wounded son and carry him from the Ethiopian lines into an Italian hospital), since he does not feel entrusted with any positive missions. The same well-known Italian actor, Amedeo Nazzari, is successively the officer (cavalryman, then pilot) of *Cavalleria* and *Luciano Sera*. He is killed twice, and each time his death closes the film. Prank does not die; he is made a national hero and asked to train those who tomorrow will fight for Germany. *Pour le mérite* is remarkable because of its emphasis on the continuity between yesterday (war) and the future. It is also part of the glorification of a crack army which is admirably evoked in other German or French films. Once again Italy is an exception inasmuch as she does not celebrate her pilots and does not make the First World War a prelude to other, more successful undertakings.

There is another aspect of the hostilities seen as a beginning – the declaration of war. In his eagerness to condemn war Milestone was keen to exaggerate the enthusiasm of those who have just enlisted and to contrast their initial burst of nationalism with the desperation into which they will soon be driven. In doing so he sticks to a literary tradition which maintains that in every country soldiers willingly entered war. Historians think nowadays that there were, in capital cities, some parades which were carefully photographed and endlessly celebrated in papers, while the general reaction – such as can be observed in small towns and villages – was a silent, dreary submission. Yet we are not speaking here of social attitudes but of images. A few pictures represent hysterical manifestations, which must be cautiously scrutinized. In this field chronology has to be taken into account. The German films dealing with 1914 were all shot before 1933. Once Hitler assumed power, the German film-makers merely concentrated on an already initiated conflict. On the other hand, the French movies which illustrate the opening of the hostilities were all made shortly before September 1939.

1914, Die letzten Tage vor dem Weltbrand (G., 1931) – that is to say, the last days before the world began to burn – takes place in Germany and evokes the diplomatic situation as well as the reactions of a few individuals. *Ultimatum* (F., 1937) is located both in Serbia and in Austria; the Danube has long been a link between the two nations but, as tension increases, it becomes more and more a borderline. Historically, *1914* is more accurate; it is a lecture on political relations magnified through the eyes of common people. History comes second in *Ultimatum*; we are only told allusively of the Sarajevo affair, and if the movie does not ignore the quick evolution of public opinion (expressed through flashes of pub conversation and street encounters) it focuses on a small crew of close friends who are citizens of the two countries. Different though they are, the films, by representing the fears and hopes of ordinary people, emphasize the dramatic character of the last peaceful days.

Beside these productions, two other films dealing with a much larger period, *Paradis perdu* and *Niemandsland* (G., d. Victor Trivas, 1931), include sequences on the summer of 1914. By showing alternately the mobilization in three fighting countries – Britain, Germany and France – the German director has chosen an editing process which seems to have no equivalent among the contemporary war films.[14] The most trite stereotypes are used in order to surround the departures with a surrealistic, absurd atmosphere. All the soldiers look perfectly happy; the French refuse to fall in, and behave as individualistically as possible, the English are only preoccupied with sporting facilities at the front and the Germans behave automatically as a perfect military machine. Amid the crowd the movie-camera selects men who will later be the main characters and lingers on the typical case of a German joiner who leads a quiet life in suburban Berlin. When called up, the man, overwhelmed with grief, is unable to talk and his wife starts weeping; both go drearily and silently towards the station, but while they are walking they fall upon more and more merry Berliners who sing, shout and sound the bugle. In a jiffy, the couple's mood changes; wife and husband begin to laugh, then to yell and finally they fall into step as if a new happiness was born from their abiding by the rules. Taken separately, the sequence could be inserted in a jingoistic film. In fact, it is a prelude to another sequence which contrasts, in a Russian style, the peace of workers' Europe with the hysterical making of weapons. Without words and through pictures, the spectators are given an illustration of the thesis which links the arms race, imperialism and world war, the civilians being unconscious victims of decisions settled far above them.

For reasons that we shall explore later, *Niemandsland* is an incomplete film which after a brilliant beginning turns into an inconsistent dream. Nevertheless, its strong criticism of the initial 'enthusiasm' fits perfectly with what is said in *Paradis perdu*: a newly married couple is walking in the beautiful, sunny landscape of Provence; suddenly a bell rings and a group of countrymen singing a patriotic song and following a flag parades in the background; the young couple look at each other in total despair. The contrast is created by succession in the German film and by the juxtaposition of two different types of behaviour in *Paradis perdu*, but both aim at questioning the so-called nationalist outburst of August 1914.

Taken together, the four films under investigation develop, with different techniques and narrative purposes, a concordant representation of the declaration of war. *Passaporto rosso*, which is short on the departure scene, pictures Giovanni and his mother's sadness, while another Italian film, *Le scarpe al sole* (d. Mario Elter, 1935), enlarges upon the topic in nearly the same manner. The film opens on a wedding during which the camera points to the three men who will be at the centre of the plot. A photograph of a mobilization order covers the screen. The spectators are then introduced to the houses of the three characters, where women and children cry and the men hardly conceal their sorrow. A patriotic song is heard in the background, as if it were sung in another place or at another level of the narration. The men go out and join their fellows.

The convergence is impressive. Three times (*Passaporto rosso, Le scarpe al sole, Paradis perdu*) it is a new couple which must part, as if all prospect of new life and fresh happiness were broken by war. In other movies, family is destroyed. The military hysteria is assigned to the mob or to an invisible, abstract power external to the small world of common people. Milestone's vision was more didactic: enthusiasm first, then disillusion and despair. In the 1930s no European cineast was ready to use Milestone's depiction of 1914, and I am tempted to make an assumption which is not based on any factual evidence but is likely to explain some seeming inconsistencies in our cluster of movies. In Weimar Germany and in France the evocation of the beginning of the conflict helped to condemn war, any war. In Nazi Germany where war was always pictured in a realistic, uncompromising light, the opening of hostilities was carefully avoided; war was already there and the soldiers had to carry it on until the end. Italy was an exception. Fascism, at a time when it was not yet involved in the Ethiopian expedition, tolerated a filmic representation which contradicted the official speeches on the 'Maggio radioso', the 'radiant May' of 1915 when Italy mastered her fate by entering the war. It must be borne in mind that fascism was filled with contradictions and that Mussolini's wavering policy alternately favoured bellicosity and international conciliation, but that is not enough. Contrary to what is often felt, even a totalitarian power may have difficulties in using films for its propaganda, since spectators are not willing to condone political parades in which leaders explain their programme with cinematic fictions. The memory of the conflict was bad enough in Italy to prevent the film-makers from transferring into their movies the official vision of the mobilization.

Nevertheless, it was not possible to question the origins of the hostilities. A fierce, consistent pacifist, Abel Gance avoided the problem; the two films on August 1914, *Ultimatum* and *1914*, are content with enumerating the dramatic events of the last hours. *Niemandsland* is the only attempt made at explaining why Europe exploded. Is it possible to account for the timidity of men like Asquith, Gance or Pabst, who hated war and knew that another threat was impending over the world? External causes – such as the pressures of censors or the fears of diplomats obsessed by the idea that an allusion to the responsibilities of a foreign country could offend a potential ally[15] – must not be underrated, but I believe that reasons internal to the world of the studios were more important.

There was, first, the weight of adaptation: Asquith and Pabst worked on the basis of texts and did not dare reshape them by adding sequences on the pre-war period since they conceived of themselves and their script-writers as mere 'translators', not originators. And, apart from delivering a boring discourse in voice-over or entrusting a few characters to talk, how could a movie enlighten an audience on the causes of the conflagration? Films were then mostly understood as narrations, and causes are not easily rendered into narrative. Another more discursive solution was offered by the Soviet cinematographers who attempted to trigger the insight of the viewers by juxtaposing in the editing-process strongly contrasted pictures, and this was the device Trivas adopted for the initial sequences of *Niemandsland*. Yet the film was not a success; it was only projected in left-wing circles while *Westfront 1918*, like *All Quiet on the Western Front*, was immensely popular. Neither the public nor the cinematographers (not to mention the producers) were ready to experiment with new cinematic forms.

BEYOND THE FRONT LINE

In 1940 Italy released her only jingoistic production on the First World War, *Piccolo alpino*. The script was adapted from one of the inane children's novels widely diffused in all the belligerent countries from 1914 through 1918. A courageous boy goes to the front line with the Alpine soldiers, shares their daily life and participates in their attacks. He is caught by the Austrians but, like all his brothers-in-arms, he is so intent on fighting again that he escapes. This dull movie illustrates the tragic inadequacy of Italian propaganda. Before entering the war Italy already celebrated her military success-to-be; even having occupied four countries, Germany did not pretend that victory was at hand. The film would not deserve a mention, were it not for the capture and escape sequences. War captivity was not often pictured in the 1930s, as can be inferred from the synoptic table which indicates merely one film for each country. Coincidences must not be overevaluated, and there is probably nothing to be inferred from the fact that the French *Grand Illusion*, the German *Patrioten* and the English *Who Goes Next?* (d. Maurice Elvey) were released almost simultaneously in 1937–8 but the thematic similarities between these movies

39

are not negligible. The protagonists are officers – in other words, strong, clever men capable of expressing their feelings and explaining why they intend to fight again, since right from the beginning there is no doubt about their longing to escape. The German, a pilot whose plane has been shot down in enemy-occupied territory, manages to pass himself off as a civilian, his journey back being mostly an obstacle race. The English and French movies concentrate on the POW camps and may be compared in the attitudes revealed by their 'talking' styles – attitudes towards individual standards in the case of the former, towards class in the case of the latter. In both cases evasion must be paid for. While the German succeeds because he is tricky and has been around, lives are sacrificed to liberate the English and the French. These may be linked to different mentalities, but it is also a result of the cinematic discourse: the German is involved in a thriller which entails that after a hard time he will necessarily survive. In the POW camps there is talking but no action, so that at the end the English or French viewers must be provided at least with a climax. Therefore an aristocrat dies for two bourgeois (French class), while an honourable man is killed to help his mistress's husband run away (English individual standards). It would be artificial to separate the cinematic treatment from the message. The German film does not chat, it shows events. The other films linger on motivations, conflict and incompatibilities; in fact, they question war without taking it for granted, while the German work takes war as a fact which has to be tackled.

Abundantly furnished with exciting American movies, English and French audiences could not be content with endless debates, they had to be offered action. Spy stories were a possible makeshift; the war was in the background, but its depiction was vague enough to allay the censors' fears. Espionage, which was ignored by the Germans and Italians, fascinated the democracies, it was the theme of nearly half of the English movies and of one third of the French ones. Secret agents ready to double-cross their fatherland or fellows and even themselves were depicted in all imaginable locations – in neutral countries, in Germany and on their national territory. Yet it must not be forgotten that spy novels were an old tradition ushered in by Le Queux in the 1890s and highly popular on both sides of the Channel.[16] The cinematic clichés were all borrowed from literature: handsome German officers who hide their cruelty behind an impressive look (Conrad Veidt, who had left Nazi Germany, was obliged to repeat the same part endlessly), beautiful but treacherous ladies (Vivien Leigh playing a French adventuress), frantic chases in U-boats and windmills which enable traitors to pass messages. Spying in films is like living in a fantasy world where everything is easy. When German baron Conrad Veidt understands he has been deceived by Vivien Leigh, who is now on the voyage home to France, he instantly finds a U-boat and stops her ship (in Victor Saville's *Dark Journey*). It is thus only by comparison that these simplistic stories can tell us something.

Let us begin with the least inane of these movies, *Deuxième bureau contre Kommandantur* which, in some respects, starts with a probable situation. The story takes place in the district of Lorraine conquered by the Germans during the first days of the war. In an occupied village all the inhabitants, be they the vicar, the countess or the poorest peasant, unite to resist the Germans, search for information on the troops and ammunition dumps and hide French soldiers. The occupiers are so upset that an officer, Heim, is especially entrusted with unmasking the resisters. This outset is rather intriguing; the national territory is no longer French, the borders have been reversed and collective spying is now the only way of fighting. Brutal though he is, Heim does not find any clue and the French are more and more audacious. This initial description which amounts to about one half of the movie is entirely seen from the point of view of the French. Eventually the German High Command, the Kommandantur, sends a new investigator, Leutnant Kompartz. While he is operating, the spectators follow his footsteps; they are no longer on the French but rather on the German side. The point of view has been turned upside-down. Kompartz finds out that Heim is a French spy and that the vicar has a twin brother, a member of the French Second Bureau, who lands at night behind the German lines, puts on his brother's cassock and spies. Who betrays whom and who is who? Confusion does not only arise from the various costumes and from the personalities attributed to the actors but also, and maybe mostly, from the shift which modifies the perspective. Who is the central character? The spy/German officer (Heim), the vicar/spy, the investigator

(Kompartz) – in other words the man who has no country, the two-faced man or the enemy? All the spy films are based on indetermination or incompatible positions. The spectators of the time were not more naïve than us; they did not believe that these films described actual spying but merely hoped to witness once more the same love-and-mystery story they had been told many times before. However, we cannot but emphasize the gap between Germany and the Allied countries. Germans on film always know where they are; the pilot of *Patrioten* who is obliged to contact French families is never tempted by the girls or interested in the local life. He only aims at returning to his fatherland.[17] For their part English and French spies are not sure they can tell where their national territory is and are tempted by love-affairs with enemies. Duty prevails after debates and hesitations which pleased contemporary audiences.

ON THE FRONT LINE

Up to now we have said very little about the fighting. The spy stories run all through the decade from *The W Plan* to *The Spy in Black* and the 'war-ending' or 'war-beginning' plots are spread through the decade with no specific relation to historical context. On the other hand, chronology must be carefully considered where battles are concerned, as the depiction of fighting was more dependent on juncture than were the other themes. Out of the twenty movies which deal mostly with war-actions fifteen were made between 1930 and 1933, and the proportion is even more striking if we add that after 1933 all the films which did not use war as a vague, unimportant background were German or, in one case, Italian. Nicholas Pronay is perfectly right when he says that there was a general interest in the First World War in Europe at the beginning of the 1930s. As we shall see, it is not hard to account for the film-making policy of the Germans under Nazism, but there is a problem with the democracies – and before 1933 Germany was a democracy. Undoubtedly the producers were impressed by the American challenge and were tempted to resist it. The influence of Hollywood is particularly obvious in the recourse to suspense and delay likely to excite the spectator. A squad, a crew is engaged in a perilous operation, they must destroy a look-out post, sink a ship or simply cheat a stronger enemy. Will they survive? How many men will escape? Like their American counterparts, most of these movies are classically ordered.

Hollywood cannot fully explain this short revival of interest. The Europeans wanted to picture some of their most dramatic experiences. Movies were used to represent aspects of what was already becoming national history – Gallipoli, Douaumont, Verdun – and the American studios were unable to meet these expectations. In contrast to an otherwise honourable but rather prosaic production, three films – *Westfront 1918*, *Les Croix de bois* (F., d. R. Bernard, 1931) and *Niemandsland* – turned out to be more ambitious and disturbing. Like Milestone, the European directors wanted to show war instead of telling it, and there are similarities apparent between their works and *All Quiet*: Pabst chooses three central characters, while Bernard chooses two with a small, less important crew around them, and we already know how Trivas detects his protagonists amid the crowd. Pabst and Bernard, as well as Milestone, alternate moments of rest during which life seems to restart, with horrifying scenes of battles. But the parallel cannot be drawn any farther. Milestone selected what he considered emblematic of the German middle class – a college – and he follows the students who have enlisted. Pabst and Bernard's protagonists have met at random because they have been assigned to the same unit. Two of the Germans are not even provided with names: they are 'the Bavarian' and 'the student'. We get little information about their previous life, and the few details which are dropped show that their past is closed for ever. One of the Germans goes on leave, finds his wife with a young man, returns and is killed; one of the French, while dying, hallucinates that his fiancée is in the arms of another.

Once Milestone's soldiers have reached the front line we guess that they are doomed to die and, in this respect, the film is not classical since the end is foreseeable before the middle is reached. But there is still a permanent group at the centre of the story. However, there is no plot – that is to say, no leading protagonist – in Pabst's or Bernard's films. The characters are so unimportant that they are killed one after the other. Both films are made of uncoordinated episodes – sometimes of extremely short sequences which seem to have been loosely edited, the logic being not narrative or chronological but emotional. *Westfront 1918* opens in a French village where German troops make a halt. A few men have been billeted in a farm, they eat, talk, play cards. All of a sudden they are ordered to move quickly. Why? Are the French arriving? Are the Germans attacking? The longest sequences devoted to military actions – the bombing of a trench, an attack in a dug-out – are divided into small series of shots which never result in a general vision of the battle. Let us look at a small bit of film. We are shown the burst of a bomb, a trench, a small portion of land (what a soldier could see from a hole; but we do not know whether there is a man who is looking with us or whether it is merely the evocation of a martyred piece of land). A soldier runs forward, falls down, rises slowly, looks in front of him. Now we start being interested in him, we glance with him at a corpse at the bottom of a well. We would like to understand how he reacts, but he is running again and we shall have no other meeting with him. Although their sound-tracks are sometimes overpowering and even frightening, Pabst and Bernard rely less than Milestone on 'echoing'. By combining a reduced number of prospects, quick editing and an absence of dominant point of view, they aim at creating a strong, long-lasting impression in the mind of the spectator, and their endeavour seems to have been effective since their films met with an enthusiastic welcome: ex-servicemen inter-viewed after the projections said that for the first time they had witnessed images matching their own memories.

In Germany the Left, while admitting that Pabst described the war without complacency, criticized him because he did not explain why there were international conflagrations and did not challenge the logic of the trenches: horror and death, bombings and attacks, war is war and that is all.[18] *Niemandsland* was an attempt to go farther. We have analysed the opening which contrasts the uncomplaining individuals resigned to die with the weapon manufacturers who need more dead soldiers in order to make more arms. The film tries then to escape the inevitability of war: five men – a Frenchman, an Englishman, a German, a Jew and a negro who has travelled throughout Europe – meet by chance in a dug-out and, instead of killing each other, decide to give up fighting. They create a world for themselves, a 'No Man's Land', where they stay enclosed until the war is over. It must be said that the film-makers had multiplied the difficulties in shooting this movie. There was a stylistic gap between the allusive, quick, ironic beginning and the more traditional continuation which, for a spectator, was merely a theatrical performance in a restricted space. As every character used his own language the dialogue was limited. Is this the reason why the film was a failure? A comparison with the two other movies suggests rather that people were not pleased with utopias, but this is no more than a hypothesis.

Westfront 1918 was a terrific success – one of the biggest of the year – and most of the other front films did very well. There was a public for this kind of representation, a public which did not care about noticeable differences of style and which paid for the classically ordered story of a commando strike as well as for the moving evocations of Pabst and Bernard. The mode lasted as long as any other fashion – three years. From 1933 onwards the democracies stopped featuring the battles of the recent war while the dictatorships went on filming them. Propaganda was, of course, at stake, but we cannot be content with saying that Rome and Berlin wanted to prepare their countries for a new conflagration, since the cinema precisely tells us there were hesitations and contradictions among politicians and cinematographers. The Nazis were keen to compensate for the effects of the pacifist movies, especially *All Quiet* and *Westfront 1918*. Although the fascists had banned these works they too were worried about pacifism. Both admitted that the early 1930s had brought something new, a critical depiction of war which no longer presented it as a rewarding, exciting experience. Hence the singularity of the movies shot after 1933, which attempt to dramatize war without condemning it.

In the peninsula only one production among the rare war films is worth being mentioned because it is quite naïve and less astute than its German counterparts. The title itself, *Le scarpe al sole*, signals the ambiguity of the project. Why are 'the shoes in the sun'? Because for four years soldiers permanently lived outdoors or because the corpses' shoes are exposed to the sun? War becomes here an ordeal which can be coped with and also an inescapable necessity. The men of a small village are assigned to the same Alpine unit. They are good at skiing and climbing up rocks and, if they miss their families and suffer cold and hunger, theirs is not an unbearable situation. During the last third of the film the Italians are ordered to retreat. Our men go through their village which will be occupied by the Austrians; clearly it is for their families that they must fight and that they launch a final, victorious attack. Some of them die, others survive and the youngest gets married immediately after he has been demobilized; the film opened on a wedding and closes on another wedding. This work is a soft, understated answer to *All Quiet*: it is a small group again but a group of simple countrymen and not of students. The men neither long for heroism nor fall into despair. Whereas Milestone emphasized the evolution of his characters by changes of style there is, in the Italian film, a perfect continuity of plot-line which illustrates the potential smoothness of classicism: a coherent, continuous, easily understandable vision is reassuring, especially if the central characters are meant to continue their fictional life after the end. War is seen as a *reasonably* murderous ordeal. Italy, which as a rule avoided picturing the war, was the only country which offered an optimistic depiction of the soldiers' sufferings.

There were various attempts in Germany to refute pacifism along the same line ('war is bearable') but with a stronger emphasis on the hardness of military life. *Morgenrot* (d. G. Ucicky, 1933) deserves a comparison with the above-mentioned *Le scarpe al sole*. A U-boat, *Dawn*, entrusted with sinking an English ship, succeeds in its mission but is in its turn destroyed. When the U-boat leaves its harbour fear and anguish are expressed by the civilians, mostly by the women who stay on the pier. Few words are exchanged, but there is no soft editing as in the Italian film – the light is cruder, people are shot in close-up and contrived smiles say more than vague gestures of farewell. Later when the U-boat approaches its target the cinematographers avoid the reassuring intercutting which would show alternately the too-quiet English and the busy Germans; they concentrate rather on a long, silent slip amidst the convoy-ships. The film plays on the spectators' nerves, but the suspense does not result in a happy ending – it precedes a second climax during which panting men try to survive.

Interestingly, other German cinematographers went so far as to have recourse to the 'showing-echoing' effects used by the pacifists, the best example being *Stosstrupp 1917* (d. Hans Zöberlein, 1934). As in *Westfront 1918* there is no story, only a succession of moments of rest and action. But there is not even a permanent group of recognizable people; anonymous soldiers are killed and replaced by other men who will be killed in their turn, and nobody speaks because there is too much noise and because there is nothing to be said. War is pictured without complacency but also without the ineluctable death of already-familiar protagonists which creates at the end of Pabst's movie an impression of total emptiness.[19] Tired, exhausted, the Germans manage to repel the enemy. War is inhuman, but Germany can take it. Yet the 'bellicosity' of the Germans must not be overrated. From 1933 through 1939 seven movies were devoted to military aspects of the First World War, but there was also a comedy using the war as a background and other movies which pictured the *émigrés*, the civilians and so on. Unlike the democracies, Nazi Germany was intent on keeping alive the remembrance of the war. The cinematographers wavered between a classic representation with central characters, and a limited, clever use of cinematic devices likely to involve the spectators strongly. If there was no official line in this field, the studios were allowed to describe the hardships and sorrows of war, which suggests that the Nazi leaders considered it a good manner of preparing their country for a future conflagration.

IMAGES IN AN UNSETTLED EUROPE

Diplomatically, politically and ideologically, Europe in 1933 was divided, but we do not need to look at the cinematic production to describe contradictions better defined by more traditional sources. Cinema, which has little to tell us about facts, can enlighten us about the building up of an image, the image of a recent past which had accentuated the contradictions of the Old World. Mobilized for a total war people had fought mercilessly and were about to struggle again. Nevertheless, the enemy was scarcely represented in movies. Here or there a few hints can be detected: in *Morgenrot* the German U-boat is trapped by an English ship camouflaged as a trawler which hoists its colours only when it begins to shell. Some of those who spy for the Allies in the English or French movies have their families slaughtered by the Germans. However, as a rule, adversaries and also allies are ignored; every nation concentrates upon itself, its soldiers and its sufferings.

I have analysed very closely obscure films with which few people are familiar; I think this was necessary in order to go beyond an impressionistic vision of the war represented in movies. I find it hard to think that, around 1930, the Europeans had forgotten. The memory of the conflagration was still deep two decades after the peace treaty, so deep that it was impossible to jest with it or to picture it in imaginary colours. Apart from the astonishing *Piccolo alpino*, which came out when Italy was on the verge of entering a war already won by Germany, no film dared insinuate that war is a game. The Italian case is a good way of measuring what was accepted on screens. The government, the Party and the head of the cinematic office continually demanded heroic, patriotic films, but the best they obtained was *Le scarpe al sole* which made war bearable, not pleasurable. The Italian film-makers avoided a conflict that they did not want to celebrate and which they were not allowed to demystify. It is too often taken for granted that spectators are passive and take what they are offered. How is it then possible to account for the reluctance of producers all over Europe to idealize war? Did it not result from the resistance of the public which did not accept triumphant war movies?

A stimulating aspect of war-cinema is that it cannot easily be labelled: there was no democratic conception as opposed to a totalitarian conception of the events. There were strong divergences from nation to nation, and even within each country, but they did not concern the characterization of the conflict. Everywhere the origins of the conflagration, the reasons for fighting, the culpability/cruelty of the enemy were passed over in silence. Almost no film tried to consider the future of the continent after the peace treaty or the reconciliation between the belligerents.[20] The war was unanimously featured as a long-lasting, practically timeless ordeal, the only moment precisely dated being the outset (pictured as a shock, a damaging interruption of life). The most common image was that of individual death, a blink between life and eternity, quickly, movingly shot – a wink of the eye, a collapsing body, accompanied, rather than underlined, by a visual emphasis (unusual framings, accentuated lighting) and by symbolical references ((broken trees, cut flowers, crosses, earth). The brutality and suddenness of a fighting death contrasts with the depiction of death in most contemporary movies where it is a pretext for endless discourse. It is, of course, a rhetorical device which must not be assigned to 'realism'; many soldiers lay in agony for hours, while others died in hospital. The cinematic figure is merely a figure – that is to say, a way of picturing one of the commonplaces of the European war film. Jeffrey Richards, who knows English cinema very well, rightly mocks its 'romanticized, class-bound and hopelessly out-of-touch' style.[21] Desperate gentlemen chat until it is their turn to get out of the trench and be killed. This is surely a reflection of the 'class-bound 1930 tradition, resolutely middle-class in tone and values'. But there is something more. What do these respectable officers say? That war is inhuman but has to be accepted and endured – which is a message conveyed by the majority of European war films; the contrasts lie not in content but in form. Most war films were audiovisual narrations centred around characters who were followed until the end. As the English films were more theatrical, they emphasized something which was taken for granted by the majority of European spectators.

A challenging aspect of the problem is the change which occurred in Britain and France after 1933. One point has to be made clear: no connection can be established between the diplomatic situation of the early 1930s and the curiosity aroused then by the war movies. The years from 1930 through 1933 were a disheartening period for economic reasons (the depression) and political ones (the threat of fascism), but until 1935 Nazi Germany did not endanger the European balance and it was not the fear of a new war which induced spectators to queue for war movies. Is it then, as Nicholas Pronay suggests, that once ten years had elapsed the memory of the Great War was less crushing than during the previous decade? It is true that in 1930 nobody objected to a film in which, just behind the front line, an English lady drives her husband and two other officers crazy (*French Leave*) but service comedies of that quality existed already in the 1920s and were much fewer than the serious films produced in the 1930s. I am tempted to think that it is the cinema itself which triggered a renewed interest in the depiction of the hostilities. On one side, there was sound, which offered unexpected possibilities. On another side, there was Hollywood with its impressive, beautifully screened stories. There were also some directors who wanted to use the emotional potentialities of sound and pictures at a time when spectators were still willing to test new experiments. And, finally, there was a public deeply concerned with the last conflict: the scene was perfectly set for a representation of war.

Why was there a shift towards other directions long before Hitler destroyed the European consensus by rearming Germany? The partial inadequacy of cinema to 'mirror' a society is particularly obvious during the second half of the decade: papers, radio, newsreels were more and more concerned with conflicts and battles in the Far East, in Africa, in Spain, but in feature films war merely served as a background for love and spying romances. Perhaps this was because people did not want to pay for a seat and to watch precisely what they feared – the trenches again and the destruction of their lives; perhaps also because the cinematic standards evolved during the period when dialogue took precedence over other sounds. There was no particular reason to stage POW camps in 1937, but the three films already mentioned are a good sample of the production of the late 1930s: noises are limited to clangs necessary to imitate a closing door, there is absolutely no 'echoing' work, the settings are filled with no more than the indispensable objects, the sequences unfold in a predictable order and everything is intended to make the public concentrate on the dialogue. In the most interesting English or French films the main themes were still the same, but they were spoken and not translated into images. Meanwhile Germany went on filming war in different manners. By using sometimes a classic narration and sometimes an 'echoing/showing' style she gave her films a dynamism which was lacking in other countries. It would be absurd to say on the basis of their films that the Germans were more ready to fight than the English, since images do not influence people directly. But there was on the Nazi side an aptitude to 'mobilize' pictures and sounds. Far from promoting an optimistic, heroic vision the Nazis understood the stimulating power of a harsh, almost unpleasant, depiction emphasizing the toughness of the battlefield and making clear that only well-trained soldiers would survive. The German cinema did not reflect any will to take revenge; it did not claim that Germany was right and had been cheated by the Allies and its themes were not significantly at variance with those of the other cinemas. But the formal use of the cinematic material, the recourse to various styles of narration, differentiated it from its English and French counterparts.

We have emphasized earlier in this chapter the relationships which existed between studios in the 1930s. Although the same people worked in several countries successively the most striking feature of the war-cinema is the isolation and self-containment of each nation. The Italian case is once more very characteristic: directors interested in war films such as Gance and Johannes Meyer worked in the peninsula where Trinker also made long stays to direct and even act, but none of these men was asked to film the conflagration. Fascism imitated Nazism in many ways, for instance in its conception of mass-meetings, but there was always a gap – or even a total incompatibility – between the Italian and the German screening of the conflict. If the distance was not as important between Britain and France, the two countries stuck to their respective visions, despite the frequent meetings of actors, directors and technicians. A conflict unanimously called 'World War' was always represented as a national event. Besides – and this is even more challenging – a conflagration that nobody could forget about was seldom filmed. If we cannot fully account for this near silence an insight into the Second World War or rather into one of its most specific aspects, resistance, will help us to make a step forward.

2

RESISTANCE

In this topic it was Britain who could provide Europe with new cinematic images. Left alone to fight Germany in 1940, she began organizing contacts on the continent, and little by little the country was pervaded by the idea that there were, across the Channel, people who still resisted Nazism. American opinion was never very interested in the secret war; Hollywood dedicated a few uninspired films to it but never believed that the topic was likely to trigger enthusiasm among its clients. On the other hand, in Europe it was an evolving theme, a theme which gave rise to many different treatments. Britain started first because she was free to tackle the problem even during the hostilities,[1] but the connections between what was featured in her studios and what was filmed later in other countries are often striking. This does not imply a direct influence, let alone an imitation. There was rather a community of concern, a similar way of looking at the question. In this respect, similarities as well as disparities have something to tell us about the re-construction of the recent past in post-war Europe.

HOW THE 'VISUAL' CHANGES

Hidden transmitters were set up on the continent and information was wired to London as early as 1940, but little was known then about these illegal, dangerous activities. Hence the value of an otherwise dull movie, *Secret Mission*, the first to deal openly with secret agents and resistance, which was made and released at a time when important changes were occurring in British military policy. Until the beginning of 1942

52

the Special Operations Executive (SOE), which co-ordinated subversive activities on the continent, assumed that it was possible to levy secret armies in the occupied countries. At the right moment these armies would rise against the Germans with the help of the British. Sabotage was still considered by many officials an unfair method of warfare. When the SOE suggested that a few men dropped by parachute in France could kill some of the best German pilots, Air Marshal Portal reacted bitterly: 'There is a vast difference, in ethics, between the time-honoured operation of the dropping of a spy from the air and this entirely new scheme for dropping what one can only call assassins.'[2] The alternative strategy of co-operation with the resistants on the continent was adopted in 1942, and the public was informed indirectly, notably by feature films. We are lucky enough to catch at its very birth a new set of images. As is generally the case, these images are neither totally feasible nor totally fanciful. There was in actuality a secret war, but film-makers had to feature it according to the rules of their job; it was not possible for safety reasons to tell the truth entirely, and it was also necessary to consider public taste. *Secret Mission* was the first step towards the building up of another 'representation' of war.

The story-line is very simple. Four British agents are sent to France, where they contact a resistance network. The Germans are easily (too easily) fooled thanks to trite devices (for example, the selling of wine to the occupiers) which will be re-used later in more serious films. The climax of the projection is the destruction of fortifications and military stores, an operation meant to deal a serious blow to the Germans. Historians still dispute whether sabotage was effective during the war,[3] but it is generally admitted that fresh data upon production figures, troop movements and military plans were much more crucial than destruction. Nevertheless, the discovery and transmission of minute data is less rewarding for a viewer than a glaring explosion which illuminates the screen and blows up a good many villains. Therefore resistance films are often conceived to culminate in just such a brilliant, exciting scene which entails some consequences for the narrative. The individual destinies, in particular the love affairs, are of reduced importance; lovers are used to fill in relaxing sequences between moments of suspense, but the spectators are not supposed to care about their problematic future. In fact, it is the preparation of the sabotage which becomes the most important – the actual – subject of the film. During the following decades gangster films would describe extensively the organization of hold-ups. This has often been attributed to the influence of Hollywood's *film noir* but, besides this unquestionable origin, the impact of the resistance films must also be taken into account.

Secret Mission pictures perfect co-operation between the British agents and their French partners: the former detect the proper target and lead the operation while the latter provide the necessary material. The only 'goody' who dies is French, but the British consider him a war-hero. The same goodwill and fair collaboration is featured in the majority of the British films dedicated to the resistance: the Greek partisans second the English officers in their mission, the Polish partisans provide the British prisoners with maps, food and everything they need for an escape, the Belgian and French resistants fight hand in hand with the English who have been parachuted in. The same is not true in the continental productions. Here, resistance is depicted as a private domestic activity, and contacts with the Allies are reduced to wireless messages about weapons supply. A character in *Rome, Open City* (I., d. Roberto Rossellini, 1945) complains: 'Will they ever arrive?' In some cases the resistance seems to develop on its own, the most typical case being probably *The Battle of the Rails* (F., 1945), the main part of which takes place during the battle of Normandy: French railwaymen aim at destroying a German convoy but no reference is made to the importance of the convoy for the Allies; the plot is reduced to a confrontation between the occupiers and the resistants. The film ends with the Liberation which is quickly pictured as if it were a mere consequence of the climactic blowing up of the train and no allusion is made to the arrival of the American or English troops.

All through the third quarter of the century the cinematic images helped to comfort the national pride of the continentals and also to deepen some prejudices. I find it necessary to give an example borrowed from Giovanni De Luna.[4] *Païsan* (I., d. Roberto Rossellini, 1946) develops an ambiguous picture of the Allies: whereas the Americans fraternize with the population and are ready to lend a hand or give clothes, the English are more problematical. In the fourth episode (Florence) they passively watch the still-occupied town from the top of a hill. Thanks to their field-glasses they see what the Italians are constantly telling them: the Germans are about to slaughter the partisans. But the British do not want to move. In the last episode (the Po Valley) the partisans and the American pilots they have rescued hear on the radio Marshal Alexander's message of 13 November 1944 ordering the Italian resistance to stop fighting until the spring. The resistants consider they have been betrayed; in fact, shortly afterwards, the Germans attack and kill them. The origins and aftermath of Alexander's message have been clarified,[5] but the visual power of Rossellini's movie is still strong. In *L'Agnese va a morire* (I., 1976), an excellent, moving film which shows how a shy, illiterate, poor country-woman called Agnes becomes an active resistant, a dramatic sequence pictures partisans, who are trying to join the Allies, intercepted and slaughtered by the Germans. Four British soldiers quietly positioned on an eminence watch the scene with their field-glasses but again keep quiet. As De Luna points out, it is a direct quotation from *Païsan*; the film-maker, who aims at reconstructing the cinematic atmosphere of neorealism, sticks to the clear-cut interpretation of the resistance which prevailed at the time. There is a gap between the cautious discourse of the historians and the simplistic version uttered by the victims, a version that films, begotten by previous films, will nevertheless perpetuate.

That Agnes will die we know from the title of the film, and indeed death is almost always the fate of partisans in movies. The resistance cinema is, as a whole, extremely pessimistic. Not surprisingly, the English cinematographers would rather sacrifice the continentals than the SOE agents. In fact, in movies, the continentals were often the counterparts of the 'faithful natives' in colonial films. But the continental directors are as merciless as the British. In Germany, where the resistance was weak and consisted mostly of individual, uncoordinated actions, a dramatic conclusion seems unavoidable. The only solutions are drawn up simultaneously (1954–5) by *The Jackboot Mutiny* (d. G. W. Pabst) and *The Devil's General* (d. H. Käutner). The resistants who wanted to murder Hitler are sentenced to death while the 'rebel' general commits suicide, and practically all the films end up along the same lines. German resistants on film are squeezed between Nazism which they hate and their country which they do not want to betray; death is their only exit. The case should perhaps be different for the French or Italians who fight for their country against Nazism, and it is true that in the two films made by communist directors[6] there is, after long suffering, a happy ending which is the preamble to the rebuilding of the country. But most movies finish like *Open City*, where the resistance leader dies under torture while the priest who helped him is executed. Even in *The Battle of the Rails* which closes after the Liberation the partisans are savagely slaughtered to the last. Undoubtedly resistance precipitated reprisals and cost many lives, but is that enough to explain why the resistance films are so sad and emphasize the dangers more than the significance of the secret war? I shall come back to this point later but I confess I have no positive answer to provide.

Resistance is a difficult, worrying problem, inasmuch as it raises unpleasant questions about people's collective and individual behaviour. The year the superficial *Secret Mission* was released the Ealing studios produced another resistance film, *Went the Day Well?* A pleasant English village is occupied by German paratroopers. The inhabitants try to alert the outside world and, having been confined by the enemy, organize an effective resistance. The movie is to a large extent a piece of propaganda, but we must never forget that cinema is primarily a means of entertainment. The idea of a sea or air landing is part of a strong collective illusion – or deception – which can be traced back to Childers's *Riddle of the Sands*, and more widely to a long series of invasion novels printed and reprinted since the end of the nineteenth century.[7] The novelty lies not in the worn-out theme but in the manner in which the danger is overcome. Traditionally it is an English gentleman, deeply rooted in the land, who foils the invaders' plans and helps defeat them. But in this movie it is the gentleman, who has been in touch with the Germans for some time, who is the traitor. Tony Aldgate, who has written the best analysis of the film, rightly limits the significance of the change: other social authorities such as the vicar or the lady of the manor take a noticeable part in the resistance.[8] The squire is, in fact, of German origin and fits in perfectly with the ancestral obsession of the invasion novels – the fear of hidden networks of aliens ready slowly to paralyse Britain.[9] The difference between this film and the antecedent stories lies in the fact that everybody in the village feels involved. The cross-class endeavour towards victory is a recurrent, and often trite, theme in British war films[10] but it necessarily entails a hierarchical division of responsibilities – in short, a military hierarchy. But in the self-defending village people decide and act in conformity with the situation they have to face; resistance is unanimous, responsible and effective. During the two decades which follow the war the continent is not at variance with that image of a strongly united country. The few traitors are aliens or outcasts, and the whole population participates or at least backs the partisans. But the distribution of authority and practical tasks is made according to a social (and military) division of ability and knowledge: in *Open City* as well as in *The Battle of the Rails* the leaders are engineers (an interesting insight into the implicit hierarchy of the time: who is the civilian counterpart of a general?), foremen are the NCOs and workers (a printer in the former, a railwayman in the latter) are the soldiers.

Fighting Britain wonders whether she would have resisted if she had been occupied – or rather she takes it for granted she would have done but finds it useful to demonstrate it. In occupied or defeated countries a common preoccupation can be detected: did we passively accept or did we resist? It is of course a moral, political interrogation, and film, as a popular art, has an important part to play in defining the way the problem was raised and solved by the Europeans.

Went the Day Well? is a violent film, at least according to the standards of 1942.[11] One of the cruellest scenes shows a lady attempting to kill a German with an axe and being transfixed by his bayonet. All over Europe the resistance films are among the crudest of the 1950s. *Open City* ends with the resistance leader, engineer Manfredi, having his fingernails pulled out and being burnt with a brazing-lamp. The partisans of *Païsan* are drowned in the Po with their hands and feet tied. The resistance leader in *Les Clandestins* (F., 1946) has his eyes filled with soapy water and put out with a stick. These were pictures made immediately after the Liberation when the memory of the tragedy was still obsessive, but even much later, horrible tortures, which I do not want to evoke, are represented, for instance, in *Odette* (1950) or *Circle of Deception* (1960). In the latter, after lengthy suffering, the SOE agent breaks down and talks. The dramatic fate of resistants and agents – the fact that they had to be trained to kill, to be caught and tortured – is extensively pictured and the consequences are never concealed. For example, the resistant in *A Man Escaped* (F., d. Robert Bresson, 1956) survives because he is ready to eliminate everybody, including his room-mate, and the SOE agent in *Orders to Kill* (1958) becomes a good friend of the man he must slay and suspects he is not a traitor (which in fact he is not) but nevertheless carries out his mission. *The Night of the Shooting Stars* (I., d. Taviani brothers, 1982) culminates in a nightmare-like slaughter: partisans and fascists who are neighbours, friends, sometimes relatives, mercilessly kill each other. The surviving fascists run away, abandoning two of their number, a father and his fifteen-year-old son. The boy falls at the partisans' knees, desperately asking for mercy. One partisan whose pregnant wife has been murdered hesitates, aims at the boy's head and shoots. Let us remember that at the end of *Westfront 1918* a wounded Frenchman seizes the hand of a dying German and whispers: 'Enemies? No, comrades.' Now let us return to Air Chief Marshal Portal's talk of 'ethics'. Notwithstanding the horrors they had gone through, some people still wanted to consider war a 'human' ordeal with so-called 'rules'. In the 1930s there was a lot of popular literature that put forward a harsh and realistic vision of the fighting, but the cinema was unable to cope with the difficulty and when evoking the First World War it limited its description to one camp, one nation, in order to avoid any kind of confrontation. It is this pretence (or hypocrisy) that the resistance cinema broke by showing how women were tortured and children shot.

Common sense tells us that systematic torture and butchery were something tragically real during the war and that resistants had to face more dramatic situations than the rank and file. Yet common sense can be misleading in providing too clear-cut an explanation. There were few resistants or agents: so why did cinematographers highlight their case? Torture was real but the cinema does not represent the whole reality. Important aspects of war were never filmed: hopeless agonies under bombed buildings, dreadful burns and wounds, smashed faces, disembowellings, dislocated limbs. We must recall how circumspect cinema had been previously: when Sanders's successor is killed by the bad natives in *Sanders of the River* (1935) we are spared the depiction of his death, and as soon as Sanders is informed of it he asks 'Has he been tortured?' to let us hear a relieving 'No'. Resistance films widen the visible; they introduce on the screen some aspects of cruelty and sadism[12] which will survive the war (think of *A Clockwork Orange*). In the films on the First World War death was dramatic but quick, decent and sometimes even clean – a final glance onto the world before the big sleep. In the resistance films it is dirty and degrading: 'I am so frightened I have pissed myself like a baby' a partisan of *Païsan* complains while waiting to be drowned: death is slow to arrive and ends painful, seemingly endless, anguish. We cannot account for this shifting of representation. What is involved in the visual part of films, the 'showing', is not as easily analysed as the dialogues or the story-line. Not only is resistance itself a complicated issue but, as has already been said and as will now be developed, its representation on the screen in many ways changed the perceptions of European spectators.

Several movies were adapted from diaries published by ex-resistants. There was nothing exceptional in this, and a character in a novel written by Graham Swift some forty years later humorously summarizes what was current in the late 1940s:

> During the war my Dad was a spy. He used to be dropped into occupied France and liaise with resistance fighters, keep watch on German installations and help to blow them up. He wrote a book about his exploits, in the fifties, and for a few years his name was well-known.[13]

Staging these stories did not cost much; there were few extras involved and the locations were still more or less as they had been during the war. The houses had not been rebuilt and military installations were maintained, with the result that they could be filmed directly. Consequently it is sometimes difficult, nowadays, to distinguish the stock-shots borrowed from newsreels and the shots made for fictions. *Open City* pictures Rome, its cold streets, its files of women queuing for a loaf, its curfew, in a manner which makes this movie a 'true' documentary on the German occupation of the city. 'Authenticity' is always questionable where resistance films are concerned. *Païsan* and *The Battle of the Rails* were made after the Liberation but actual countrymen and railwaymen who had resisted, repeated in front of the camera what they had done previously. Are these films fictional? *Canaris* (1954), one of the first German movies on resistance, cleverly intercuts newsreels with enacted sequences showing the 'secret fight' of Admiral Canaris: are the authentic documents anything but a trick used to tell the viewers that the film is faithful and that its arguable version of Canaris's permanent opposition to Hitler is 'the truth'?

The problem is even more complicated if we take a glance at the cast. There was a general attempt among film-makers, in the late 1940s, to use non-professionals. Italian neorealism has generally been credited with this tendency which existed in other countries and which was especially strong in works dealing with resistance. Various purposes intermingled in such a choice. The participation of resistants playing their own part in the film, as was the case in *Now It Can Be Told* (1946), was good publicity. At the same time, resistance was considered too serious an involvement to be staged by professional actors. Many years after the war the casting of important films like *A Man Escaped* or *The Night of the Shooting Stars* was still mostly non-professional. Since amateurs cannot learn lengthy lines their parts have to be reduced to a few cues and they must follow the director's instructions as closely as possible. Hence the impression of *naïveté* or clumsiness conveyed by *Now It Can Be Told* or *The Battle of the Rails* in which characters seem to try too hard to be convincing. Only strong directors such as Rossellini or Bresson succeeded in restraining this goodwill by adopting a distanced way of filming. Rossellini himself in *Open City* used professionals, since actors understand quicker and eventually cost less than amateurs. But stars inevitably modify the meaning and message of films. When director Alfred Weidenmann decided to screen his version of Admiral Canaris's actions he wanted his main character to be convincing. He selected a well-known actor, Otto Eduard Hasse, a tall, reassuring, serious-looking fifty-year-old. His image having already been created, Hasse *had* to be a good German, *the* 'good' German, the rebel. In other films, he was the general who does not accept Nazism (*08/15 in der Heimat*, 1955) or the doctor who never gives up (*Der Arzt von Stalingrad*, 1957), and when he was not available Curt Jurgens played the same kind of role. Wittingly or unwittingly, voluntary resistance was thus equated with maturity: those who were supposed to have reflected upon and rejected the excesses of Nazism were strong, intelligent, experienced men. It is something which is not implied in the narratives but which appears clearly on the screen. Even from a purely cinematic point of view resistance is a highly problematical topic which wavers between a biased use of real documents and a forging of 'authentic' fakes, between an awkward representation of actual resistants and the building up of a mythical figure for the 'perfect' secret fighter. It is true that the same contrast can be detected in other series of pictures – for instance in films dealing with sport – but resistance, especially in an international context, is much more challenging than football.

People resist when they no longer accept foreign domination. Resistance to Nazism is a historical fact and as a subject appeals to many people, but in the track of Nazism other forms of resistance have emerged: African and Asiatic natives against colonialism, Vietnam, Afghanistan . . . Europeans have been concerned with the two specific cases of Algeria and Eire. The French cinema has almost totally self-censored the Algerian war. Indirect hints can be spotted in a few movies, and there were two courageous, short-lived films featuring the reactions and behaviour of French soldiers entrusted with 'pacifying' the mountain regions. But apart from Algerian films the resistance is only pictured in foreign productions. In a German melo-drama, *Madeleine und der Legionär* (1958), a French teacher, shocked by the brutality of her fellow citizens supports the Algerians, while Pontecorvo's *Battle of Algiers* (I., 1966) is an excellent reconstruction. Made in black and white it attempts to recreate the impression produced by newsreels in the late 1950s; it is staged as if it were a television report of the fight between the resistants trying to terrorize the French population and the French paratroops who track them down. Accurate though it is, the film was not a big hit since it could not seduce the Italians who were not involved in the case, the French who did not accept such a precise depiction or the Algerians who found it too pessimistic with regard to the consequences of their hidden struggle.

There is an amazing contrast to be drawn between the French cinematic treatment of Algeria and the British cinematic treatment of Eire. The same year, 1947, witnessed the release of *I See a Dark Stranger*, in which an Irish patriot is ready to support German plans of sabotage in Britain, and of *Odd Man Out* (d. Carol Reed) which depicts uncomplacently but without hatred the last hours of an IRA fighter. Shortly afterwards, *The Gentle Gunman* (1952) went back to the same topic: the IRA has to choose between hopeless violence or negotiation. The fictional treatment is of course biased: the 'good' IRA fighter who visits London in 1941 is impressed by the courage of the British. At first he is regarded as a traitor but contrary to his brother, girlfriend and best friends he renounces violence, and other IRA men join him. My point is not the final message, but the fact that the IRA is named, described and presented in some of its daily activities.

Even twenty years after Algerian independence a French equivalent to *Ryan's Daughter* (1970) could not be shot in France. It may or may not be possible that David Lean was influenced by resistance films. At any rate, the frankness with which the relationship between the Irish and the British is treated can be compared to situations or images used in previous resistance films. I will focus on two points. The first day, in Ryan's pub, the two English soldiers are depicted visually like occupiers in resistance films. It is probably because the cinematographers aim at describing the point of view of the villagers, but the result is that the English are kept at a distance, repelled to the farthest part of the room. One of the Irish starts speaking of the freedom fighters recently slaughtered in Dublin, and the soldiers, far from remaining silent, frankly confirm the facts. Later, when the 'resistants' go and fetch the weapon-coffers on the beach, the unanimity of the Irish folk is beautifully represented, thanks to a series of pure cinematic devices, a quick editing of shots filled with various contrasting motions. At first the scenery is empty, and all of a sudden the whole village is present. We are shown the faces of people we already know and everybody is frantically involved in picking up the coffers. National unity, typical of resistance films, has been transferred to Ireland. Why did no French film dare present an Algerian village backing the National Front of Liberation? Why did the French not make any film on Algeria built on their actual experience of resistance? The answer lies probably in the fact that a certain time-scale is involved before a topic becomes less painful and also sufficiently unknown to a new generation to excite not only interest but also acceptance. From 1922 through 1947 no English film pictured 'resisting' Irish. Lean's movie[14] was made more than half a century after the events it describes – the time for memory to fade and for the past to become 'historical'. Later, in the 1970s and 1980s, when the 'Troubles' had resurfaced, other films probably more pertinent than Lean's one were made, and we shall revisit the question of 'historicity'. Resistance to a foreign occupier is what concerns us here and the contrast between two attitudes, the English and the French, is striking.

AN ENGLISH MODEL?

I have tried to synthesize some of the complicated problems inherent in the representation of resistance in film. I have surely missed important factors, and further research could be carried out on the same topic. It is certain that resistance modified the common conception of war as inherited from 1914–18, as did the very nature of World War Two itself. Although the British, French, German and Italian experience varied widely, it was a war involving everyone. Every able-bodied man and woman was liable to enlistment in the war effort, and civilians became legitimate targets of attack on a wide scale. But what is it that explains the shared features apparent in films about the secret war? Screened resistance was pessimistic, consensual and widened the horizons of the 'visible' by banalizing the representation of cruelty. It contributed also to deepening the demand for more 'documentarism' in the depiction of events. The main trends which have just been summarized were generally not developed simultaneously in movies; some films emphasized one aspect, while others focused on a different point. There was in fact only one movie which combined pessimism, documentarism, amateur-acting, cruelty and consensualism. In this respect *It Happened Here* made by two newcomers, Kevin Brownlow and Andrew Mollo, deserves a close examination.[15]

In 1960 stock-shots were usually inserted in war movies, and *It Happened Here* begins with what could have been a cinematic

It Happened Here: Film as historical evidence?

summary of recent events, intended for a foreign audience: maps with moving arrows, short sequences on various fights illustrate the successes of Germany while a serious, neutral voice-over explains how Britain was invaded and occupied and how resistance began thus to provoke reprisals from the Nazis and their allies. Later, faked documentaries present a German-ized London. The characters enter a film-theatre where newsreels show the burial of a fascist official filmed in the style of the 1940s. The shots are so good and convincing that if other pieces of evidence were not available future historians could prove beyond doubt that Hitler got hold of the British Isles during the Second World War. In fact, the 'documents' do not demonstrate anything. It is the commentary which explains, clarifies, informs. Here the directors question the technique used in *Canaris* and in some other films. Their 'stock-shots' seem feasible because they have the characteristics (framing, lighting, rhythm) attributed to the films of the mid-century, but clearly realism or even reality do not imply truth: in itself the opening sequence of the film is a wonderful lecture on historical criticism.

Witnesses provide resistance films with another warranty of authenticity. *It Happened Here* goes as far as to follow an anonymous lady, Pauline, instead of a famous resistant, as if she were one out of millions who went through the same tragedy. Another film, *The Sorrow and the Pity* (F., d. Marcel Ophüls, 1969), tried later to represent French collaboration and resistance by means of interviews with unknown individuals. Nevertheless, this film is extremely 'classical' inasmuch as the chronologically ordered events which occurred between 1939 and 1945 constitute a 'plot-line'. The witnesses complement the spoken commentary, creating a secondary, less important theme which is the daily life of a French town, Clermont-Ferrand, during the same period. On the other hand, there is no chronology, no story, no well-defined ending in *It Happened Here*. Some sequences are devoted to Pauline's activities, but what does an anonymous nurse do even during a war? Nothing but survive. She lives first in a village. As partisans threaten the countryside she is transferred to London where she sleeps, works, goes to the pictures, visits friends. She also joins the fascist party, Immediate Action, and is obliged to undergo a special training. Later she is sent to a country hospital, arrested by the fascists, then by the resistants. Some hints are dropped that Britain will eventually be liberated by the Americans but the film avoids one of the tritest climaxes of the time – the explosion of joy and excitation provoked by the Liberation which closes so many stories. We shall never know whether the fictional Pauline survived or how Germany was defeated.

Pauline Murray who took the part of Pauline was not an actress; she did not learn a text and was content with participating in short passages of dialogue. The information conveyed by words is restricted to two fields: propaganda expressed in political talks by fascists (pre-war speeches of Sir Oswald Mosley are astutely introduced in this context) or resistants (hence the recourse to a professional actor – the only one in the film – who explains why some people have not capitulated and resist the Nazis) and also 'historical' references transmitted by the voice-over. Far from being hampered by the absence of words, the film cleverly resorts to the devices of mute (but not silent) movies: faces, expressions, gestures communicate impressions which would not necessarily be accurately transmitted by words. Pauline goes to bed. We see her serious, tired face looking at something – following shot: close-up of her worn-out shoes. It is not hard to infer from this traditional figure that she is upset about her shoes, and that this worry will be of some importance later. When she has joined Immediate Action, another close-up presents her new shoes. Now we cannot decide whether her longing for better clothes had played a part in her joining the collaborators or whether she is happy or ashamed to be so different from the miserable, ill-dressed people she meets in the bus. In the same way, the sound-track is used to convey something which goes far beyond pure factual information. While Pauline spends her last night in the village before being transferred to London, partisans raid the Germans and collaborators. Initially the village is silent – an upsetting, heavy silence generating fear rather than quietude. Then there is the shooting. The pictures, taken in low light, tell little. One shot of a German fired on by the partisans gives the sequence its significance: it is an attack, not a drill. The subsequent shots are almost indecipherable; they are pure motion, surface tumult, and it is the cracking of the rifles which 'echoes' what is happening. The technique is not by any means comparable to Milestone's in *All Quiet on the Western Front*. The latter overwhelms the spectator with shocking bursts of light and sound. *It Happened Here* does not aim to move the public but to create an impression (suddenness, rapidity, difficulty in understanding for those who, like

Pauline, are not involved in the event) without delivering a lecture.

The participation of non-professionals is consistent with the tendency of many resistance films to have ordinary people play some of the parts. However, the directors also aim to challenge previous films. A few references are made to neorealist movies, but the most important quotations are borrowed (rather, 'derived') from Helmut Kautner's *Last Bridge* (1954; the film was made in Austria by a well-known German director, with two German stars as the main characters). The story, which takes place in Yugoslavia, tells how a German female military doctor is kidnapped by partisans who want her to look after their wounded. She is first terror-stricken but after spending some time with them she willingly cares for them, not because she is now anti-Nazi but because they need her. On one occasion when she is short of drugs she obtains them from German supplies. Nurse Pauline is also kidnapped by partisans to tend the wounded. Although she is a member of the fascist party she is moved when she hears that the resistants have no sedatives for their death and she tries to get morphia at the German hospital. Just as the German lady is told by the chief partisan why he and his comrades fight, so Pauline has the aims and ideals of the resistants explained to her by a partisan leader. However, the obvious similarities only tend to create a strong contrast. The part of the German doctor was played by blonde, good-looking Maria Schell, who two years before in *So Little Time* (d. Compton Bennett, 1952) had played the part of an anonymous lady who, after becoming conscious of the Nazi oppression, helped the resistance. She was already associated with a certain part, and by focusing on her, by contrasting her paleness with the darkness and roughness of the partisans and by emphasizing her reactions, *The Last Bridge* shifted towards a psychological description – a description of how a decent person behaves when confronted by wounded enemies. But Pauline is too average a lady to be such a star. We are given no clues about her motivations. Why does she join the fascists? She acts on the spur of the moment after being unwillingly involved in the aftermath of a partisan attempt. Later she revolts when she realizes that the Nazis kill the incurables. She has sensitivity, but no psychological evolution can be traced throughout the film. *The Last Bridge* reduces resistance to an individual problem: once faced with truth people must choose (or sometimes die, which, as has been said, was often the issue in German films). *It Happened Here* says that individuals do not exist as pure, detached, independent wills and that they are never confronted with unquestionable evidence. In other words, taking advantage of one trend of resistance films *It Happened Here* questions another trend, the introduction of stars which, it is argued here, diverts the movies towards the most classical traditions and obliterates the problems raised by the secret war.

There is considerable violence in *The Last Bridge*, but it is entirely perceived through the eyes of Maria Schell who looks, suffers and thinks. However, Pauline does not deliberate; she is equally upset by the partisans' bomb which results in bloodshed as by the liquidation of the incurables, but she sees very little. If the film goes very far towards the description of a reciprocal murdering fury, it does not involve the reaction of individual consciousnesses and merely settles murder as a part of life. The final shot (which does not include Pauline, who has vanished without explanation) is taken in long distance. While English collaborators are fired on in the foreground, lorries and people circulate in the background. A passing American soldier seizes his camera and takes photographs of the execution.

Not surprisingly, *It Happened Here* was not a big hit. In fact, it did not even get a national release and so was hardly given a chance to be judged in the usual commercial way of things. On the one hand, it participated in a new trend of European cinema, discussed later, which attempted to destroy the classical Hollywood narration and which was often considered too abstract and intellectual by the spectators. On the other hand, it expressed a period of history – resistance – which was no longer very popular. Nevertheless, for our inquiry it is an extremely interesting work. First, it synthesizes the various features which had been used separately to picture resistance in previous years. It also raises a question which is expressed implicitly rather than explicitly in other movies: was not resistance first and foremost civil war? The general outburst of violence in resistance films is better understood in a context of domestic conflict, but many movies resist the idea of civil war and, in the tradition of *Went the Day Well?*, with the help of surviving witnesses who were ordinary people, tend to assume that the Second World War was 'a people's war'. By challenging star films, unilinear films, climactic films, *It Happened Here* suggests that an involving narration and an extensive use of personal psychology helped to obliterate a fundamental aspect of resistance. We are not obliged here to decide whether Brownlow and Mollo were closer to the reality of resistance than other directors, since we are not dealing with facts (resistance as it was) but with images, and there is no 'correct' interpretation of images. An analysis of many films made in the late 1940s and in the 1950s detects immediately a perpetual representation of consensus. *It Happened Here* tells another possible version: when a movie shows all classes united against the common enemy, is it not trying to conceal the fact that there were many collaborators? And this is mostly expressed thanks to the particular style of the film. By focusing on a small group of well-delineated characters a classical film such as *Open City* unambiguously indicates the protagonists, that is to say the goodies and the baddies. There is not much room for uncertainty or doubt, whereas the mostly non-narrative technique of *It Happened Here* opens a breach in the seeming unity of resistance.

It Happened Here, which was not appreciated by the public, interested cinematographers and was a prelude to changes in the depiction of resistance. We must not speak of direct influences (which are hard to prove); the film was rather a sign that the Europeans were ready to take another look at the secret war. When Pauline arrives in London the lorry goes slowly through the town, giving us enough time to glance at shocking scenes like the Jewish ghetto enclosed by barbed wire. The link between resistance and the Holocaust, the fact that many people resisted by hiding Jews, had hardly ever been evoked, not only in English films but even on the Continent before 1960.[16] During the following decade, not because of *It Happened Here* but in accordance with it, the Jewish drama was introduced in all the European cinemas. The notion of civil war was also explored by film-makers, and behind the occupiers who were the only adversaries in the 1950s collaborators began to appear, thus destroying the illusion of consensus. Let us reconsider *Ryan's Daughter* which depicts so brilliantly the cohesion of the Irish community: one of the fiercest patriots (Ryan himself) is a traitor, and the unanimity results in the boycott and nearly in the murder of a girl who is different. And *The Sorrow and the Pity*, a pessimistic film in which an echo of *It Happened Here* is easily detected, emphasizes the limitations and weaknesses of the French resistance, a theme which will be further explored in later years.

Britain helped to develop a new vision of the secret war after 1960, and we must not forget that she had inaugurated the series of resistance films long before the Liberation. Twice in the century she determined the fashion in the representation of resistance but she did not take it further or develop it because the producers did not realize that there was throughout Europe a real interest in the theme. So many pages have already been devoted to the policy of the 'circuits' uniquely anxious to get the Hollywood products necessary to feed their theatres[17] that we do not need to expand on the topic. It was suggested, around the middle of the century, that contacts could be made to arrange permanent exchanges between the British and continental film companies, but it is far from clear that the resistance films produced in the different countries were likely to find a positive response among the various national publics. Doubtless there was a general curiosity regarding resistance; there were also local prejudices which could not be easily overcome. After underlining the similarities we must take note of the chronological and idiosyncratic variations throughout the decades which followed the war.

RESISTANCE, FILMS, POLITICS

I have listed some two hundred films in which resistance plays a part. It would be tedious to enumerate them so I have chosen the most important according to their impact or their influence (Table 2). My selection is subjective and arguable; it merely tends to situate the above-mentioned movies in a context and to show that there were successive 'waves' in the depiction of the secret war.

Between 1942 and 1964 there was no significant gap in British production, whereas on the Continent there were alternately periods of intense curiosity and moments of silence, France and Italy following approximately the same lines and Germany standing well apart. France made about twenty

Table 2. Resistance films

UK	France	Germany	Italy
1942			
Secret Mission			
1943			
Went the Day Well?			
1945			
	Le Jugement dernier		*Giorni di gloria*
	Peleton d'exécution		*Open City*
			Due lettere anonime
1946			
Now It Can Be Told	*The Battle of the Rails*		*Païsan*
	Jericho		*The Sun Rises Again*
	Les Clandestins		*Un giorno nella vita*
	Le Père tranquille		
1948			
Against the Wind			
1950			
Odette	*Le Grand Rendez-vous*		
1951			
			Achtung, banditi
1952			
The Gentle Gunman			
So Little Time			
1954			
		The Last Bridge	
		Canaris	
		The Jackboot Mutiny	

Table 2. continued

UK	France	Germany	Italy

1955
The Man who
  Never Was
		The Devil's
		  General
		Der 20. Juli
		Himmel ohne
		  Sterne
		Verrat an
		  Deutschland	

1956
Ill Met by
  Moonlight
	A Man Escaped	08.15 in der
		  Heimat	

1957
Seven Thunders
Count Five and
  Die
		Der Fuchs von
		  Paris	

1958 Orders to Kill Carve Her Name with Pride	La Chatte		

1960
Circle of
  Deception
	Babette s'en
	  va-t-en guerre
		Kirmes
		Soldatsender
		  Calais	

1961			Un giorno da
			  Leoni
			Una vita difficile
			Il tiro al
			  piccione

1962
The Password
  is Courage
			Le quattro
			  giornate di
			  Napoli

1963			Il terrorista

Table 2. continued

UK	France	Germany	Italy
1964 *It Happened Here*			
1966	*Paris brûle-t-il?*		
1968			*I sette fratelli Cervi*
1969	*The Sorrow and the Pity* *L'Armée des ombres*		
1970			*Corbari*
1972		*Studenten aufs Schafott*	
1973	*Lacombe Lucien*		
1974			*C'eravamo tanto amati*
1976			*L'Agnese va a morire*
1977			*1900*
1982		*Die weisse Rose*	*The Night of the Shooting Stars*

fictions or documentaries between 1944 and 1955. Italy started later and produced the same number of films until 1951. Then there was an interruption until 1957 in France and until 1960 in Italy. In Germany everything was made during four years in the middle of the 1950s. The early 1960s witnessed a revival in France and Italy, more concentrated in the latter (1960–3), more diffused in the former. After 1966 isolated movies were released every now and then, Italy being the only country where producers dared invest in the depiction of the secret war. In fact, during the latter decades of the century, resistance was pictured more by television with the intervention of witnesses or the introduction of photographs, newsreels and even fictions made in the 1940s. For the new generations the secret war was an often ill-known aspect of an almost forgotten history, too close to be intriguing and too distant to look familiar. Resistance was the concern mostly of the third quarter of the century.

The first years, 1945–50, were the time of testimonies. The three films which to my mind are the most typical – *Open City*, *The Battle of the Rails* and *Odette* – deal with 'true' stories, or rather stories inspired by actual facts: Don Pietro in *Open City* recalls a Roman parish priest shot by the Germans, the derailment in the French movie has a precise reference in the battle of Normandy and *Odette* is adapted from the memories of a war heroine. The latter two gained praise from the critics, but *Open City* was a terrific hit and remains nowadays the most admirable film ever made on resistance. Basically didactic, the English and French movies aim at illustrating as clearly as possible a succession of related events. There is always someone to explain to the specators what they are seeing; at times it is a voice-over but more frequently it is one of the characters who, seemingly addressing another protagonist, in fact informs us. Both films are mostly narrative and tell distant, vaguely involved, public well-defined, happy-ending stories. *Open City* is much more emotional; instead of telling, it involves the viewers in what is happening and offers them room or space in the narration by using simple, effective tricks. When the characters meet they are not face to face but rather side by side; the background is closed, while the open foreground includes the spectator who is, in addition to the protagonists, the addressee of the discussions. *Open City* is stronger than the others, not because it is more faithful but because it does not have recourse to the tricks used in average films. We inevitably feel frightened when Odette is tracked by a Gestapo agent, arrested and sent to a concentration camp since the plot has been conceived to be exciting. By contrast, there is no suspense in *Open City*; things are pictured simply, with no delays, no startling shadows in the dark, no terrifying noises. The parts of two of the main characters, the priest and the lady, were played by popular actors previously used to acting in light comedies and the device works wonderfully: these familiar, smiling faces are now scared, tired, hopeless. We learn little about the dead of the Italian resistance but we cannot avoid being impressed and touched.

Why did Italy and France stop filming the resistance in the 1950s? Historians often account for this change in political terms. In 1944 everybody was keen on celebrating the secret fighters, but when the Cold War began in 1947 the communists broke with the democratic coalitions which, in their turn, integrated conservatives and even ex-collaborators. Producers no longer spent money on a potentially biased topic. Without ignoring this explanation I am not satisfied with it since the theme exploited for just two years (1945–6) disappeared before the beginning of the Cold War (since a film released in 1946 had been made or at least planned the previous year). The inability to make another *Open City* is not surprising: there were few opportunities to make a movie as involving, as deeply rooted in the atmosphere of the moment, after 1944. No actors could feel again so totally submerged in sorrow, fear and despair as had been the case at a time when half of Italy was still occupied by the Nazis. As for the other resistance films, producers and critics found them too slow, too intent on describing small details, too respectful of the continuity of time. We cannot decide whether spectators would have liked to be offered more products of the same sort; the public is never asked to give its opinion. The fact remains that other rules, other patterns prevailed in the 1950s.

The shift is perceptible in Carol Reed's *Odd Man Out* and *The Man Between*, which are not resistance films but which illustrate aspects of different secret fights in a style more elaborated, less flatly descriptive than the one adopted for *Against the Wind* or *Odette*. But the best example is provided by Bresson's *A Man*

Escaped, which far from trying to revive the forgotten series of resistance films took advantage of a general silence to offer a difficult, challenging work. If *Open City* is the most touching movie ever made on resistance, *A Man Escaped* is the definitive film on the topic, a work which does not depict exciting events but which attempts to express, through pictures, the spirit of resistance. In occupied Europe few things could actually be done because the Germans were too strong, and therefore resistance meant mostly silent hope, persistence, waiting. We know nothing about the main character of Bresson's film, a French lieutenant arrested by the Gestapo. Why has he been sentenced to death? Was he an important leader? Was he involved in some precise action? Instead of answering, the film is content with showing how a man behaves. Right from the beginning we are introduced to another rhythm of time: we are inside a car; three men sit in the back; we see what they see – the driver. The car slows down, stops, starts again. Something should happen but nothing happens. Later, at another stop, one of the men tries to run away. We stay in the car while we vaguely hear a gun, then a shriek. No words – they would be indecent in this universe of death, where people withdraw into themselves and merely attempt to survive. Slowly the film builds up a space of absence which prevents spectators from concentrating on actions and makes them look at the pictures. Bresson's work played its part in the revival of the European cinema which we shall examine later, but it was too demanding to attract large audiences and give resistance its cinematic rebirth.

During the 1950s, while Britain stuck to a traditional vision of the secret war, Germany alone produced linear, classical, exciting stories, brilliantly pictured. It is not by chance that her films were popular on the continent. Unlike their British counterparts the German movies emphasized the characters and their psychological evolution rather than the details of their training and missions, and consciously had recourse to visual devices which introduced touches of fantasy in the narration. Arbitrarily, but in a pleasant manner, camera motions linked separate locations, thus suggesting possible connections; symbolical images cleverly photographed were mixed with historical evocations or fictional sequences to make the story-line quicker and less heavy. The German studios were in a position to fill the gap of the mid-1950s, but their series of resistance films was uniquely a commercial attempt intended to exploit the situation. Defeated Germany was being progressively reintegrated into the concert of western nations in the 1950s, first by entering the European Coal and Steel Community, by experiencing the end of the Allied occupation and finally by becoming a member of NATO. During this period the Germans were anxious to prove they had not been entirely infected by Nazism, and in this respect films celebrating the persistence of a strong individual opposition to Hitler were apt to please domestic opinion as well as those foreigners who did not conceive of a European future without the integration of Germany. The films made in 1954–7 were not blatant propaganda but were merely adapted to the circumstances.[18] Once Germany was rehabilitated the producers abandoned the field.

The return of the theme in the 1960s has often been referred to political events. In Italy the Left summoned up all the resistants at a time when the Christian Democrats contemplated a parliamentary coalition with the neo-fascists. In France resistance was again fashionable when De Gaulle came to power in 1958. Yet far from praising resistance, most of the new films either mocked it by depicting stubborn, harmless, easily fooled occupiers or questioned the significance of the secret war. *Circle of Deception* which opened the decade is an exemplary production which assembles all the features characteristic of the period. It is primarily a psychological study partially based on a moral dilemma. The beginning recalls many previous films with the SOE agent sent on a mission, but later the plot focuses exclusively on the central protagonist who finally gives up and runs away to Morocco. Endless conversations explain the changes in his behaviour. Whereas the films of the 1950s were mostly action, those of the following decade consisted more of talks and discussions. And this leads to the central question raised in nearly all movies: what is a hero? what is a traitor? Is the SOE agent who betrayed, because his commitments programmed him to betray and give the Nazis false information, a coward or a victim? Similar questions are to be found in other well-known, very controversial films such as De Bosio's *Terrorista* (I., 1963) and Malle's *Lacombe Lucien* (F., 1973). In Venice, the heads of the resistance stop the attempts against the Nazis because the Gestapo kills too many hostages. A man who believes that terrorizing the enemy is part of war does not abide by his orders: is he a traitor? In rural France young, illiterate Lacombe Lucien joins the Gestapo because the resistance leader treats him scathingly. Who was wrong? Considered 'scandalous', Malle's film won success which was also a reward for its quality: the atmosphere of 1944 is pictured with great care and enormous attention is devoted to small, typical details. Malle inaugurated what was then called the 'retro fashion', a nostalgic look taken at a remote, almost forgotten period, at a history ignored by the two generations born since 1944.

If I had to choose two resistance films among those produced since the early 1950s I would select *It Happened Here* and *The Sorrow and the Pity*: in fact, two non-films. Both are extremely valuable for their critical interpretation of the secret war, but the former which mixes up all sorts of material is neither a fiction nor a documentary and the latter seems to avoid pictures while concentrating on carelessly shot dialogue. Here lies the decline of filmed resistance. After 1970 the secret war was still evoked, but almost exclusively on television and in a controversial, polemical way which pleased the viewers but which could not be easily introduced in a movie. Yet previously, for twenty-five years, resistance was frequently represented in films and the works made in the four European countries met on the whole with a good response. Everything seemed to be at hand to create a mythical image likely to balance the mythical American West: there were the goodies and the baddies, the past and the future, totalitarianism and democracy, the unity of all the well-intentioned. The differences of approach which were so strong before the war and which account for the contrasts that can be detected between the various national productions, no longer existed after 1944. On the contrary, there was a common conception of filmed resistance, a common way of showing it. What is more, the resistance films contributed to modify the 'vision' of the Europeans by screening views which were previously unthinkable, unacceptable. Despite the diversity of their situations during the war, the four countries succeeded in sharing a common depiction of the secret war, and to a large extent films played a significant part in popularizing the memory of resistance in the Old World. Yet, despite all these characteristics, despite a strong interest among the viewers, resistance did not become the epic of modern Europe.

So why was this? First of all, there were the specific needs of film production which had to renew its narratives and technical devices as often as possible in order to seduce a fluctuating, unstable public. The film-makers who were keen on filming the resistance had to abide by the rules of their producers. Therefore the secret war which was still present in people's minds in 1950 was scarcely represented during the following decade. A purely emotional representation, as given by *Open City*, could not be repeated and the cinematographers had to look for another solution. A few of them tried to require more from the spectators, to force them to see and think. Their films were appreciated but remained far beyond the capacity of the average viewer. The issue was, of course, good narration and the attempt to find a balance between psychological involvement, thrill and fun – exactly what the Germans did around 1955. But at that time the theme was too urgent, too serious to be depicted astutely, in cold blood and with an eye on the box-office. The German attempt, which was no more than an adoption of Hollywood's recipes, came too early. Shortly after, in the late 1960s, a 'talking' (which means, in fact, less expensive) version of the secret war triumphed on television and few financiers wanted to venture their money on a resistance film.

Economic factors explain why film-makers who aimed at illustrating their idea of the resistance were obliged continually to move on instead of deepening their personal conception of the question. How did the spectators react to these changes? Recent research[19] has emphasized the importance of what some historians call 'dominant memory'. Competing constructions of the past are offered to the public by institutions such as political parties, unions, newspapers, film-companies which try to win consent among their fellow citizens. The variety of images prevents any of them from ever being fully accepted, but some are steadier than others – they are 'dominant'. Until the mid-1960s the resistance was part of the social memory inasmuch as it was still understood as a close past, almost a present. Yet, given the fact that there was a constant shifting in the representation of the secret war, no 'dominant' memory could be built up. The different pictures of the resistance were merged among other constructions. Later, in the 1970s, the resistance was already history – that is to say, a past time recognized as such.

Resistance films have a lot to tell us about some images common to all the Europeans after the war but they belong mostly to a limited period in the history of European culture, the 'golden years' of the movies.

3

A GOLDEN AGE

The decade which followed the Second World War was a Golden Age for the film exhibitors. Let us forget for a moment that in Britain film attendance began to decrease as early as 1948. In Europe 1955 saw the peak of cinema admissions: more than 3,000 million tickets were bought, which means that, statistically, every European, including the new-born, went to the movies sixteen times. I must admit that my figures are to a large extent artificial since they combine those of different countries. Contrasts between nations regarding entertainment as a whole, and more specifically film consumption, are important and extremely instructive. But seen from outside – say from Hollywood which at the time was losing a large proportion of its domestic clients[1] – Europe was a wonderful market, ready to swallow an enormous quantity of cinematic productions. As film history is generally organized according to the divisions between languages and national boundaries, little has been said up to now about this extraordinary juncture which Europe went through in the 1950s, and it is hard for us to realize that this passing fancy (it did not last more than fifteen years) was common to the whole continent. Also it is said that the movies made at the time were not exceptionally good. However, we are not concerned here with judging their quality but with understanding the relationship between the Europeans and their cinemas, and as soon as we take a look at the statistics we guess that something unusual happened during these years. This is what I would like to throw some light on in this chapter.

VISITING THE PICTURE-HOUSES

In the 1930s the 'circuits' – the big or small companies which owned the film-theatres – had built in the American fashion luxurious picture-palaces, the famous 'domes of pleasure' in which the patrons were supposed to have dreamt, for a few hours, of a brilliant, exciting life which in fact was not theirs. At the end of the 1940s the cinemas which had not been redecorated for a long time looked a bit dilapidated, they were badly heated in winter, their seats were often defective and their carpets worn out, but the circuits did not bother to restore them since there were long lines of clients waiting outside the doors. The Europeans were so anxious to go to the pictures that new picture-houses appeared even in the smallest towns; in the 1950s an extra 1,000 cinemas opened in France, another 1,000 in Germany and 3,000 in Italy. Researchers have excavated the archives of the local cinemas throughout the continent so that we now have a reasonably good vision of film exhibition in the post-war era.[2] The most striking aspect of these inquiries is the resignation and the persistent goodwill of the spectators who accepted the most incredible, scandalous conditions. We are told of rooms so small that only 100 or 150 people could be admitted, but in which, in contravention of the rules, patrons were allowed to stand at the back if there were no more seats available. To increase the capacity of these 'theatres' a wooden balcony was sometimes hastily erected. The viewers had to climb up and down a narrow staircase, so that at the end of the projection the two waves coming from the ground and from the balcony merged in the entrance and, blocked by people trying to get into the next performance, could not get out. There were of course no sanitary arrangements, no lounges, no fire-escapes. When no theatre was available the local town hall was used to show films a few nights every week. Even in England the security regulations were not always respected as the authorities could not be too strict about closures that might have driven to despair a population which lacked other forms of entertainment. As for the exhibitors, most of them were not rich enough to invest in repairs. The seats were permanently booked, but because all countries attempted to control inflation the prices were kept artificially low and went up much more slowly than the cost of living. In the provinces it was not exceptional for the front seats to be priced at six pence and the back seats at one shilling. This may have been enough for the exhibitors to make a living but it was not enough to cover refurbishment.

What must be borne in mind where this decade is concerned is how strongly the public longed for its movies. In Britain, before the war, despite the 1932 Sunday Entertainment Act, many picture-houses were closed on Sundays or presented only 'harmless' documentary programmes. At the beginning of the hostilities it was suggested that it could be useful to provide a mobilized population with more amusement. The local councils felt obliged to test public opinion about the projection of feature films on Sundays. Generally a large majority opposed the reform. But owing to the presence of servicemen, the wounded and war-workers the authorities had to bypass the rules. By the end of 1944, as the war drew to its end, local churches, backed by some politicians, campaigned for the Sunday closure. Polls were undertaken again and this time up to 70 per cent of voters were in favour of feature films being presented, which proves that cinema-going had become a social habit that people were no longer prepared to forgo for even one day a week.

As the love for movies at that time is unquestionable attempts have been made to explain this sudden, rather short-lived passion, always within the framework of national borderlines. It has often been suggested that the gloomy, cold atmosphere of the war prompted hungry men and women to try and forget their actual condition, be it only for a few hours. There is surely some truth in this assumption, but it is not wholly satisfactory. Why did the British begin to desert the pictures in 1948, that is to say half-way between the end of the war and the moment when their standard of living began to improve in the early 1950s? Economically, 1948 was neither worse nor better than the previous years; the dream could have ceased earlier or continued until 1950. And how is it possible, if we stick to the hypothesis, to account for the fact that it was only in 1956–7, long after the 'boom' had started, that the German and Italian audiences reached their peak? The number of cinema-goers was already increasing throughout Europe in the late 1930s. The war merely accelerated a trend which had existed previously and which survived it; therefore we cannot be content with putting forward the notion that it was the hostilities which provided the motive for cinema attendance.

Much has been written by novelists or writers of memoirs about their cinematic experience of the 1940s. People become lyrical on the subject and tell nice anecdotes about it, but one suspects a measure of complacency in their recollections. Some of these accounts are very moving but they do not provide us with a good starting-point. Luckily enough we have another very different source of information at our disposal. In 1947 an English sociologist, J. P. Mayer, who was worried by the damaging effect of pictures on children and adolescents advertised in a film magazine asking readers to send him what he called their 'motion picture biographies'. The wonder is that more than 400 film-buffs answered. Many of them were factory-workers or housewives who had no scholastic background; some could not even write properly (Mayer was fair enough to avoid correcting their texts) but were keen to explain what films represented in their lives. In itself this burst of enthusiasm is extremely revealing: that so many English men and women thought their relationship with the cinema was worth sweating over a sheet of paper.[3] The book has rightly been criticized. Mayer was biased since he wanted to prove how dangerous horror films were. His questions were naïve, and he was not able to draw any statistical conclusions from his material because it was not based on a rational sample but on a cluster selected at random. Sociology must be founded on precise, verifiable computations, and it is obvious that we would never have noticed the peculiarity of the post-war decade if we had not been provided with reliable figures for the whole of Europe. Yet, for a sociologist, quality is as important as quantity and Mayer adds what is lacking in statistics – the feelings and personal impressions of contemporary viewers. Therefore I suggest a fresh reading of the volume taken less as a series of data than as a sort of collective dream, the dream of the film-fans of the late 1940s.

Most correspondents trace their cinematic life back to their childhood. Families from the surrounding districts used to go to the movies on Saturday afternoons with their children, grandparents, cousins and other relatives. To be in a cinema meant to 'feel at home'. At least four hours were to be spent there from their arrival – as early as possible to reserve the best and most comfortable seats – to the end. After the B movie, trailers and anything else came an interval which was followed by the main feature. This was typically English. On the continent two-film shows no longer existed after the war, but the programmes included (as in Britain) documentaries, newsreels, and various shorts while the feature was divided into 'epochs' (in fact, two different parts) which provided regular breaks in projection, making the show last nearly as long as in Britain. Between the projections the spectators liked to move around, discuss, eat, go to the toilet, get out for a drink: to a large extent the cinema was a place to spend pleasantly one's time off.

If cinema was first experienced with the family it soon became a step towards independence. The 'biographers' told Mayer that at school or even in the factory the youngest children who were still accompanied by their parents could hear their older siblings who had gone to the movies on their own bragging about the 'hard' films they had seen. To visit a cinema with a group of mates was a way of seemingly splitting from father and mother without changing one's life and without entering an unknown world. In fact, the cinema was a place which was approved of by parents. There were thus two different kinds of attendances: the 'gangs' of youths who could go to the movies as often as four times a week, generally in the evening, and the family groups who preferred the afternoons. A highly significant figure is the proportion of adults among the cinema-goers. In the 1960s visiting a cinema would increasingly become an affair for adolescents, with up to 70 per cent of spectators being under twenty-five. In the 1950s 50 per cent of the viewers were over twenty-five.

When Mayer suggested that the public, and especially the young, could be strongly influenced by films and that when they sat 'spellbound in darkness' – as the title of another book puts it – they were in danger, he was not saying anything new, since intellectuals had for a long time considered cinema to be a threat for the 'uneducated'. In the same post-war period two German philosophers, Adorno and Horkheimer, denounced the cultural industries (radio, cinema, press) which produced standardized objects and prevented their clients from criticizing what they were offered.[4] More recently analysts influenced by psychoanalysis have compared film-reception and dream. The spectators are presumed to be motionless, deprived of most of their muscular reactions and therefore ready to accept that what they see is a product of their own fantasy. It would be unfair to reduce the above-mentioned works to one dimension, but it is clear that scholars, who are used to organizing carefully their own cultural activities and to discussing them, cannot understand forms of apparently casual consumption. Mayer's correspondents are not stupid or blind; they admit that they can be influenced by the movies. They even describe the indirect influence of the film-characters on their behaviour and explain why they imitate their favourite heroes. It is true that some young people like to repeat endlessly in their minds those scenes which have struck them, but most of them are easily able to sever the screen dream, and a few viewers are capable of detecting those shots which are faked or have been taken with different backgrounds. The public as a whole was not ready passively to accept deceptive images – even if only because it was just as much interested by the relationships which could develop in the cinema as by the film itself. Speaking of the Italian case, Giovanna Grignaffini makes remarks which apply to the other countries:

> Going to the cinema was predominantly a group habit . . . The cinema was the centre of social life, the place to be seen in public, to meet members of the opposite sex, and where different generations mixed. Even the ritual of actually watching the film deviates surprisingly from the theoretical model of spectatorship. Due both to the arrangement of halls and constant interruptions in the flow of the images as the audience continually moved and changed seats in the rituals of communication that took place during screening, viewing was subject to a series of intrusions and interferences by the real world that made distraction a significant part of the experience of visiting a cinema.[5]

In the 1950s cinema must be regarded first and foremost as an extremely 'popular' form of entertainment. We tend to look suspiciously at the highly ambiguous adjective 'popular', but it is not as misleading as we might fear if we define the sense in which we understand it. Something is popular when it plays a significant part in people's lives, when it is often mentioned and used as a reference. On this point Mayer's correspondents are perfectly clear: chewing over the film at length afterwards was a pre-eminent part of the pleasure cinema provided. In these years, outside the cinemas, there were many reminders of film. There were the posters as well as the stills which anticipated the excitement of the projection and prolonged it after it ended. More importantly there were the papers. Before the war the local press was short on movies, and the specialist magazines expended more space and time on the stars than on the films themselves. In the 1950s the general press could no longer ignore the cinema and reserved an important space for it. Besides the star-magazines, other reviews were launched which discussed productions, and many of Mayer's 'biographers' were keen on cutting out clips or collecting photographs. The importance of this press, more or less comparable to *Sight and Sound*, indicates that analysing and debating had become a habit even for those who were not regular attenders. It is significant for instance that France, which statistically was the country least interested in movies, had the most publications and gave Europe, in 1953, what would soon become the most influential of her film-monthlies, *Cahiers du Cinéma*. Film societies also played a noticeable part in inducing viewers to ask for information and to choose their programmes. An Italian witness of that period, Isidoro Canari, explains quite well what was happening: the novelty with the film societies, he says, was 'the debate in the viewing-room. Discussion had been introduced shortly after the war. The first thing we wanted was to understand perfectly what we had seen and the organizers began to analyze the films with the spectators.'[6] Film societies did not develop as quickly in Britain as on the continent, but the foundation of the National Film Theatre in 1952 was a significant example, and thanks to the British Film Institute the film-buffs could find the necessary material. Cinema had now become a respectable topic, and a collective discourse on film spread all over Europe.

'Popular' also connotes that which concerns the poorest and most numerous. From that point of view cinema was undoubtedly popular. However, country people must be left on one side. Except in Italy where the parish priests and organizations of the Left were competing to gather as many viewers as possible into their respective picture-houses cinema was almost exclusively an urban activity. It is not by chance that in France and Germany where the rural population was still considerable, 40 per cent and 30 per cent respectively of the inhabitants never saw a movie. Yet statistics are not fully reliable, and we must tackle them with care (what is the precise meaning of an expression as vague as 'heavy manufacturer' and where does – an everlasting question – lower-middle class part from middle class?). However, the numerical importance of the working-class audiences in cinemas is unquestionable. Italy apart, 40 per cent of the spectators earned low wages and worked in industrial districts or in suburbs.

It is even possible to distinguish two different attitudes regarding the consumption of films. 'Learned' viewers were selective. They were those who had received a secondary education, but social distinction is also implicit since they were predominantly middle class. Nevertheless, education seems to have been the determining factor. The 'learned' insisted on knowing what they would see and did not go regularly to the movies. They were the best clients of the film-magazines and they liked to display their expertise on cinematic problems. On the other hand, workers were as a whole perfectly regular spectators accustomed to visiting the picture-houses at fixed intervals. Among them it was money, not taste, which made a division; a good third of wage-earners could not even afford a ticket. Money was in fact the dominant factor for the popular audiences who were extremely sensitive to the variations in price. In Britain where the diminution of attendance was permanent after the peak of 1946 a spectacular loss of 20 per cent was observed between 1956 and 1957. This is partially explained if we look at the prices which had not risen above one shilling ten pence, as a mean, until 1956 and then jumped to over two shillings. In France, where the public was less developed but where it remained rather stable after its summit of 1947, a sudden increase in price in 1953 was immediately followed by a loss of attendance. The same happened in Germany, as will be seen later. Only Italy escaped these erratic variations because the exhibitors did not try to regain too suddenly what inflation had cost them. The exceptionally numerous attendances of the early 1950s are closely linked to low prices. The 'popular' spectators who liked their cinemas were not film-buffs. Therefore, after they deserted the cinemas, either because they did not want to pay more or for many other reasons that we shall examine later, they did not come back. Numerically, the crisis of the cinema is a direct effect of the disappearance of its popular public.

What is it possible to discern regarding the preferences of the popular viewers? One of the favourite questions in opinion-polls is 'Do you like [this or that, candy, western or motorbike race]?' Consider this question which can be found in a German poll of 1952: 'Are you expecting from films a reproduction of actual life?' Not surprisingly, as many said 'yes' as 'no', which makes the answers useless. Nevertheless, there are a few hints in opinion polls, which are not negligible. When they were questioned about their preference for genres the 'learned' were keen on giving an elaborate list, whereas the workers gave all genres the same value. Is it not because the latter were not bothered much about the programmes? Let us remember that the cinemas located in industrial areas were among the meanest, that there was generally only one picture-house in European factory-towns and that individual means of transport were rare at the time. It was a question of 'take it or leave it'; in the absence of any other sort of entertainment people had to accept what they were offered. In this period the film prints had a long life. In Germany, in 1951, 174 out the 609 films in distribution had been made before 1944, and the case was not exceptional. Needless to say, these copies had been broken many times and hastily repaired, which implied the suppression of numerous shots. The worn-out prints went to the poorest cinemas, and the spectators did not object since they had no idea of other conditions. Choosing was the privilege of those who could reach the town centres where there were numerous cinemas. The popular cinema was something strange and it is not surprising that it faded so quickly in the 1960s.

We have first emphasized the features common to the various European publics and we must now take a look at their specific characteristics. Statistics provide preliminary informa-tion: at its peak film-attendance reached 1,600 million seats in Britain (1946), 800 million in Italy (1955) and Germany (1956) and 400 million in France (1947). Beside the numerical differences a noticeable point is the rapidity with which the national publics became fond of films and then deserted the cinemas. The evolution was extremely slow in Britain and

France. There the ascending trend began well before the war and the declining one was very prolonged. It took Britain twelve years to fall to half of its peak (which was still much higher than the Italian or German maximum) and, as we have seen, the decrease was aggravated by the rise in prices. In France the same evolution took place over more than thirty years. On the other hand, German and Italian attendances developed quickly in less than ten years after the war. The German cinemas were then deserted within eight years, while Italy followed, but ten years later, the slow pace of Britain and France.

The British were precociously film-minded; going to the pictures was for them a cultural habit which developed considerably when during the war people were moved around to strange places so that the cinema made an unfamiliar place feel more familiar. However, the number of cinema sites did not change as attendance grew, which means that the profits of the exhibitors were probably considerable. The word 'crisis' was uttered very soon at a time when, in fact, the theatres were not yet abandoned. The reaction of the cinema owners was severe. It must be recalled that exhibition was almost the monopoly of just two circuits, Rank and Associated British Pictures Corporation (ABPC). The dispersed independents could not survive unless they accepted the conditions of the big circuits. Rank and ABPC, which had lost a great deal of money in trying to produce expensive films, decided on savage cuts in exhibition; from 1950 through 1960 nearly 2,000 picture-houses were closed, and no cinemas were opened in the new towns or big housing estates built throughout the 1950s. Television has often been blamed with deterring its viewers from going to the pictures. Nevertheless, in Britain, during the first five years of television (1947–51) the number of licences increased only slowly while the number of spectators decreased by 3.5 per cent per year. Then, between 1951 and 1953, the number of licences jumped to two million,[7] while the diminution in attendance reduced to 2 per cent per year. The television challenge had only a lateral, secondary effect. It was an accident, the American embargo to which we shall return later, which struck the first blow; at the same time, from 1947 onwards, workers and clerks began to move towards the new urban districts where opportunities for jobs were better. The

300 million spectators lost in the late 1940s were never regained, and the policy of the circuits worsened the situation. When television became 'adult' the decline of the cinema was already well advanced.[8]

Television had no automatic effect; in some cases it strongly influenced frequency of attendance but in others it was harmless. Germany illustrates the first point.[9] There, regular daily television services began in 1952 but, as had happened in Britain, the Germans were at first reluctant to buy expensive TV sets. The success came between 1957 and 1960, a period during which 3 million sets were sold. Throughout the same period admissions diminished by 200 million, that it to say, one fourth of the peak of 1956. However, the competition with a domestic form of entertainment does not fully account for the decline of the movies and we must also consider the cultural context of the Federal Republic. The defeated Germans were not film fanatics in 1946; they were not disposed to spend their money sitting in cold theatres where the features, mostly foreign, were accompanied by moralizing American documentaries on the 'reconstruction' of their morality. The American distribution companies which wanted to conquer the market granted exceptionally good contracts to the exhibitors who built new cinemas and set low prices so that Germany was the only country where the tickets cost less in 1950–1 than in 1946–7. Attendance boomed within a few years, and the exhibitors took advantage of it; within five years they had raised their prices by 33 per cent. The mid-1950s saw the massive introduction onto the market of cars, domestic equipment and radio and television sets. Many Germans who were not as film-addicted as the British easily renounced the more expensive entertainment. But France,[10] which can be compared to Germany, contradicts the supposed importance of television. There it was only in 1960 that the number of TV sets exceeded 1 million (at that time there were more than 10 million sets in Britain) and cinemas were already losing slowly but regularly 4 per cent of their clients every season. Film attendance being less developed in France than in the other countries, the decline was not spectacular but, as in Germany, it was directly linked to the availability of rather expensive individual goods. On the other hand, Italy[11] was still relatively poor in the 1950s and cinema was the only luxury many people could afford. There were many more cinema sites in the peninsula than in any other part of the Old World: in 1956 Italy had 10,000 picture-houses while Britain in her peak year, 1946, had fewer than 5,000. The Italian cinema became a battlefield between the communists who attempted to promote Russian films and the Christian Democrats backed by the Church who replied with American productions and edifying, 'harmless' movies. The Italians were constantly prompted to see more films at cheap prices, which explains why audiences were still considerable in 1960, not much below the maximum of 1955.

To a large extent cinema was *the* popular art in Europe after the war. The general interest in movies is impressive. In 1945 cinema, which was only fifty years old, still looked young; it was more alive, more immediate than radio and it provided people with more direct information. All the Europeans participated in an enthusiasm for an art-form which conveyed an idea of modernism, of permanent motion and excitement. Later, other forms of consumption would excite the same curiosity, but films were the first to point to a common need for a new style of leisure. In this respect we may speak of the creation of some sort of cultural uniformity. Nevertheless, the European countries were extremely different and their strong national traditions determined the behaviour of their respective publics. Beyond their striking similarities we can observe different, often contradictory responses. However, there was another factor of unity: the beloved/hated American cinema.

HOLLYWOOD, BUSINESS AND MYTHOLOGY

It is difficult nowadays to imagine how strongly people felt in relation to Hollywood, but their violent feelings are understandable. On the one hand, ruined European countries were not disposed to waste their precious dollars buying American pictures but, on the other hand, given the weakness of domestic production, it was impossible to do without the world's biggest dream factory. The Americans were well aware of a situation that they intended to exploit. The powerful Motion Picture Export Agency (MPEA), forcefully supported by Washington, was active, and its arrogant deputies did not hesitate to introduce themselves as official representatives of the US government. In London it was reported that they called themselves 'the little State Department'.

Before the war the Europeans had attempted to limit the invasion of their screens by establishing 'quotas' – that is to say, a maximum of American films to be permitted annually in the picture-houses. In 1945 the situation was extremely complicated. Distributors and exhibitors badly needed the American movies since there was no other way for them to fill their programmes. Rank and ABPC, which controlled some 1,500 cinemas, could not survive without Hollywood, and even though the circuits were smaller on the continent the problem was the same. But the domestic film-makers who worked in difficult conditions were not in a position to compete with the already paid-for, and therefore cheap, American films. On both sides, businessmen lobbied in public offices, ministries, parliaments and in the papers. The conflict was worsened by the equation 'Hollywood = United States'. This could be translated as 'Hollywood = Liberty' or 'Hollywood = Imperialism'. Everywhere there were harsh debates and even street demonstrations. For the first time cinema became a political issue – which is, after all, another form of 'popularity'.

Germany could not hope for very much from an occupier with no interest in limitation. Until 1960 more than 40 per cent of the films distributed in the FRG were American. Despite this competition domestic production restarted in 1947. There were too many film companies which were often unable to finish their movies, but with the help of the government the steadiest ones could survive. Between 1951 and 1960 Germany made a hundred films annually – in other words, one fifth of the average distribution and one half of the American importations. France was not an important market, and the American government signed in 1948 an agreement which granted the domestic companies a yearly minimum of two fifths of the schedule. During the following decade the production figures were more or less the same as in Germany: 120 films every year and an importation of 200 American pictures. In Italy the Christian Democratic government did not want to oppose Washington in any way and allowed the exhibitors to infringe the very reasonable quota (one sixth of the schedule for the Italian films) established in 1947. Yet at the same time substantial help was granted to the national studios which worked quickly and effectively: the 200 movies made in 1960 (an exceptional year) equalled the number of American importations.

The British case deserves more attention. The United Kingdom was considered central by the MPEA which, rightly or not, saw it as a model of what would happen subsequently in the other countries. As it seemed impossible to come to terms with Washington, the Labour government decided unilaterally, in 1947, to put a 75 per cent tax on the value of the imported films. Had it succeeded, the number of American films would have been noticeably reduced and the duty produced would have subsidized the manufacture of national movies. But the MPEA replied with an embargo on its exports. The exhibitors, now unable to fill their schedules, asked for mercy and Britain capitulated. We have already noted that the immediate result of the crisis was a fall in admissions, resulting in the closure of many cinemas. The only thing the government could do was to prevent the American firms from re-exporting their takings. The money was reinvested in the British studios so that by 1956 one third of British films had American backing and were American products with an English label. Despite this financing and despite the distribution of public funds to the film companies, production fell to seventy films a year. The American movies filled more than half of the programmes, while the British ones could not reach a third of the distribution.

By 1955 the situation on the continent was not very different from what it had been twenty years before; 30 or 40 per cent of the films offered to the public came from Hollywood. But the ideological contexts of the two periods cannot be compared. After the war the Hollywood products carried stronger implications than ever and were a constant source of scandal and discord. Interestingly enough, the opposition to them was not merely political, although politics were strongly involved in the debate. Even the 'Atlanticists', those who thought that the Pentagon was the shield of the free world, complained about the damage caused to the best European traditions by American modernism, while those who feared US imperialism nevertheless admired the youthful vitality and technical quality of American films. Let us take a look at two magazines, the French *Paris-Match* and the Italian *Hollywood*. *Paris-Match*, the most popular French weekly, staunchly backed American foreign policy but seldom alluded to Hollywood productions, while overpraising all that was made in the French studios. *Hollywood*, whose title seems to guarantee total allegiance to California, was filled with details on the lives of American stars, while criticizing the shortcomings of the American films which it judged inferior to the first-class Italian productions.[12] Hollywood was mocked for its puritanism and for the narrow-mindedness of the Hayes Code. A film like *The Girl Rose-Marie* (G., 1958) in which the sex-appeal of a fast woman is willingly used as a basic element of the plot was obviously something America would not accept. At the same time the puritanism of Europe could not cope with the so-called immorality of Hollywood. Everywhere in Europe the Catholic priests prompted their 'flocks' to avoid seeing *Joan of Arc* starring the divorced Ingrid Bergman. In various directions Hollywood was a challenge to Europe's moral values.

There was also an aesthetic side to the question. The communists and socialists who despised the representation of a society where money and success were synonymous could not help admiring the style of many American films and the capacity of the Americans to tackle problematic, difficult issues. They celebrated *The Grapes of Wrath* and were happy to note that *On the Waterfront* was a top hit in Europe, especially in conservative Germany. At least Hollywood was able to show the police backing the bosses against the workers or the unemployed. Among the conservatives the vision of an affluent society was appreciated but the lack of respect for the Establishment was felt to be unpleasant; American movies were taxed with vulgarity, unhealthiness and elementary Darwinism. What is more, the big hits such as the movies mentioned above were not typical US productions and had not met with real success in America.

What did European audiences admire most? The 'realism' of American films was often spoken of but, apart from the fact that the word 'realism' is a minefield and cannot be defined adequately, it is impossible to say in what way the American productions were more realistic than the European ones. In these years an Italian director, Pietro Germi, attempted to adapt American recipes to an Italian context. His style was neorealistic but his themes and plots were borrowed from America. He made a Sicilian western, *In the Name of the Law*

(1947), and transcribed *The Grapes of Wrath* into *The Way to Hope* (1950). What differentiates his movies from contemporary Italian films is clear; there is more violence on the screen, the competition is harsher and the class-conflicts are described more crudely. The same elements exist and are powerfully exposed in other films, but they are never visually developed to the same extent. For instance, in *The Earth Quakes* (1948) the fishermen attack the bosses who exploit them, but while they are fighting the camera takes us to the police headquarters so that we do not see or hear the struggle. The policemen intervene and stop the scuffle. On the other hand, in *The Way to Hope* when the strikers assault those who still want to work their harsh battle is filmed extensively and it takes the police a long time to separate them. The European cinema was in many ways freer than its American counterpart; it was allowed to go deeper into problems but it was too accustomed to understatement. It was unable to represent things which were considered crude or filthy. Compare *Boys in Brown* (1949) which deals with a Borstal institution in Britain and *Blackboard Jungle* (1955) whose action takes place in a difficult college in downtown New York. If you merely look at the plot you can say that the latter, with the good-looking, good-intentioned Glenn Ford mastering a gang of tough guys is more 'unrealistic' than the former in which Richard Attenborough has to suffer punishment for petty theft and is finally sent to the detention block. But, visually, everything is stilted and artificial in the English movie; the boys look like inoffensive Boy Scouts, whereas a true sense of revolt and excess overwhelms the screen when the New York guys mock, blackmail and even physically attack their masters. From a purely cinematic point of view Europe had much to learn from Hollywood, and the audiences were sensitive to the difference.

Hollywood was such a controversial topic that even nowadays it is difficult to tell what influence the Americans had in Europe. The question seems a very simple one: who saw the Hollywood productions and liked them? However, we have no positive answer to the question. We know how many films were in distribution, but distribution and exhibition are not the same thing. Roughly speaking, there were more American films available on the market but they were less successful than their European rivals. An interesting hint is provided by the division of the takings: everywhere the financial rewards from the domestic movies were higher than their share in the distribution or, to put it another way, while two spectators were looking at two US movies, two others were seeing one national film. Nevertheless, this information is insufficient, since the prices varied depending on the cinema and the town. Generally one fifth of the newly released films received four fifths of the total takings, the last fifth being divided between the old prints and the short-lived new releases. We would like to have precise figures regarding admissions to the different films, but in those days nobody was interested in gathering that sort of information since the only 'worthwhile' films were the big hits. I am not suggesting that we have no information, I am merely saying that our knowledge is partial. Our best source is the list of the ten top money-makers which is available for the four countries, but it only shows us the preference of those who could choose, not what the public as a whole actually saw.

Hollywood sold Europe films covering five fields: war, western, detective stories, comedies and 'blockbusters'. The Europeans did not like the war films much, and there were only two successes, *From Here to Eternity* (1953) which was appreciated for its critical view of the army and *The Bridge on the River Kwai* (1957) which won a prodigious response (top money-maker in Britain and France, second in Italy where it came immediately after *The Ten Commandments* and in Germany); despite the latter's partially American financing it cannot be labelled other than typically British. There was a limited, steady public for westerns and many film-buffs did not disdain seeing a detective story occasionally. Nevertheless, no film was pre-eminent in these series; it was the 'genre' which was of interest rather than any precise work. About a half of the movies sent by Hollywood belonged to these first three categories, which were neither really appreciated nor totally ignored, so that while some films made money others were flops. Comedies were another case on which we shall expand later. The only American films which were always unquestionably successful were the 'colossals', the prestige spectaculars with a huge budget, a thousand extras and a supposedly 'historical' background. C. B. de Mille's *Ten Commandments* is probably the best example but others such as *The Robe*, *Quo vadis?* and *Samson and Delilah* won the same praise. The critics

97

may have been savage, incisive, sharp and stinging about these movies but their opinions were of no avail. The public knew what to expect and took no account of the contemptuous opinion of the learned. Hollywood had found a pattern which was recurrent in all these productions until the end of the 1950s. Primarily there was a batch of stars. But there were no characters in the ordinary sense of the word, that is to say, no protagonists whose psychology would evolve with the progression of the narrative. The stars were introduced in the initial sequences and provided with a few, simple features they would never lose during the projection. The luxury of the sets was also emphasized at the beginning and was displayed as scenery, as artificial, expensive and surprising. Realism was not sought; on the contrary the film had to be understood to be an artefact exclusively made for the pleasure and delight of the spectators. The structure of the story was carefully calculated. Every ten minutes or so an event (battle, race, chase, celebration) would happen and last two or three minutes so that the movie would be a regular succession of short moments of sheer excitement and intervals filled with a rather elementary plot. These films have to be understood as total spectacles combining movement, music, colour, noise, amazing settings and large crowds, or else as brilliant exhibitions aimed at people who never had a chance to visit a theatre or circus. To a large extent they were a prelude, an introduction to the big live-shows of the 1960s. The blockbusters represent the most conspicuous aspect of American influence. They were not by any means the only Hollywood productions but they made much more money than the others and pleased the 'popular' public. Unsurprisingly, they did not survive the decline of the large audiences in the 1960s. They were unmistakably 'made in Hollywood', although a few Europeans attempted to imitate them; Rank lost a great deal of money with *Caesar and Cleopatra* (1945) and the other films at best only covered their costs. Given the huge investments which were necessary only America with its double – domestic and foreign – market could find the capital. The unexpected triumph of *The Bridge on the River Kwai* signalled the end of the 'colossals'. The film was expensive but no hint was dropped about its cost; it looked simple and dealt mostly with an individual case, a purely psychological affair.

EUROPE, TRADITIONS AND DIVISIONS

The Bridge on the River Kwai was also important because it was a European film which caught on everywhere in the Old World and revealed the efforts made by Europeans to get rid of American influence. Chapter 5 will enlarge upon these attempts which were merely in their initial stages before 1960. However, during the 'Golden Age', Europe was not uniquely fascinated by Hollywood and she even tried to compete with American cinema. Imitation was a fundamental issue which can only be traced in thrillers. Detective stories had widely developed in the 1930s with a dominant pattern akin to the tradition of Conan Doyle: an enigma exposed at the outset will be solved at the end. After the war, American gangster movies or *films noirs* were presented in the cinemas and it is not hard to detect their influence. Take *The Blue Lamp* (1950) and the French *Jenny Lamour* (1947). Both deal with national institutions, a police station in the former, a police inspector in the latter. They provide a familiar, 'popular' depiction of policemen and take advantage of the situation to raid the inside of Scotland Yard or its French equivalent, Quai des Orfèvres. However, there is something new in the cinematic treatment of the two stories. We are offered no riddle and the police do not conduct a real inquiry. Small incidents perpetually break in on the plot, thus focusing the viewer's attention on the protagonists rather than on their job. They are good policemen, of course, but, like their American counterparts, they have their problems; they are human beings. The relationship between the two English cops is peculiar, half sentimental, and the French inspector is upset by his son's difficulties, but the social background of big-city policing is not forgotten; *The Blue Lamp* concentrates on the young thugs, petty criminals or dangerous murderers, who terrorize the town, and *Jenny Lamour* introduces car-breakers or petty criminals. A seemingly documentary style helps, thanks to grey, flat lighting, to suggest visually a gloomy, dull atmosphere. The conclusion may be naïve or over-optimistic (the truth revealed by chance in the French film, the petty criminals uniting with the police to catch a murderer in the English one), but the daily activities of the policemen are described in a sceptical, critical way which recalls many Hollywood productions.

Rather than competing with the USA Europe preferred to stick to old, well-established recipes. Germany went back to the fashion of the 1930s, with the *Heimatfilm*. Literally *Heimat* means 'country', but there is much more than this basic significance in the German word, which conveys the idea of a place where one feels fine and at home. The *Heimat* literature began in the second half of the nineteenth century and then gave rise to a long series of movies which was extensively developed under Nazism.[13] All through the 1950s the *Heimatfilms* got a good response in big towns as well as in small villages and remained in distribution for a great many years. Nature, or more precisely high mountains, are central to the *Heimatfilm*. It is the setting which determines the characters (forest-rangers, guides, outlaws), action, drama. Mountains, which signify stillness, permanence and faith, get involved in a direct, simple conflict between past and present, maturity and youth, country and town, but this opposition does not work up to a climax, and the forces of evil disappear almost unnoticed since the only thing which really matters is the landscape and its beauty. *Heimatfilms* should be labelled 'documentaries' were it not for their length, their absence of didacticism and the perfection of their music, which fits in perfectly with the quality of the pictures – all elements which make the best of these movies poetical variations on an unspoilt, soothing wilderness. The generation of the 1960s reacted violently against the *Heimatfilms*, taxing them with crass conservatism and obliteration of the most blatant social conflicts; this criticism was relevant in a Germany that was becoming increasingly industrial. Yet, despite the poverty of their plots and the weakness of their protagonists, these movies succeeded in maintaining a vanishing tradition of popular, well-made and artistically shot films. They were the domestic equivalent of the American spectacular and they pleased the spectators because they offered them (together with complete oblivion to the problems of the day) excellent, highly entertaining shows. The Italian counterpart of the *Heimatfilm* was melodrama. Melodrama – understood as a family story with mysteries, hidden births, substitution of children and so on – is deeply rooted in Italian literature. During the first half of the century it was revived by the cinema, which endlessly restaged *The Two Orphans* and other similar stories. The point is that if family dramas remained much appreciated in the 1950s the film-makers were clever enough to make their characters shift from an ill-defined nineteenth century to the contemporary world.[14] The protagonists were now garage-managers, farmers, mine-owners and doctors, involved in incredible, sentimental relationships with their girlfriends and wives but trying at the same time to find the money to improve their business. The spectators could weep about sad stories but at the same time could appreciate a social progression which was their dream but which was still far from their reach. So while urban Germany was pining for her wild, empty mountains, rural Italy was contemplating her domestic comforts to come.

Britain was loyal to comedies, which still filled the main part of the programmes. During the decade 1951–60 five out of the top money-makers were comedies, three of which belonged to Ralph Thomas's *Doctor* series, starring Dirk Bogarde, and one to the everlasting *Carry on . . .* series. The plots which merely dealt with private affairs were humorous, harmless, sometimes nostalgic and always deprived of authentic social background. In this respect something unprecedented occurred when Michael Balcon's Ealing studios began to release comedies. Charles Barr and John Ellis have explained extremely well what happened then. To quote the latter:

> Ealing Studio's post-war productions were innovatory within realist cinema. The films were recognised as fresh and new, and yet at the same time were easily watched and enjoyed by the mass audience. This is because their innovations preserved many of the fundamental methods of classic cinema (preserved them as part of the unconscious practice of the film-makers): they shifted the terrain of, but did not alter, the basic aim of realism, that of showing the world as it 'naturally' appears to be.[15]

While fully accepting this analysis, I find it possible to re-view Ealing in the light of Hollywood and the European cinemas. A comparison between four contemporary films, *Jour de fête* (F., 1949), *The Man in the White Suit* (1951), *The Return of Don Camillo* (I., 1952) and *08/15* (G., 1954), will provide us with the necessary material for a re-examination of the comedies of the 1950s. Why shall I emphasize the comedy? Because it is the only 'genre' which was equally popular in all four countries but also because Hollywood's productions combined an exceptional capacity for laughter with a sharpness, a sense of satire and social criticism which were often missing in the Old World. A few directors were able to learn something from the American experience, and this is what I would like to illustrate.

The German and French films are the only ones which openly refer to Hollywood. In 1954 *From Here to Eternity* was the second most successful film in Germany (it was also the American movie that made most money throughout the decade). In 1955 *08/15* captured first place. The structural similarities between the two films are striking: a good fellow is confronted with an evil, sadistic NCO. The hero is strong enough to resist the villain who rounds on a weak, inadequate guy whom he tortures until he dies or (nearly) commits suicide. The goody wreaks vengeance on the baddy. There is no question of imitation since the German film is adapted from a previous novel,[16] but there is a strong closeness of spirit. *08/15* is the first violent, straight attack against German militarism with its stupidity and its cruelty. The almost unbearable scenes of humiliation, notably the passage in which exhausted men are obliged to creep in mud, were inspired by the American movie. The arbitrariness and uselessness of the rough jokes are clear; the NCO does not attempt to train his men but merely wants to compel obedience from them, thus destroying their goodwill and personal talent. Today this sounds commonplace, but at the time only Hollywood could criticize military institutions and it was in its wake that a European production dared to follow. The French film is not so tense. In a small township the inhabitants get ready for the village fair which gives the film-makers a pretext to explore the streets, visit the pub, linger on the talking and chattering. The American mythology is present thanks to a few GIs and thanks to the movies. US documentaries are projected; spectators are told that American methods work wonders. Nevertheless, apart from postman François who would like to adopt American rationalization, nobody believes that it is possible to compete with the giant: France admires American dynamism but submits to her own backwardness.

The other films do not refer directly to US productions. The *Don Camillo* series is generally considered rather stupid since it stages the artificial conflict between a parish priest and a communist mayor who seem to hate each other but are in fact very good friends; an imaginary opposition is created to suggest that in Italy the political struggle, which was in fact extremely harsh, was less important than local relationships. Besides this trite story *The Return*, second in the series, deals with a serious and even dramatic problem, the impending threat of the Po. The river runs fast over the flat country and when there is too much water at the end of the winter it overflows. The priest and the mayor are aware of the danger. The latter would like to have a dam built, but general incompetence and a tendency to postpone any decision prevent anybody making a decision. The expected happens; the village is flooded. The county is unable to give assistance to the inhabitants who are obliged to flee on foot to camp under canvas. So, at the beginning of the 'economic miracle' this film depicts an antiquated, isolated, poor portion of land. It is not an Italy for tourists but a country which survives in water and mist, which depends on the elements and which does not care about progress. In contrast with the modernity portrayed in American movies Italy is, according to this movie, still deeply rooted in her past.

The English story takes place in a textile centre near Manchester. The domestic industry looks as inadequate and behind the times as the Italian village. The equipment is old-fashioned and dirty, the goods are still conveyed by hand-drawn carts, there is no real research laboratory and genial inventor Sidney can order all he wants without anybody noticing how much he spends with no immediate results. Charles Barr, who compares the film with contemporary American movies centring on inventions, concludes that 'the stagnation soon reasserts itself' and that 'what stands out most sharply' is a 'built-in code of amateurism'. Bosses, unionists and workers of all sorts agree on a common programme: 'nothing has to be changed'. Houses are cold, streets gloomy and dark, but that is better than any novelty. Since we are shown industrial surroundings the contrast with American dynamism is sharper than in *Don Camillo*: there is no possibility of resisting American competition.

From a purely thematic point of view the four films illustrate the heaviness of history without taking any pride in it. Other films like *The Maggie* (1950) or some Italian comedies try to suggest, after all, that the European is much more clever than the naïve, stubborn American, but this indirect humour has no room in the movies we are discussing which describe an existing state of affairs. *Jour de fête* indulges in evoking a happy, peaceful community. The others are sharper and say that something is wrong; people suffer because they are not allowed to move or because they are pressured into staying where they are. The criticism arises from a comparison with the USA or has been triggered by American examples. However, the films do not stick to Hollywood's lessons, and it is their stylistic interpretation of the American models which is noteworthy.

The German and the French films are again closely related in their use of the most classical Hollywood gags. The bad NCO of *08/15* is a giant who persecutes a slim guy. A couple typical of American comedy perform what people like to see; the small one tries to hide while the bully outsmarts him. But here the conflict is tragic since there is no hope for the weakest who is regularly defeated. An excellent joke is turned into a nightmare. In the same way a long sequence shows a group of NCOs taking off their trousers, but far from making spectators cry with laughter the scene makes them feel as uneasy as reluctant peeping-Toms. All the elements, be they the gestures, the clumsiness of the protagonists or the musical background, are borrowed from slapstick's repertoire, but the fact that there is no possible reversal, that nothing will turn what is staged into a farce, prevents the spectator from relaxing. *Jour de fête* is not as astute (or perverse). Here the film-makers use the American recipes without attempting to modify their meaning and even follow the trick which consists in accumulating the jokes. When François decides he will deliver the mail 'American style' there is a surprise every second, but the letter put into a hat or under the tail of a horse, the bell which lifts up the bell-ringer, the rope handed round, the bicycle that runs by itself, have been around for ages. The actor who plays the part of François (the director himself, Jacques Tati) looks like some of the best American actors, Harold Lloyd or rather Buster Keaton whose earnestness and seeming inadequacy he shares. Imitation creates a strong contrast here; the signs are American but the background is French, and the spectators start laughing because the gags are inefficient in this context. There are few letters and people do not care about them. An American postman should hand out a big quantity of letters and his ability to do it as quickly as possible would be funny; on the contrary, François is wasting his time and efforts but it is the constant reference to Hollywood which is absurd and therefore enjoyable.

The American quotations in *The Man in the White Suit* are more subtle. The various phases of Sidney's research which ends up with the creation of a fibre that will not wear out are filmed in medium shot with long dialogue in the English literary fashion. These rather 'theatrical' moments are intercut with short American-like inserts which quit the main story-line to develop a more critical side of the film. Let us look at a few examples. Once the mill-owners have decided to suppress a dangerous invention which threatens their factories they get hold of Sidney and take him to a house belonging to one of their number. We are then offered a quick shot (ellipsis of time between the factory and the house) with a dull, depressing housing estate as the background and wonderful, luxurious cars which come past in the foreground. A trite cliché of the American cinema which, this time, does not for once contrast the rich with the poor but, on the contrary, advertises their alliance since they unite against Sidney's formula. In another passage we can observe a file of black cars with dubious, menacing men inside them. A gang of Chicago killers heading for some murderous expedition? Not in the least, merely the executives hurrying to a meeting – but after all what is the difference between them and a criminal gang? In comedies the most pleasurable scenes are chases and there are many in *The Man in the White Suit*. It would be easy to edit them together in order to demonstrate their kinship to Hollywood, but I shall be content with taking the last occurrence. Sidney has run away; we are inside the house where he was trapped and we have a Hitchcock-like picture with the dark, disquieting staircase of a haunted abode and a couple in the twilight (remember Dr Edwards's house in Hitchcock's *Spellbound*, USA, 1947). The gangsters (sorry, the union men and bosses) jump into their cars and start. Sidney in his white suit is Superman or the saviour angel of the serials, but he is also ridiculous since everybody can easily spot him. The chase is therefore simultaneously absurd, derisory and tragic. An ironical use of devices which are known to all the viewers results in a possibility for the public to catch the message and to enjoy the alteration of the signs inherited from the USA. The effect of parody is all the more perceptible if we make a comparison with another English film, *The Ladykillers* (1955). Here, at the outset, the devices of gangster films denounce a man who is really a gangster and it is hard even to smile since the pictures do not say more than what is implied in the conventional signs – danger, that is all. *The Man in the White Suit* is grounded on the very 'modern' idea that the most familiar images can generate, provided they are not shot in the expected manner, surprising and even disturbing effects. Since cinema-goers saw American films almost every week, they were familiar with their conventions. Consequently when they were 'twisted', diverted from their traditional use, the audience responded immediately. If we merely look at the pictures we could jump to the conclusion that Ealing imitated Hollywood, but if we concern ourselves with the re-shaping of American banalities we realize that the British cinema created something new with old tools.

Derision operates also in *The Return of Don Camillo*. When the priest comes back to his village he is present at (and then intervenes in) a boxing match. This classical image of the American movie is turned here into a mad demonstration of local hysteria. A frenzied crowd gets rid of the rules, there is no more fair play and the most vicious blows are loudly cheered. Yet I do not think that this is the most surprising aspect of the movie, and I am more interested in its representation of the flood. The film was made at the time of neorealism, the influence of which is perceptible in the shooting. The movie-camera first records, in medium shot, the forced migration of the villagers and then pans slowly over the devastated land. It is in a documentary style, impressive in its gravity, in contrast to the quick, nimble editing of American movies that describe a collective drama. I am not suggesting that the Italian film is better: we are confronted here with two different conceptions of cinematic language. But *Don Camillo*, even if it deals with a tragedy, remains a comedy and the film-makers have not forgotten that the public has paid to smile. The funny part of the plot, the duel between the two champions of religion and communism respectively, is re-inserted as a side episode into the long sequences devoted to the swamping of the valley. In the flooded church, alone, Don Camillo celebrates mass while his flock have gathered on the bank to listen to the bell. The scene could be agonizing were it not for the fact that the mayor, who has not left the village but who does not want to attend mass, takes a turn around the church in his small boat. Is the attempt to make fun of a dramatic event very effective? Opinion is divided on this point. Still the process is noteworthy: starting with a critical vision of rural life in the Po valley the movie mocks the futility of conflicts which merely tend to perpetuate a local hegemony. It certainly takes advantage of the situation to please its viewers and does not offer any solution to the problem. But it is not content with celebrating progress; it suggests a truly Italian atmosphere and helps us to understand why things cannot change in a day.

The four films are fairly different. *Don Camillo* pretends to ignore the Americans and thanks to the patterns established by neorealism adopts a genuine style to make a satire which implies, in fact, a reference to America. The other movies avowedly have recourse to Hollywood's textual systems, well known to the public, in order to subvert them. In the four cases the modernization of an old country is at stake and from that point of view the USA is not far away. But there is something in the films which is not American: a capacity to leave the plot aside and make gratuitous, purely poetical pictures. In an American comedy there is forever something new, the spectators being conceded no free, empty moment, whereas our films do not hesitate to 'waste' time. For example, one morning Don Camillo meets a boy at a school and goes for a long stroll with him. Why? There is no link between this passage and the fight with the mayor or the building of the dam; it is a sequence of pure pleasure that the film-makers have shot for themselves and finally edited because the film-goers were likely to enjoy it. The first pictures look a bit uncanny, there is a great deal of mist and we are surprised to see the gigantic priest walking beside the tiny little kid. Slowly, while the background music shifts from gravity to happiness, they get out of the village and enter the countryside. It is spring, the boy starts running, the priest leans against a parapet and lets the sun beat down on him. A break, an instant of rest, interrupts the flow of a rather tense movie. The tokens brought into play are simple but they succeed in creating a feeling of freshness and giving the viewers the impression that a comedy is not necessarily a concatenation of jokes or surprises.

The Man in the White Suit tends more towards pastiche. Sidney has found an ally, Daphne, the daughter of his boss, who believes in him and his invention. When he escapes from the house in which he has been trapped he climbs through the window down a rope held by Daphne. The picture taken in long shot is extremely romantic, somewhat reminiscent of Romeo and Juliet, with white, slim Sidney silhouetted against the darkness of the night. And indeed, before pursuing the fortune of the hero, the film concedes us a shot of the girl lingering voluptuously on a sofa. In an American comedy there would be a romance between the poor, inspired inventor and the rich heiress, and although obliged to part they would never forget their love. The Ealing film appropriates the American ingredients but denies their sentimental implication: it is not a love-affair since neither of the two protagonists can conceive of such an impossible misalliance. Daphne thinks artificial thread has a future and Sidney is ready to accept any kind of help. The beautiful nocturnal pictures are therefore redundant except that they provide us with the pleasure of sharp, inspiring photographs.

It is no accident that in *Jour de fête* poetry and night are confounded. Visual tokens traditionally used to signify softness and rest introduce something different in the course of the narration. The characters in this film are unimportant, and apart from François we do not see them twice. The movie does not need to deter its viewers from misinterpretation, and instead of challenging the stereotypes (which is what *The Man in the White Suit* does) it can present them directly and unrestrictedly. However, the romanticism of night is not spectacular, it merely signifies peace, silence; in the half-darkness people go home quietly while through the windows boys look at the girls as they get undressed, and the pictures themselves seem to drop off to sleep. The scene could look prosaic but does not because it has no narrative purpose and is uniquely intended to create a distance, an impression of diversity.

Film-makers who worked in different countries for fairly different publics resorted simultaneously to mystery (mist, darkness), low lighting, silhouettes, and the interruption of the general trend of the plot to intrigue their spectators. They also mixed up the 'genres' and diverted the social comedy dealing with public problems towards private issues. However, it is true that none of them dared organize his movie on a permanent contrast between poetry and laughter, satire and pure visual pleasure. Audiences could accept an inflection of the established rules but were not ready to have them totally overturned. Hollywood offered many European cinematographers a 'pretext' – in other words, something which came before the text, not a model but, rather, a possible source of inspiration. In some cases imitation prevailed, but there were also innovations in a field in which Hollywood was strong and had accumulated long experience.

Neorealism and what else? Nearly nothing. Europe did not give world cinema many masterpieces during the fifteen years that followed the war. Victorious America believed she could exploit the situation but after a short while it turned out that she would simply restore the pre-war situation. Hollywood may have won first place on the European market but was not alone; the various national cinemas developed well throughout the period.

The most important fact which gives these years their specificity was the tremendous expansion of the public. Viewers were never as numerous as during these years. Old habits became even more imperative as young and old, families and individuals, haunted the picture-houses. Is this the reason why the productions were so poor? I do not think so. The spectators were not stupid. Some of them were given no choice but others expressed well-defined tastes. They wanted to be entertained and informed but not to be disturbed. The eclipse of resistance films after 1947 is best understood in this light: the political and ideological implications of the secret war were too strong for the large audiences who wanted enjoyment rather than earnest enquiry from their weekly incursions into the theatres. Cinema had to be cinema – that is to say, a good story told with plenty of action which combined artistic photography and exciting sounds. This did not fit in with the experience or tradition of most European cinematographers and Hollywood made its best profits in this field. But the viewers were also interested in films dealing with their own world or surroundings, the world of factories, the army, the countryside, in middle-of-the-road productions with no artistic pretensions. It was not great art but the films of the period are a valuable document on the concerns and hopes of the reconstruction era.

4

THE BLURRED IMAGE
OF CITIES

Hollywood, which would later become a mythical city, was initially chosen to make movies because it was a convenient place in a wonderful location. The European film-makers contemplated the idea of building their movie studios on the coast, in Brighton, or Nice, or Naples,[1] but the capital cities prevailed and the fate of European films was very soon linked to London, Paris and Rome. And also to Berlin but, when the city was isolated inside the German Democratic Republic, Munich took over its function, and the attempts to create other studios in Wiesbaden or Freiburg were not successful. In Europe cinema has always been an urban activity. Actors said they could not earn their living unless they were close to the most important theatres, but distances were not so big in the Old World that it was impossible to move quickly from studio to stage. In Britain or France the centralization of theatrical activities could be an explanation but not in Germany or Italy where many provincial cities are, and were, culturally as important as Munich or Rome. In fact, politics provide the only real reason; film producers constantly need the help of the state and have to be in close contact with governments. Nor is Germany an exception, since in this decentralized country rich Bavaria is the *Land* most likely to give cinema substantial help.

For almost a century films made in towns have been offered to prevalently urban audiences, and it is no wonder that a great many cinematic narratives have taken place or still take place in towns. Nevertheless, an urban background does not necessarily mean that a town is featured on the screen. If *This Happy Breed* (1944) and *Family Life* (1972), to take two very different examples, are located in urban surroundings spectators are given only a few, elliptic images of the city. In the former, establishing shots evoke London briefly and then a street near Clapham Common, but the story develops inside the house of the Gibbons family. In the latter when Janice, the central character, goes back to her parents' home, glimpses of jerry-built houses suggest only an ill-defined urban district. The plots would be fairly different if the Gibbons or Janice's parents lived in the country or in a small town; the fact that these people have settled in a big city is important for the understanding of the narrative but does not result in any representation of urban activities.

The depiction of a town in films is the consequence of a deliberate choice. A side-effect of such a decision is that it contributes to estranging European movies from Hollywood. The Americans have attempted to 'film' European cities, but their reconstructions are generally fanciful whereas the Europeans can easily recreate their own world visually. This does not imply any reference to 'reality'. Shooting on actual location was important in some periods inasmuch as this implied noticeable changes in technique and style, but a setting is not more 'true' because it exists in actuality. The film which will introduce us to the subject, *It Always Rains on Sunday* (d. Robert Hamer, 1947), was entirely made in a studio as was Fellini's *Roma* (I., 1971) which is a wonderful exploration of the most unexpected aspects of Rome recreated in plaster and painted cardboard. This book is centred on images not on realities; it aims to detect the vision offered to spectators and not the cities themselves in which these spectators lived. From 1950 onwards Europe witnessed considerable urban development and the creation of entirely new towns. Yet we want to study neither this extraordinarily quick change nor how it modified the life of citizens. The theme we would like to explore is the reflection of cities, real or artificial, in European cinema.

A POLARIZED IMAGE

It Always Rains on Sunday was set in London's East End. Nevertheless, unlike *This Happy Breed*, the film does not begin with a comprehensive vision of London. We are in a small street, Coronet Grove, and the very first shots inform us that it is a Saturday night, that it rains and that the plot will be

It Always Rains on Sunday: Town centres – the locus of social activities

centred around George Sandigate, his wife Rose and his family. The initial sequence, which introduces us to the Sandigates and to Rose's previous affair with Tom Swann, is interrupted by a narratively unmotivated incursion into a pub. Two locations are thus delineated right from the beginning: on the one hand, Coronet Grove presented as a distant, suburban area; and on the other hand, an urbanized street which will later turn out to be Petticoat Lane (people have to be given a lift to go between the two, the outset of the film tells us twice). This Sunday could be as boring as Sundays customarily are, but Tom Swann who has escaped from Dartmoor asks Rose to help him hide. Interesting though it is (the problematic relationships of a woman with her husband, her step-family, her neighbours in a working-class district), it is not the story which concerns us here but the depiction of the town. The film is entirely structured by an alternation between Coronet Grove and Petticoat Lane. The former is explored right at the beginning. The first sequence describes the street, the second adds the yard and the dumps so that spectators are now familiar with the district. On the other hand, Petticoat Lane is revealed little by little as viewers are successively given glimpses of various places such as an amusement arcade, a pub and several shops, before the market and finally the street itself appear on the screen. There is always something new to be expected in this area and even in the second part of the movie other aspects of the urbanized districts are disclosed. The film purposefully plays on this strong opposition and delineates the contrasts of the East End.

Alternation is particularly clear in this picture, but the same device is common to a great many movies from the 1920s to the 1960s. Representations of towns were frequent in European cinema throughout the 1920s: 'avant-garde' cinematographers attempted to show as many pictures as possible in order to make their public understand the infinite variety of cities.[2] Sound, and the influence of Hollywood's narration, modified the trend. From 1930 onwards towns were depicted as spatial wholes divided into contrasted areas which defined each other by opposition: centres versus outskirts. Let us remember that we are not speaking of geography but of images. For four decades the outskirts were 'somewhere else'. Films did not try to give accurate descriptions of suburban areas but to point out a few of their specific characteristics.

Distance, emphasized by necessary recourse to means of transport, was a primary feature. Cars are convenient cinematic tools which often have a function in plots as well as being social symbols. Now, where suburbs are concerned, cars are mostly used to emphasize the length of the journey. A car drives along endless streets or, inside a vehicle, impatient people chatter nervously. In city centres, changes are instantaneous and almost motionless so that we jump from the music shop to the amusement arcade and then to the market. If the film lingers somewhere it is because an event is to happen there or because new information will be provided to the spectators. In contrast with city centres, the outskirts are not socialized spaces. They look empty and deprived of places where people can gather. Everybody is thus presumed to long for something different, for centres. George Sandigate's two daughters would do anything to leave Coronet Grove, George and Rosie are expected to visit the centre when they have some time off – and it is precisely because, on this Sunday, Rose does not conform to her 'normal' behaviour that the police suspect she has hidden Tom. Celia Johnson and Trevor Howard cannot have their *Brief Encounter* (d. David Lean, 1946) in the places where they live; they have to move toward a centre where they will find pubs, restaurants, cinemas, libraries, public parks (and also hospitals) – in short everything which, according to the film, is necessary to initiate and develop a love affair.

However, if the outskirts are strange they are not repulsive and, after presenting them at the outset, films go on exploring them with an amazed curiosity. Centres, on the other hand, appear in flashes which never result in a coherent whole. It seems that 'town' (not this town or that one but *town* as such, the notion of town) is already known and does not deserve a systematic representation. There are, of course, locations which cannot be avoided, those which are precisely filmed in *It Always Rains on Sunday*, such as pubs, dance halls, clubs, markets and shops which are necessary to the plot. Where will the police inquire? Where, if not at a pub, will the journalist discover that Rose stayed at home? These warm, lively, crowded places are convenient to make the story progress, to shift the development of narration from one direction to another. Yet this does not imply any systematic exploration whereas, with the outskirts, a visit seems unavoidable. An anonymous movie-camera (I mean a camera which is not meant to reproduce the gaze of a character) or more often a protagonist looks at the scenery which we see with them. Abodes are carefully described so as to provide viewers with small details – corridors, stairs, furniture, a wash-basin, some clothes. The striking fact is the lack of fictional relevance of these trifles. The plot stops for a while but it is not the kind of suspension which is likely to make spectators shiver. Nothing but curiosity will arise from these short breaks. The oddity of the outskirts is well exemplified by what could be called 'multiple exploration'; the same images are offered successively through the eyes of different visitors. We see Rose's home with a neighbour, then with a detective, later with the journalist. Angles vary slightly (a mere repetition would be boring), but the camera seems to be fixed on these peculiar, almost uncanny surroundings.

It would be absurd to reduce the films dealing with towns to this extremely simple polarization. For instance, the silence and desolateness of Coronet Grove underline wonderfully the loneliness of Rose who wants to betray neither George nor Tom, while the activity of Petticoat Lane emphasizes the indifference of her family. But the film is moving because it uses cleverly, for a fictional purpose, a cinematic commonplace. In the films of the 1950s the contrasted images in cities were powerful. First of all, they fitted in very well with 'classical' narration. For instance, in *It Always Rains on Sunday* the main theme is Rose's dilemma. Once the initial problem has been exposed, the situation could not evolve if people, moving between Petticoat Lane and Coronet Grove, did not disturb and threaten Rose. The story is sustained by the intrusion of visitors who constantly renew the difficulties. What is more, the central plot is complemented by side-stories (the respective love-affairs of George's two daughters and the robbery by petty thieves) which are, typically, generated by the city centre. Implicitly it was admitted that the outskirts cannot provide a story. But this partition was not only fictional; it was also visual. The two components of towns were filmed in different manners, and their pictorial representation had a different status. The outskirts were conceded an almost documentary description while centres were represented in a more elaborate and synthetic way. Sometimes (think of *Knave of Hearts*, 1954) short glimpses were given of London daily life so as to create a poetic background. In other cases a few shots were sufficient to make spectators spot a cheerful little street-market, a row of shops, children loitering under a tree, a peaceful square or a busy crossing. The centre contrasted strongly with run-down suburban areas where small factories and closed churches squatted among semi-detached houses. In the middle of the century cinema thus developed an elementary but coherent conception of urbanization according to which a city was exclusively a place where trade and entertainment existed. Towns were seen as circles, the centre of which people were longing to join. Most films dealing with urban areas were unquestionably concerned with citizens' social life but tended to enclose it within a restrictive statement: 'Look at these people living in suburbs, how depressing their fate must be.' What has just been written is not intended to play down the dirtiness of slums or the extension of poverty in the outskirts.

There was a reality behind the screens, a reality that film-makers often wanted to represent. But the strong opposition between two totally impermeable spheres was an image, a cinematic manner of interpreting and even emphasizing an actual difference. This implies not only that some shots give valuable glimpses on mid-century towns but that the movies must be questioned from the selective point of view which structures them.

NEOREALISM OR THE COMPLEXITY OF URBAN RELATIONSHIPS

Neorealism is a label that film-buffs and specialists stick onto a limited cluster of Italian films shot during the decade that followed the war. No clear-cut definition can be offered for the word;[3] it is even hard to decide whether a film was or was not neorealist, and estimates waver from sixty to eighty films (out of a total of 1,000 Italian productions). Neorealism was short-lived but had a strong impact on European cinematographers during the second half of the century. The quality of these movies explains, at least partially, their influence. They were carefully made with good scripts, elaborate dialogue, excellent shooting and editing. Plots were not original but were developed against a background which, instead of being merely an evocative setting, played an important part in the stories. Emphasis on the social, cultural context was another significant aspect of neorealism and distinguished it from the dominant Hollywood style of production. One half of the neorealist movies had their story located in rural surroundings and evoked the problems of farm-workers, fishermen or members of co-operatives. These pictures of typically Italian situations had no counterpart in other European countries, whereas her 'urban' films were comparable to other foreign productions while offering, at the same time, an original, unprecedented vision of cities.

Open City, generally considered the first neorealist movie, takes place in Rome, as do some twenty important neorealist films, among which is De Sica's trilogy of *Shoeshine* (1946), *Bicycle Thieves* (1947) and *Umberto D.* (1951). I want to focus on these three movies and find it necessary to sum up briefly their respective plots. The Shoeshines are two young boys, one an orphan and one the youngest son of an extremely poor family who survive by cleaning GIs' shoes. They become unwittingly involved in a robbery, and the police send them to Borstal. In *Bicycle Thieves* unemployed Guido Ricci is offered a job as a bill-sticker which requires the use of a bicycle. The very day he begins working his bike is stolen. He searches for it hopelessly throughout Rome. As for Umberto D. his pension is no longer sufficient to afford the room in which he has lived for ages and he is obliged to leave it. There is, in these movies, unemployment, misery, loneliness – in other words, the crisis of post-war Italy – and there is also the city, Rome.

Rome is the largest city in Europe with a municipal territory almost as wide as Greater London. In *Shoeshine* the two boys often sleep in a barn with horses and on one occasion they enter the centre of the city on horseback. This was 1946, but four decades later there were still farms, barns and small groups of houses which could only be reached along unasphalted roads but which were nevertheless 'in Rome'. The Italian capital has for a long time been a city, plus suburbs, plus a no man's land.

When the kingdom was unified in 1871 Rome had only 200,000 inhabitants. The city, kept inside the Roman wall, was divided into three sectors. The West was the traditional, popular, overcrowded district, and it was there that the parents of the second shoeshine boy lived in 1946. The South was composed mostly of Roman ruins. The East was occupied by sumptuous mansions surrounded with parkland. The regal government decided to transform the old, half-ruined city into a modern capital. As it needed ground to erect a central station, offices and blocks of flats it spent enormous amounts of money to buy the parks and lay out rectangular streets. It is in this district that Umberto D. lived in 1951. A retired civil servant, he was unwilling to leave the abode he had been used to for such a long time. We easily follow him on his daily strolls and note that he is closed inside a sort of magic circle (say from Marble Arch to Charing Cross), the boundaries of which he is unable to pass. From the point of view adopted here (spatial relationships in a town) his drama is simple: he can no longer stay in the centre but he does not want to admit that like his former colleagues he should find a flat in the suburbs.

Before the war Rome had 1,200,000 inhabitants, many of whom were unemployed immigrants settled in shanty towns hastily established all around the city. Fascism, irritated by this unpleasant image, had promised to demolish all shanty towns and build proper housing for everyone. Some construction sites were set up quite far out from the city walls, because land was cheaper there and also because this would remove the proletariat from the city centre. Val Melaina, where *Bicycle Thieves* begins, is a full five miles from the Roman wall. Later, the entire stretch along the road was built up, but in 1947 this was an urban desert, a gap of several miles. Distance is a fundamental feature of the film. There are no jobs in a new neighbourhood, a neighbourhood that is not even finished yet. The distance from the centre prevents the men from going into town to look for work. From this point of view fascism has been successful and even in 1947, three years after the Liberation, the administrative delegation at Val Melaina checked all proposals and controlled the labour force. Two sequences, the opening one and the scene of a meeting in a cellar when Ricci goes to pick up a friend after the theft, provide us with further information. Among the unemployed there are many bricklayers but there is no work for them. All available jobs are for highly specialized workers (turners, for instance, but this category does not exist at Val Melaina) or totally unqualified men. At the outset of the film we are told that an unskilled labourer is needed, and shortly afterwards Ricci, who has no qualification, gets his job. The Val Melaina estate is not finished, there is no running water in the flats, the streets are not paved, but there is no money and no will to complete it. In the mean time entertainment and luxury stores grow up in the city centre where there is the requisite clientele. The owner of the picture-house in the building where Umberto D. lives restores his theatre, and Ricci is urged to cover the walls with posters.

The Val Melaina residents wait. They will be ready at the beginning of the 'economic miracle'. Without over-emphasizing it, without making it the main topic of the story, the film outlines the conditions of this future development. On the one hand, businessmen long to exploit the tourists' need for entertainment and the enjoyment of middle-class people; on the other hand, the unemployed are impatient to get work.

De Sica shows us very clearly that the latter are poor but not indigent. Abject poverty is portrayed in *Shoeshine*, where families evacuated from the countryside because of the war live in huge barracks, four or five people to a room, with no money or clothes, and are obliged to beg or steal. Family ties are very loose, young men and even children living independently. This permanent promiscuity gives rise to hatred, to wickedness and, paradoxically, also to a sort of mutual self-help, a feeling of solidarity (although they are not guilty, the two boys do not want to denounce those who have stolen and are therefore sent to Borstal). The condition of the Ricci family is totally different. They have the basic minimum income needed in order to survive decently thanks to welfare cheques and to what the son earns working at the petrol-pump. Their flat is fairly large with a kitchen and two rooms. Cinema here offers us a comparison. In the first sequence of *Four Steps among the Clouds* (I., d. Alessandro Blasetti, 1942) a scene rather like the one in *Bicycle Thieves* shows us the home of a travelling salesman and his family near Rome's central station. It is not different from Ricci's flat since the same standardized model was used in all housing blocks built for the lower-middle class in the 1930s and 1940s. There is a social distinction between the travelling salesman, who has a job and lives within the city walls, and Ricci, but it is less of a difference than that which separates Ricci from the people portrayed in *Shoeshine*. In both flats family life is very rigidly structured, and this is clearly what allows the families to survive the harshness of everyday reality. Throughout the entire story the Riccis are always doing things in pairs, either husband and wife or father and son. On the other hand, they have practically no ties with their neighbours; the wife tells no one that Ricci has found a job, and when the latter comes back home he hardly even says hello to the woman he meets in the hall. It never crosses Ricci's mind to borrow a friend's bike and he really appears to have only one friend, Baiocco, the head dustman.

In other words, De Sica is depicting a very peculiar group, a close nuclear family which certainly existed in Italy at the time but which was much rarer on the screen than an open, wider family pattern. I shall come back later to some of the sociological aspects of the contrast between the two types and would just like to add for the moment one suggestion. Since the main actors were not professionals the voices were dubbed, so that it is dangerous to rely on the dialogue. Yet, the characters do not speak in Roman dialect, not even in the fragmentary expressions spoken by the extras that create the sound-track background for the sequences shot in Val Melaina. It is possible that the inhabitants are not from Rome or even from the surroundings. Nothing brings Southern Italy to mind. Hence my assumption that these people could come from central Italy. They could be an entire resettled population or perhaps a combination of Romans and peasants.

Ricci enters the city three times. On the Friday he has the job of registering at the workers' office; the following day he begins work and has his bike stolen and on Sunday he tracks the thief. On none of these occasions does he go through Roman Rome or classical Rome and he never goes past an ancient monument. This is one of the indirect but very accurate indications that the film gives us. Umberto D., on the other hand, walks past ancient buildings. He does not look at them, but they are a natural background for a man who has lived for so long a time in the city centre. Ricci's Rome is much more limited, and it is not by chance that he is generally filmed in close-up or in medium shot. For him Rome is not a familiar place, and he appears almost to be 'blind' to his surroundings.

On Friday, apart from the journey from Val Melaina to the city centre, Ricci and his wife Maria merely go through popular neighbourhoods all located in the West. Maria appears to be at ease in this part of the city. They visit first the pawnshop to get back the bike and she is the one that does the talking and succeeds in getting the best conditions. Then they go to the flat of a fortune-teller where Maria has already been once before on her own. She would not be so self-confident if she came from a village. While he is waiting for her in the street Ricci is extremely nervous. Is he jealous? Or is he rather ill at ease in a district which is so different from the one he is accustomed to? Let us assume that Maria is Roman, for she is more lively, more at ease than Ricci who is probably an immigrant. In all matters that do not concern work she is the one who decides. And yet, when Ricci goes off to get his uniform at the workers' office she stays outside and is only allowed to see the room through the window.

On Saturday, in uniform, Ricci enters with more authority

into the official Rome, the eastern district with its wide streets, the neighbourhood of the ministries, of clerical workers and of Umberto D., a world full of noise and crowded with cars. Other contemporary films show the same areas, but here De Sica is especially good at contrasting in a very light-handed way this ministerial city with the Val Melaina estate where there was not a single car at the time. Ricci is lost, confused and gets his bicycle stolen right away, just 200 yards from the police station. Irony, although obvious, is not enough to explain his visit to the police. The police station and thefts are two commonplaces of the Italian cinema of the 1940s. The police are everywhere and appear immediately whenever there is a threat of a riot (at the beginning of *Umberto D.* they prevent retired people from having a street demonstration), to the extent that Ricci finds a *carabiniere* every time he feels tempted to do something wrong. But the police are totally inefficient. In another film, *Under the Sun of Rome* (1949), they fail to arrest the thieves and are content with catching a poor, weak boy who has no parents and no home. Everyone in the city knows perfectly well that the police are powerless, and the only ones who trust them are people who come from the provinces, for instance the newly married man who has been abandoned by his wife in Fellini's *White Sheik* (1952) and believes that the cops will find her, or Ricci, neither of whom know anything about the rules and rituals of the city.

The loss of the bicycle changes Ricci's situation. On the Sunday when he goes into the city to look for it he leaves his uniform behind and as he does not dare explore the western area without a guide he follows Baiocco the head dustman, who is wearing uniform. Together they walk across Victor Emmanuel Square, a characteristic part of the straight and orderly official city. Here Baiocco displays a certain amount of authority and he directs his group of dustmen like a captain. Yet he does not want to go beyond the official district. He avoids the working-class market at Porta Portese, and it is the driver who takes Ricci to this place before leaving as fast as he can. For a few years after the war, on Sunday mornings, people could come freely to sell their wares on Victor Emmanuel Square. The market was so open that the police had no trouble keeping everything under control, and it was extremely unlikely that a stolen bicycle would be sold there.

The man Ricci suspects and who is not in fact the thief, shouts at him that in Victor Emmanuel Square 'people are honest', and this is not just an empty boast. A visit to the Porta Portese market would be more useful but dangerous as well. Baiocco and the others wait until it is too late. The driver can only say 'We should have come here earlier this morning.'

The second part of Ricci's search is a walk along the Tiber. Father and son follow the river as if it were a sort of Ariadne's thread leading through a mysterious country. They do not know that for centuries the life of the city has developed far away from the banks of this dangerous river. The climax is reached when Ricci finds the thief who forces him to go back home to Panic Street. This is not a fanciful name and it was certainly not chosen by chance. Ricci is really panic-stricken when he is confronted with a world he does not understand – a very close-knit community in which everyone knows each other and is willing to help.[4] This network of alliances, connivance and relations is very tight; the entire street rushes to support the thief against an outsider, a stranger. At first, Ricci seems to be prepared to get back his property but then he gives up and, through his panic, the film shows how for a man from the suburbs the traditional city centre is an insurmountable obstacle. Obviously this is the biased vision of an immigrant. In this movie, as well as in *Shoeshine* or in *Under the Sun of Rome*, theft (and also prostitution, although in a less obvious, openly admitted way) is a normal practice, a necessity in poor neighbourhoods. But in these films the thieves do not succeed. They try to steal from the inhabitants of the traditional city centre but city-dwellers know how to defend their goods. If they want to make money thieves have to fool tourists or strangers. Stealing is a profession and an amateur cannot become a thief just like that. The idea that comes to Ricci, when on the evening of the Sunday he sees a bicycle leaning against a wall and decides to steal it, inevitably ends in failure.

The last sequence of *Bicycle Thieves* is not a moral lesson, it is not a condemnation of the second theft. It simply records the fact that criminality is also a way of organizing oneself, a means of survival. It has often been noted that this conclusion is highly ambiguous: is it optimistic (Ricci and his son leave hand in hand, closer than ever to each other) or pessimistic (the bike has been definitely lost)? In fact De Sica avoids 'messages' in order to provide us with an interpretation of contemporary reality. The boys in *Shoeshine* attempt to recreate a family environment among themselves in order to be able to get out of the dreaded city; yet they are so much involved in their surroundings that they cannot escape. In 1946, for those living in the poorest areas, there was no hope. Umberto D. wants to die in the house where he has lived for decades, but the centre is being modernized and there is no more room for those who do not have enough money. Both these films explain how the city is destroyed by its problems, its backwardness and by the invasion of a rich and ambitious new population. Ricci's case is not that simple. This man has all the qualities necessary to become a good employee: he is serious, he has no connections with other workers, he is determined to improve the condition of his family. But the traditional Romans are not going to allow themselves to be thrown out. Ricci is potentially valuable to bosses for he is a newcomer but he has none of the necessary connections and he does not know how to go about entering the city. He must wait but he will succeed because Rome is changing.

To consider neorealist films as documents in no way implies diminishing their artistic value. In fact, it is the quality of the photography, the interest of the story, the sequence construction that push spectators to look beyond the purely factual and discover the potentialities of the situation. Most neorealist movies suggest and allow for several interpretations and let the public discover contrasted aspects of contemporary life. De Sica's Rome is not merely a constructed area divided into a centre and outskirts. It is instead a space where habits or traditions intermingle with new needs and ambitions, thus creating a complex network of social relationships. There is a difference, or rather a distance, between the centre and the periphery, but entering the city does not only require means of transport. Townsmen participate in regulated exchanges, and the immigrants must learn how to behave before being accepted. Neorealism does not exhaust the subject of urban life and social changes in cities but it offers a coherent, moving vision of some problems which accounts for its long-lasting success.

Its influence can still be traced more than a decade later in films which seem to have little in common with it. To a large extent Antonioni's movies and especially *The Eclipse* (1962) get rid of the neorealist inheritance. For instance, there is practically no story in this film. A young lady, Vittoria, who lives in Rome, breaks off with her lover. She visits several people. She meets a bill-broker, Piero, and begins an affair with him. That is all. No emphasis on the social/economic background, no psychology, but perfect pictures and a stress put on time, on duration suggested through a wonderful matching of images and sounds. Yet Rome is still there.

Interestingly the film helps an understanding of what happened between 1947 and 1962. In 1947 the relationship between outskirts and centre was more conflicting than complementary; the traditional population rejected the inhabitants of the marginal areas, whereas the new ruling class needed them. Fifteen years later suburbs were no longer isolated and the middle class was bound to emigrate there. At the outset of the film we follow Vittoria, who has just left her lover, along a deserted district with empty roads, mean trees, no passers-by. The place is soon identified; it is the EUR – that is to say, Rome's Universal Exhibition, the district chosen and baptized by Mussolini for an exhibition which was never organized. After 1950 the town council built new residences there, but owing to the tradition of living inside the Roman wall middle-class people were reluctant to move. The opening of the film is then easily understandable. Vittoria, whose job was by no means common at the time (she is a translator), belongs to the new economic/intellectual élite. She lives in the EUR because she cannot afford a convenient flat in the centre but she ignores and hates her surroundings. Every time she has a few spare hours she goes to the centre. Piero, Vittoria's mother, and their respective dwellings stand for the traditional, pre-war Rome. When she visits the magnificent apartment of Piero's parents Vittoria nearly loses her way and we, following in her footsteps, see a fantastic mansion. The mother, who is the widow of an officer, lives in a street built at the end of the nineteenth century, beside the Vatican. The old aristocracy and the civil service were the component parts of the Roman upper class until the middle of the century – and the film emphasizes purposefully the contrast between the lively, animated centre and the EUR. But, little by little, hints are dropped that the centre is doomed to die. The mother's flat is covered with dust, the parents' apartment is empty, Piero's office is about to tumble down. Vittoria still dreams of the old Rome but her future – the future of her class – is in the EUR. In short, the film tells us about an eclipse, the eclipse of Rome.

In 1980 or 1990 it was easy to say that the centre of most European towns lost inhabitants to the suburbs. In 1960 that was not clear at all, especially in capital cities where well-off people hoped they would get rid of the lower classes (sent to the outskirts) and stay in the historic districts. In contrast to their wishes, *The Eclipse* pictures a radical change which seemed overstated at the time but which squares with what was to happen during the following decades. Using documentary material (we could describe the progress in the building site during the shooting by a close study of the pictures), the film tells us about the fears and expectations of the Roman middle class at the peak of the 'miracle'. The same feelings could be found in other sources such as newspapers, but it would be difficult to find documents which grounded the expression of those fears and expectations on a picture of what was actually happening in the towns at the time. In this respect cinema cannot be balanced by any other source of evidence.[5]

SHANTY TOWNS: A THIRD WORLD?

The Eclipse ignored the shanty towns which were also the most manifest blank in the neorealist depiction of Rome. When De Sica decided to show a suburban area he went to another place (*Miracle in Milan*, 1950), and it is not before 1956 that he dared present, in *The Roof*, Roman suburbs built out of old tin cans and boxes. By this time European cinematographers had begun to take another look at their towns. I find it necessary to digress here and emphasize the fact that there is no clear-cut chronology in the cinematic representation of cities. Roughly speaking, the coupling of centre/outskirts was more common during the 1950s while shanty towns were often represented in the 1960s but both existed, in films, from the 1920s through the 1980s. No big change took place at the end of the 1950s; there was rather a slow shifting towards new images. I suggest we call the vision which developed after *The Roof* the blurring of cities. The strong system which associated the centre and outskirts, presented as complementary entities, vanished, and the picture of towns began to lose focus. Two points are worth noticing. The first is that this change spread throughout Europe. There were, of course, differences in time, and the pictures were never totally comparable. Nevertheless, despite obvious discordances, comparable trends can be detected in the four countries which are under examination here. The second important aspect of this evolution is that many film-makers – the most noticeable among them – were affected and moved from the classic polarization towards less structured and even towards destructured visions of cities.

In 1945 throughout Europe towns were severely damaged. If many films alluded to the destruction (in one of the establishing shots of *It Always Rains on Sunday* we are presented with a bombed church), only Germany developed the theme over a long period. Nevertheless, in Fassbinder's *Marriage of Maria Braun* (G., 1978), which is temporally imprecise but which follows a German lady from 1945 to the mid-1970s, the image of Maria's smashed house recurs frequently. When she feels worried by one of her relatives she takes them to the ruins which had, long ago, been their home. As the story tends to be more and more enclosed indoors as Maria is getting wealthier and wealthier, the town is finally reduced to a few dismantled walls. Private life and the economy have been restored but the wounds of the city cannot be forgotten.

This might explain why the German cinema indulged less than its counterparts in the centre/outskirts pattern as well as in the depiction of roughly built shacks. While suburbs are dependent on more urbanized areas and are linked to them, cinematic shanty towns exist by themselves and have identifiable characteristics. They are, first of all, half-void spaces with long patches of empty ground spread between ill-built huts. Here, people constantly move on motorbike or delivery tricycles or even on foot. The one-way track towards the centre has been replaced by permanent local exchanges. Displacements, small turns, random meetings, give way to an intensive collective life. In fact, films re-enact some stereotypes of the 'popular' neighbourhoods previously developed in the nineteenth century's popular novels with open-air dances, feasts, games of chance and violence. Life is supposed to be hard but free in these faraway districts. Doors are never locked (how would it be possible to close them?), everybody can enter

A Taste of Honey: Suburbs – dirt and dereliction

everywhere and, if necessary, take what they need. Theft does
not exist since no property can be guaranteed. Unemployment
or short-term work is the normal fate so that there is plenty of
time to linger, chatter and drink.

Shanty towns are huge, uncoordinated areas where towns
are allowed to pile up their garbage. If anything is typical of
these places, inasmuch as it was filmed again and again, it is
the junkyard, the dumping ground filled with metal or
worthless objects and unwanted rubbish. Scrap iron, discarded
appliances – bent, rusty, heaped-up, hideous – are bitterly
fought over and, despite their seeming uselessness, turn out to
be marketable. In *The Knack* which is, among other things, a
film on London, the characters go to a junkyard and find an
out-dated iron bed, which conquers the city before becoming
the most important item of the house. Those living on the
margins of towns are especially good at making bargains out of
scraps.

Shanty towns, where people know each other perfectly well
and are used to making the best out of nothing, look like

spaces of liberty and friendship. Nevertheless, the inhabitants cannot survive except by cheating. Characteristically, one of the countless Italian movies dealing with the topic is entitled *Dirty, Mean and Nasty* (1976). Generally, hatred overflows and becomes the reality of daily life. But cinematic shacks are separated from the centre; they are deprived of the vital road which provides the outskirts with a window onto the outer world. Shanty towns threaten only themselves. Oddly enough, while cities generate thieves and criminals (see *Boys in Brown*, *The Blue Lamp* or De Sica's films), the cinematic shanty towns are too distant and too primitive to be dangerous. The best adjective to qualify them would be 'savage' with its double meaning of being fierce or cruel and of being still young, not yet civilized. The films seem to warn their spectators: 'Take a look at them but you had better not visit these places.'

The filmic version of the poorest neighbourhoods which developed mostly in the 1960s and 1970s was ambiguous. It tended to give a realistic, critical vision of derelict areas excluded from the benefits of contemporary welfare in countries where prosperity was increasing. At the same time, shanty towns were presented as fairly different, as another world, what I would like to call a third world. The social function of images is manifest in this case. The cinema disclosed something that most viewers had good reason to be unfamiliar with because neither the politicians nor the media wanted to unveil them; it described the terrific growth of depressed, abandoned areas. While providing accurate pictures, it played them down by inserting them into funny stories and by using stars. The most wicked protagonist in *Dirty, Mean and Nasty* was Vittorio Gassman, an actor famous throughout Europe, whose face implied fun and irony rather than crass poverty. Obviously nobody had asked film-makers to conduct research on shanty towns, and I am not criticizing them. All I want to suggest is that their depiction, starting from direct observation, did not result in the shooting of documentary films but in an imaginary representation of an outer-world – a world people could not know, although it existed beside them.

The best way to explain what I have in mind is to look at Pasolini's two first films, *Accatone* (1961) and *Mamma Roma* (1962). *Accatone* is one of the most implacable films devoted to outlying districts. The main character lives in a total wilderness and is obliged to accept everything, including the sacrifice of those he wishes to survive. *Mamma Roma* starts in the opposite direction. A prostitute, Mamma Roma, decides to give up her business and live with her son Ettore, who has been brought up in a country family. They settle in a nice, well-lit fiat in the middle of a newly built suburban area. While his mother becomes a respectable stall-holder Ettore meets clean, polite boys who become his chums. Since suburbs can produce nothing but swindlers, these friends are petty thieves who induce Ettore to steal. There is nobody to prevent him from imitating them in this isolated, selfish, middle-class district, and as he is not trained he is quickly caught. This is only one aspect of an extremely complex movie. Strong though it is in contrasting the various aspects of suburban Rome, the film cannot be reduced to the description of a social failure. Both Accatone and Ettore are Christ-like figures redeemed by their sufferings, who reach a mystical level of self-oblivion through abject misery. But here we are mostly concerned with Pasolini's conception of shanty towns as a separate universe where people are obliged to face, painfully, their responsibilities. Between capitalist and proletariat, between exploitation and theft, they inhabit a third world.

THE END OF CITIES

Shanty towns which played such an important part in European films of the 1960s must not be seen in isolation. They were the counterpart, or the backlash, of an equally significant feature of the time, the cinematic destruction of the towns. A series of films initiated in Britain, later extended to the continent, annihilated urbanized areas and reduced them to ugly rows of blind walls. London or other capitals which had been previously the commonest location for films were replaced by depressing industrialized towns of Yorkshire or Northern England. In general, Arthur Marwick has convincingly explained that the 'cultural revolution' of the 1960s accounts for the changes which can be spotted in films and also that films helped their viewers to become aware of what was happening around them. With *Room at the Top* (1959), *A Kind of Loving* (1962) and *This Sporting Life* (1963) people usually absent from films were given faces, hopes and wishes. Accountant Joe

Lampton becomes a middle-class man and miner Frank Machin buys a sports car. For the first time in the history of cinema 'the possibilities for mobility and change' were represented on the screen.[6]

While this is perfectly true, it is true also that film-makers took a desperate look at the surroundings with which their characters were merged. Boasting about his new car, Frank invites his lodger and her kids for a ride. They drive up a hill and contemplate a desolate ocean of uniform roofs and black chimneys. Then they turn back to the sinister line of terraced houses where they live. Joe Lampton will marry the daughter of an industrial boss but he will also stay in the depressing atmosphere of Warnley (Bradford) with its morning rush to the bus stop, its mean buildings, its bleak dog-track. And in *A Kind of Loving* gigantic building cranes tearing down old semi-detached houses forecast an even more inhuman environment for tomorrow. What was at stake here was not only a cultural twist, however important it was. Cinema confronts us also with a crisis in the representation of towns.

Let us remember that the problem did not exist before, since describing a town was seen as a very simple task.[7] Take two cinematographers who had their share in the subsequent blurring of cinematic cities, Antonioni and Godard. Antonioni's *Adventure* (I., 1959) is framed between two towns, Rome at the outset and Noto (Sicily) almost at the end. These towns are important locations inasmuch as they are related to different activities (and love-affairs) of the main protagonist. But there is more. Antonioni enjoys exploring Noto; he makes the wonderful classical buildings, the streets and the squares become entities which frame the plot but which extend far beyond it. Spectators are asked to wander from the story to the purely hedonistic pleasure of contemplating a beautiful urban scene. Godard is less sophisticated in *Breathless* (F., 1960). He guides his public into two districts of Paris whose contrasting architecture evokes different periods, activities and styles of life.[8] It is the town which speaks and, by displaying its front, its windows, its pediments, it tells the viewers where they are and what they should feel. In these films the town is self-evident, it is as solid as its stones, as evident as the regular design of its streets. It is also alive and glamorous enough to add some supplementary meaning to the story, to characterize the protagonists and to provide the public with the joy of discovering new monuments or hidden aspects of well-known surroundings.

Ten years later a concerted, systematic representation of an urbanized space seemed so hazardous that few cinematographers attempted it. The destruction, or maybe the negation, of cities had various aspects, but was a general tendency in all European countries. Both Antonioni in his English film *Blow-up* (1967) and Godard in *Two or Three Things I Know about Her* (F., 1967) dared not do what they had found so easy at the beginning of the decade. Different though they are, these films share noticeable similarities. Their plots are vague, loosely told and inconclusive. The first relates a day and a night in the life of a London photographer, Thomas, while the second presents a day in the life of a Parisian lady, Juliette. When *Blow-up* was first released critics objected that the dolly birds, the Rag Week students and the rock concert gave a fanciful vision of Swinging London.[9] The point is that there is no London in the film. At the outset we are given the only precise clue when Thomas, getting out of a doss-house (he wanted to take photographs of the tramps), finds his car in Consort Road. This could be the first sequence of a realistic movie, but we are immediately transported to another, anonymous district of newly erected multi-storey buildings where dressed-up young things shouting with laughter pass in a vehicle. Where are we now? Nowhere or anywhere. A strongly emphasized rupture affects the settings, the characters and the sound. *Breathless* had already contrasted two kinds of environments, but a link was created by the permanence of the central character and by the correspondence between what was seen and what was heard. The outset of *Blow-up* sets off two ill-matching series of shots – a naturalistic one focused on the protagonist and a mannered one fixed on unknown young people who will only reappear, briefly, before the end. There is nothing mysterious in Thomas's occupations; he simply moves from his studio to various places and vice versa. If he drives a lot no precise itinerary can be drawn up. We are offered glimpses of an unidentified English town, and buses or lorries cross our field of vision, preventing us from pinpointing any recognizable site. Long rows of brick houses, coloured buildings, waste grounds and now an antique shop in a small, decayed structure: a town, for sure, but more a skeleton, an idea of a town rather than any defined place. The same year Godard went even further in the destruction of the surroundings. Juliette, when she moves outside, is filmed in close middle shot so that the setting is almost imperceptible. The town is artificially introduced, thanks to stills or long shots taken from above which are not related to the protagonists.

A simple, indisputable interpretation of these representations could be that Thomas and Juliette are so used to their daily universe that they no longer see it. This means that, contrary to what they did shortly before, by 1967 Antonioni and Godard no longer wanted to exploit the attractiveness or the singularity of famous cities, especially diverse and interesting ones such as London or Paris, to seduce their public. Instead of being played as a counterpoint, as a supplementary delight, cities were flattened, reduced to prosaic clichés. There was surely a 'message' underlying the pictures, something like: towns become increasingly humdrum expanses crossed by indifferent drivers and damaged by greedy property developers. Spectators either caught these implications or they did not but they could not miss the dullness, the anonymity of the urbanized areas.

In many films of the late 1960s towns were no longer presented in an appealing, pleasurable manner. They were purely fictional, though. Thomas and Juliette are imaginary characters inasmuch as the hours they are meant to live through are concentrated, summed up, thanks to a few synthesized actions. Their rides throughout the city are also condensed: a few shots are given as an equivalent to miles of street. Realism is not the point here, the films of 1967 are neither more nor less realistic than those of 1959–60. Godard, by separating the life of Juliette from the city in which she lives, emphasized the artificiality of the story. The outer setting, the city, became thus an independent part of the movie, almost an autonomous character.[10]

The distance separating setting and plot got even wider during the following decade. Wenders' *Alice in the Towns* (G., 1973) offers, together with other movies by the same cinematographer, a striking example of the resistance of cinematic cities to penetration by human beings. Felix, the male protagonist, is also a photographer who is unable to capture with his camera the gist of American towns. As he flies back to Europe a lady entrusts him with the care of her daughter Alice. Starting from Amsterdam, Felix and Alice drive through Germany in search of the girl's grandparents. The narrative is flimsy, but there is a narration, a fictional world that the characters travel through and which is almost exclusively urban. During the longest part of the movie Alice and Felix, in a car or on foot, literally file past an indifferent, but carefully differentiated, urban background. The setting is neutral, invisible for the characters who do not care about it. Nevertheless, even Amsterdam, one of the Meccas of European tourism, is never filmed for itself, as was often the case in the 1950s. When the protagonists drive somewhere, for instance down a street, the place is entirely shot, and spectators are not granted the ellipsis which transforms an actual location (a street) into a setting (the editing of a few glimpses). Yet, the background is not annihilated. On the contrary, it is seen alternately from the point of view of the camera which follows the car from outside, from the point of view of the characters who chatter while looking for their way and also, more specifically, through the eyes of Alice who picks up some details and inserts them inside her own vision of her life. Unlike Noto, Amsterdam or the cities of Ruhr are not flexible material; they can neither be forgotten nor be used according to the evolution of the plot. The partition between the centre and the outskirts is no longer effective and the movie-camera films in the same, seemingly unconcerned, manner wherever it is. The urbanized space stretches away endlessly into the distance. Local distinctions might be detected but they would be irrelevant, uninteresting. Such notions as urban atmosphere, city life, which were central to the cinema of the 1950s, are abolished. Cities have vanished, leaving behind them only monotonous lines of dwellings.

Describing a town is always a difficult task. Where shall we start? Shall we go along the streets? Or rather trace the various phases of the urban expansion? The guidebooks written many centuries ago in ancient Greece or medieval Rome had already faced the same difficulty. Speaking of Victorian cities, Steven Marcus goes so far as to say that they are 'illegible'.[11] Cinema tried to solve the problem by developing a sophisticated vision of urbanized areas. Cities became human landscapes likely to enclose and sometimes to influence the fate of individual characters. In Carol Reed's *Odd Man Out* (1947) and *The Third Man* (1949) Belfast and Vienna combined reality and mystery, death and wonder; they accounted for the lives of their inhabitants, while offering the viewers something which could not be easily expressed – the strength, beauty and misery of a man-made environment. Cinema never gave up this tradition, and still at the end of the 1980s *A Fish Called Wanda* was, among other things, a long ramble through a refurbished, glittering London.

Beside the dominant pattern other representations of cities spread after the war. We have followed some of the attempts which were made throughout four decades and we are now in a position to arrange them under two headings. Some film-makers, particularly those who have been labelled 'neorealist', were aware of the blossoming of urban areas and tried to express, cinematographically, the complex relationships between old town centres and new outskirts. After 1965 or so other cinematographers were no longer able to tell, or see what towns were and created a blurred image of cities. In this field obvious correspondences can be established between the films and their historical context. The first decades after the war witnessed the expansion of 'greater' towns which developed around the traditional centres, but later the ancient districts tended to be deserted in favour of hastily erected, disordered conurbations. These connections, which are unquestionable, tell us very little about the visual depiction of urban areas in films. If we speak in terms of images and not in terms of social issues what is to be learnt from the movies made during the second half of the century?

The cinema of the 1950s was directed toward large, mostly 'popular', audiences formed of people who used to leave their dwellings and gather in town centres on Saturday evenings. It aimed to make its viewers think over problems which were sometimes complicated but which always had some connection with the sphere of family life and social relationships. Spectators wanted to be entertained; they wanted surprise but not sophisticated novelties. Hence the technique used to introduce a topic as important as the town. City centres were explored in easy stages and were filmed according to the simple, contrasted pattern of activity/stillness. During this period the cinema contributed more than any other means of communication to reinforce the mythology of the town centre conceived as a sphere of pleasure and animation. However, it brought in simultaneously another area – less defined but crucial for most of its clients – the outskirts. I have dwelt upon the considerable difference between suburbs and shanty towns, but here I can also focus on their similarities: by showing both of them, films pointed a social distance. If the centre was such an enjoyable place all those who lived elsewhere were implicitly disadvantaged. The cinema offered its public a problematic, if not very critical, vision of towns.

Even during that period the cinematic representation of cities was already fading, but the transformation was not perceptible. In fact, the first films which blurred the images of cities used unattractive pictures to reinforce the legibility of their narrative. Hostile though it was, De Sica's Rome remained a wonderful capital, whereas in the English movies mentioned above workers had to face not only a scornful middle class but also a squalid environment. It took, then, some time to realize what was happening – which was very simple: towns were no longer depicted as beautiful, admirable places. I must stress, once more, two important points. The first is that realism is not the point here. Is the visual synthesis of a town created by clever editing more or less realistic than an endless tracking-shot along an ordinary street? There is no answer to this question. The second point is that narration is not involved here either. Truly, there was a crisis of the classical narrative style from the end of the 1950s onwards, and we shall examine it in Chapter 5. All the movies cited here told a story but, in them, the representation of towns was neither perfectly congruent with the plot (as was the case in *This Sporting Life* for instance) nor totally alien to it. If towns were unavoidable and served as a setting for more and more films they were not filmed with pleasure, as if they had lost their appeal. A change occurred in the realm of socially constituted images when film-makers ceased to view cities as potential works of art. Assumptions can be made regarding the origins of the modification, but explanations enlighten only a precise moment – the beginning of events or evolutions – and say little about the long-lasting process of change. What interests us is the long-term trend. Over a half-century an identical, unchanged word, 'city', was automatically referred, at least in movies, to different, inconsistent images. Other significant shifts relating to racial communities, nations, work, welfare and so on could be detected throughout the same period, and we shall emphasize, later, the discontinuities in the representation of sex and gender. This book does not aim to accumulate information but rather to pinpoint noticeable transformations of collective visual references. The effacement of cinematic towns was one among many changes but it was surely not one of the least interesting.

5

CHALLENGING HOLLYWOOD

The opening credits of Fellini's *Vitelloni* (I., 1953) are printed upon a photograph taken by night, from above. It is of a cross-roads but is first and foremost an artificial setting, a replica of Rimini's central square erected in a studio for a film.[1] Other settings similar to that one had been used in American or European cinema from the beginning of the century; the presence of the junction at the outset and its frequent return throughout Fellini's movie was therefore a way of informing the spectators that they were going to see something with which they were familiar, a cinematic fiction. Faked settings are reassuring – remember *Brief Encounter*. The story is simple and involving but everything has been so obviously shot in a studio that it is impossible to get totally immersed in Celia Johnson's desperate quest for love. The 'classical' cinema does not conceal the fact that it is merely an 'imitation of life' (as the title of a famous American movie of the 1930s reminds us) – a close, faithful imitation, but not life. Later in Fellini's film, at dawn, after a foolish night of feasting and pleasure, the public is taken back to the crossroads and this time, unexpectedly, it is the actual setting – stones and cement instead of cardboard and plaster. Fellini, who could have chosen either a real or artificial representation, decided to play on ambiguity. The story is not 'truer' when it is shot in Rimini itself; it is still the same fiction but the viewers are asked to distinguish artificial from real. Of course, they can ignore the distinction. They can also try to puzzle out its meaning; it is up to them to concentrate on the plot or to allow their attention to waver from the story to the setting and vice versa. *I Vitelloni* is, in many respects, a classical film, with an introductory sequence, some episodes, a climax and an ending. It is also something different. There is no central character, no problem which must be solved, no love story. There is also an important part of the film which is purely visual; a great many shots were taken because they were interesting or enjoyable, even though they were not directly connected with the narrative. Fellini emphasized the fact that he was showing a film; not just a fiction, but also a text, an audiovisual artefact which owes its qualities to its physical components (photographs and sounds). As early as 1953 Fellini was at variance with the dominant cinema in at least three ways: some of his movies lacked a leading strand and, at the same time as including purely pleasurable shots, drew attention to the fact that they were artificially made. There was nothing new in this use of cinematic language since film-makers had already had recourse to the same devices, especially during the 1920s, but the triumph of Hollywood between the wars swept away all these experiments and imposed 'classical' patterns which were accepted by the largest audiences. Stephen Heath[2] rightly notes that the narration (the fact that a story is being told and that what is shown on the screen is not *really* happening) is not necessarily hidden in the classical cinema; as he says: 'the narration may well be given as visible in its filmic procedures; what is crucial is that it be given as visible *for the narrated*' – that is to say, for the story itself, as it is told – 'and that the spectator be caught up in the play of *that* process', for instance, the process and conventions characteristic of a genre; the film does not conceal its operations but it offers them as a transposition of a pre-existent reality. An important change occurred in the realm of cinema when movies began to confess that they were constructing the story – that the narrative did not exist outside the narration.

THE WATERSHED OF THE 1960s

This mutation was what we may call an event, but events do not have the same status in cultural history as in other fields. A political event such as the British adhesion to the EEC in June 1971 is precisely dated and has had traceable consequences, but it is impossible to say when the European cinemas started to change in this way, and it is perfectly clear that the modification was limited; most films made in the 1960s and

1970s kept to the traditional models established at the outset of the sound era.[3] Cultural innovations develop over a long period of time and once they have reached their full expansion they often become a new classicism. Technically there was no important novelty in the 1960s (nothing which could be compared, for instance, to the advent of sound). It is true that some cinematographers tried to order differently the basic components of cinematic language, but already in the late 1940s and early 1950s film-makers such as Bresson in France and Antonioni and Fellini in Italy had reconsidered the formal organization of their pictures and offered their viewers unconventional adventures in perception. Why then can we speak of an 'event' having taken place? Because contemporaries, instead of merely remarking on a few uncommon movies and labelling them 'modern', strongly emphasized the idea that something was happening.[4] In cultural matters, where tastes and opinions are determinant, the reaction of immediate witnesses must be taken seriously.

The classical style was criticized and rejected by the innovators, but what was at stake was not a total rupture with Hollywood; it was rather a challenge, an avowed attempt to make better films than America on the basis of previous American achievements. Most film-makers of the 1960s or 1970s had been film-buffs in the 1940s, were fond of US productions and admired the intelligence of the stories, the equilibrium of the narration, the quality of the pictures and the art of the performers. They borrowed many of their plots from American literature, particularly from detective stories (which were adapted by Godard, Chabrol, Truffaut, Wenders, Fassbinder and others). Numerous allusions to Hollywood were deliberately spread throughout their works. Look at Godard's *Pierrot le fou* (F., 1965). The theme – a naïve guy taken in by a pretty girl – is akin to gangster films or melodramas; some sequences in which the girl sings while the guy talks are treated like moments in a musical. The walls are covered with film posters. References are made to *Johnny Guitar*, *His Girl Friday* and other big hits. The central male character asks a passer-by: 'Have you seen a Hollywood-like, technicolor young lady?' and during one of the initial scenes he meets the American director Samuel Fuller with whom he talks about cinema. The same Fuller has a part in Wenders' *American Friend*

(G., 1977) where director Nicholas Ray is also one of the protagonists. After *Pierrot le fou* Godard shot *Made in USA* (F., 1966), the plot of which takes place in a French town called Atlantic City, the site of film studios; it might perhaps be seen as nothing but a huge film studio where people, unknowingly, recreate bits of American movies. As we have already seen, Wenders' *Alice in the Towns* begins in the USA, and although the story of one of Fassbinder's later movies was located in Germany it had an English title – *Despair* (G., 1977) – and overtly imitated an American pattern. More importantly, the young cinematographers wanted to be professionally as good as any US director. Their dream, which often became a reality, was to be invited to the United States and entrusted with making a movie there. Analysing the cinema of Fassbinder, Thomas Elsaesser emphasizes its ambiguity. It is highly formalized and likely to bewilder unprepared viewers. At the same time, as Elsaesser says, Fassbinder 'wants to make Hollywood pictures, his audience-effects keep a balance between recognition and identification through genre-formulae and the use of stars'; Elsaesser concludes, following Tony Rains, 'Sirk taught Fassbinder how to handle genre which became an important facet of his audience-getting strategies.'[5]

However, it must be understood that while admiring the art of Hollywood most of the young film-makers did not like the USA, which for them was the country of imperialism. Wenders' American friend is a gangster who exploits the gullible Germans. Godard's films, at least until 1972 (later he was less interested in political debates), were filled with what must be called a trite anti-Americanism; all the Yankees who happened to cross his screen were pictured as fat and easily taken in. In *One + One* (1969) the main female character, Eve Democracy, writes on a wall: 'FBI + CIA = TWA + Pan Am'. Godard's forceful hatred is exceptional, but the same distrust of the American way of life, the same fear of Americanization of European culture, is to be detected in many movies. This feeling is well expressed in Fellini's *Ginger and Fred* (I., 1985) where an image of the good America of the 1930s is contrasted with the schizophrenic, impersonal Italy of the 1980s totally subjected to American standards.

It has been suggested that, given their cultural background in which cinema had an important place, the cinematographers who began working in the late 1950s were tempted to 'fetishize' the technical side of their work, to consider it the most relevant aspect and even sometimes the only significant part of film-making. It would not be hard to prove that, in their films, many images are pure replicas of antecedent American ones and have no other purpose than to remind viewers of films they had seen before and probably enjoyed. Recourse to Hollywood's devices was considered a good trick to seduce a public which admired American productions and had begun to be fed up with the low quality of many European films. The watershed of the late 1950s must be analysed in its context: audiences were vanishing and for European producers the only way of finding other patrons was to seduce a good many fans of Hollywood. 'Change or perish'; as is often the case in cultural history, the innovators wanted to go back to the roots of their art and restore them. They thought that routine and stereotypes were destroying European cinema, and their conviction turned their attempt into a conflict between generations. 'I don't see how you can define the New Wave except by age,' Truffaut one day challenged the contributors to *Cahiers du Cinéma*, who had nothing to say in reply. Everywhere in Europe, film production was monopolized by mature or even elderly people. Just take a look at the British feature directors around 1960: 16 per cent of them were over sixty, 77 per cent between forty and sixty,[6] which means that the large majority of these cinematographers had been trained before the Second World War. Some of them such as Carol Reed (born 1906) were able to give classical patterns a personal touch, but they did not try to modify the dominant trends of the cinema. The young were quick to accuse their predecessors of lack of imagination but observing the situation from hindsight we can say that in fact the mid-century film-makers provided audiences with what they had enjoyed for two decades: entertainment. There was no demand from the viewers for another style of movie. The watershed was surely an important event in the evolution of European culture, but it was more the result of a clash between two conceptions of production and film-making than an answer to the needs and hopes of the spectators.

Italy did not develop polemics against the old guard. There, producers were accustomed to engaging unpaid assistants who hoped that after a long stint in the studios they would be allowed, one day, to shoot their own film. It must also be noted that the stability of film audiences in the peninsula prevented the cinematographers from looking for fresh, unknown recipes. In the other countries the renewal extended over the decade 1956–66. Britain came first. In the middle of the 1950s the 'Free Cinema' was an attempt to revive the English tradition of quality documentaries, and in its wake a few film-enthusiasts succeeded in making feature-length movies. They were associated by journalists with the 'Angry Young Men', whose plays and novels had strongly shocked the British intelligentsia; this was because their biggest hits – Karel Reisz's *Saturday Night and Sunday Morning* (1960), Tony Richardson's *Loneliness of the Long-distance Runner* (1962), Lindsay Anderson's *This Sporting Life* (1963) and other less famous films – had been adapted from their literary texts. *Saturday Night and Sunday Morning* was top money-maker the year after its release, and this was amazing at a time when, as has already been said, hits were generally comedies. Historians have been critical of the English 'New Wave'. 'What one feels most strongly is not anger but envy – the envy of a have-not for what he wants to acquire', Alexander Walker comments.[7] It is true that the cinematic Angry Young Men did not form a coherent group, that they did not innovate technically and that they parted very soon. Nevertheless, they contributed to making European cinematographers break with the theatrical conventions of mid-century productions.

The French 'New Wave' was not a school either, but it lasted longer than its British counterpart, and the new directors, although working in totally different (and often contradictory) manners, shared some basic convictions. They endlessly reiterated that it was necessary to give the camera complete freedom and, by an illusion of 'direct' shooting (as opposed to shots taken in studios), to improve the emotive quality of movies. They devoted close attention to the form, had little interest in the reaction of general audiences and were keen on finding tricks likely to interest cinephiles. In short, there was no programme, and the New Wave was mostly an idea, a sign. Once the young film-makers, who had begun by merely inveighing against their predecessors, were gathered under the same flag by newspapers, they felt obliged to question their own practice and – at least the most interesting of them,

Chabrol, Godard, Truffaut – permanently to modify their approach to the cinema.

In 1960 there was no room for the newcomers in German studios. At the beginning of 1962 some thirty angry film-lovers launched, from the small town of Oberhausen in the Ruhr, a violent manifesto denouncing the collapse of the cinematic old order. 'We declare our object to be the erection of the new German feature film. This new cinema needs new freedom . . . We are ready to cope with the economic aspect of the work.' There was no question of style or art, and it was not specified that any particular topic such as contemporary social issues should hold a privileged place in films, since the Germans were less interested in film theory than the French. Their main task was to obtain the necessary facilities and, under their pressure, an office was set up in 1965 to provide young directors with interest-free loans. The following year, for the first time since the war, a German film, Alexander Kluge's *Yesterday Girl*, won an award at the Venice festival and gained international praise.[8] The new German film-makers formed an even less coherent whole than those of Britain or France; theirs was mostly a fight to give a younger generation a right to film.

The European directors visible by 1960 had little in common but they shared some social characteristics, not least that they were descended from well-off families and had a strong cultural background. Reisz graduated at Cambridge, Anderson at Oxford, and both contributed to *Sight and Sound*.[9] In Germany Kluge was a barrister as well as a novelist; Straub and Schloendorf had university degrees,[10] while in France Chabrol, Truffaut and Godard wrote in *Cahiers du Cinéma*. Most of these men had little, if any, technical training and they reacted precisely against the idea that a long preparation in the shadow of admired directors was necessary to become a film-maker. Having bitterly commented upon the ordinary cinematic products, they considered their critical work a sufficient background. They were keen on writing their scripts themselves and claimed to be 'authors', not simply stage-directors. They were rather arrogant but eventually they proved that they could do as well as many well-trained cinematographers.

The polemics developed by the young film-makers have obscured other relevant aspects of the 1960 revival. Besides the cinematographers, young actors played a considerable part in seducing the public. In 1959 Richard Burton, born after the First World War, starred in the first of the 'angry' films, *Look Back in Anger*. The following year the leading part in *Saturday Night and Sunday Morning* was given to Albert Finney, born during the Second World War: this was an amazing jump of nearly two decades, a real change of generation which had been initiated in Italy some ten years earlier. When neorealism began to decline, *Bitter Rice* (d. Guiseppe de Santis, 1949) was an attempt to keep social problems in the background (the film tells how poor women gather to work in rice-fields of the Po valley for a few weeks), while propelling to the foreground the young, beautiful Silvana Mangano who displayed her outstanding features, making her body thus become the focus of the screen. She opened the way to a series of new actresses, Sophia Loren, Monica Vitti, Claudia Cardinale. Giovanna Grignaffini has explained well what happened then:

> The cinema of the 1950s refers to a femininity understood as *naturalness*, body 'of the earth', in harmony with the landscape . . . This had the effect of diminishing the importance of actors' interpretative skill. The 'new' professional skill of the actor essentially meant the need to keep to his or her nature: firstly on the figurative plane, then on the attitudinal and behavioural plane. This happened starting from the premise that a face and a body can tell a story, demonstrate what had led to it and show what happens next . . . New actors were trained and film actors of the 1930s were retrained on the basis of the assumption that *face and body are language*.[11]

In Italy the old generation was able to adapt to the fashion of the day, which may explain why there was no 'anger' – no sharp contests – in the peninsula. With Finney, Tom Courtenay and Rita Tushingham in Britain, Brigitte Bardot and Belmondo in France and later with Hanna Schygulla and Bruno Ganz in Germany, the external appearance of fictional characters, their looks, their behaviour, their physical presence on the screen, were modified. Brigitte Bardot was not, at least during the first years of her short career, a terrific actress but she did not care; she did not try to perform, but only to be herself and she introduced into movies a naturalness, a whimsical grace which were unknown previously. Alexander Walker evokes beautifully the 'young bodies doing acrobatically all the contortions denied to the hardened attitudes of their elders', adding that with the ascending generation 'there was none of the awful English vice of well-mannered but low-voltage characterization'.[12] Compare Celia Johnson in *Brief Encounter* (she was nearly 40) with 18-year-old Tushingham in *A Taste of Honey* (1961). The parallel is perfectly reasonable since, against an urban background, two women renounce a frail happiness which cannot be tolerated by their families. In the former, David Lean focuses on Johnson's mental reactions; we participate in the drama through her eyes or her heart, we read it on her face. Her body is almost invisible, and during the most moving scenes such as the final parting it is her facial expression which matters. On the other hand, Tushingham, except when she cries, seems unable to manifest her feelings. But she uses an extraordinary variety of attitudes and postures which make her look one moment a nasty adolescent, next a mature woman and later a small girl. She can run, leap, then stop, linger, stay idle, or erect, or bent, her head down over a banister, her chin aggressively pointed toward her interlocutors. What is involved in this contrast between two actresses is not the meaning of different stories, it is the way spectators are positioned in relation to the narrative and are invited to make sense of what is shown on the screen. Johnson provides them with an explanation: it is sad, hopeless, but what else could be done? The progression of her feelings from excitement to resignation is perfectly clear. Tushingham varies constantly; she jumps from one impression to another and she jumps in the proper sense of the word, thanks to the incessant motion of her legs, arms, head. The public cannot decide what the 'lesson' of the movie is. To put things differently, characters are more important in the first film, actors in the second. I am not trying to oppose two styles: it is up to everybody to decide which is the better or to think that both were good in their particular context. The point is that viewers were addressed in contrasted manners which entailed different responses.

Brigitte Bardot was discovered when she had the part of a maladjusted, inadequate girl in *And God Created Woman* (F., 1956). Her lines were short, almost onomatopoeic; she seemed to be outside a story which did not interest her but in which she was physically present on the screen, delighting in exhibiting her body. The discrepancy between her fictional absence and her material closeness fascinated contemporaries. Later, Tushingham's and Bardot's careers diverged but, in the early 1960s, they both featured fantasy and liberty, and their images seemed to extend beyond the frames of the screen. Anthony Aldgate remarks that the irruption of young actors into the studios was a 'short-lived love affair',[13] since the English actors turned back to the stage very quickly, while the continentals were all too happy to sign contracts in America. Now, as it happened, the outburst of new talents was another challenge to Hollywood which had just lost its idol, James Dean, and had trouble in selling its 'ageing' stars, Marilyn Monroe and Montgomery Clift. The case of Brigitte Bardot indicates that exporting European youth could have been an excellent bargain – but Bardot was the only decisive case in this field.

The Germans were especially intent on providing the new film-makers with money. Here again, Hollywood was directly concerned. Despite the fact that cinema attendance was still considerable, German cinematic production was in a permanent state of crisis. Hastily created independent film-companies did not get sufficient loans from the banks and collapsed one after the other. The distributors who made big profits were not keen on financing new films since it was simpler for them to invest in traditional productions or to buy American films. As there was no restriction on the export of profits the takings of American films were exported to the USA. No alternative cinema could develop unless another financial policy was adopted, and such was the reason why the newcomers, in their Oberhausen manifesto, insisted on the economic side of the matter. Britain seemed in a better situation since most American earnings were blocked and had to be spent in the country. But the British products financed by American companies looked and sounded like Hollywood, and when they were exported nothing could prevent the Americans from recovering the external takings.

The young cinematographers attempted to escape American pressures. The German office set up in 1965 helped to finance some twenty movies. In France director Chabrol created his own production company in 1959, and Godard imitated him shortly after. In Britain director Tony Richardson participated in an independent company which produced *Saturday Night and Sunday Morning*. Having little money, these small companies dropped the idea of making films with elaborate settings and thousands of extras. There were aesthetic motivations for their decision but also more practical limitations. The film-makers were content with few locations which were always actual ones and with a small cast of less than ten people, one or two leading figures dominating the movie. Expenses were practically confined to the wages of the most important actors who were little-known newcomers. With a small cast it was hard to stage events, and the films were deprived of significant action. Most of the time the protagonists were seen living an ordinary life, talking, walking, making dates, waiting for their friends to come. Most of the indoor sequences of *A Taste of Honey* were shot in an empty building which spared the producer the price of a studio. Tushingham was the centre of the whole story, and there were only four less important characters around her. The new cinema succeeded in offering a range of fresh experiences because the film-makers faced the problem of financing and solved it, albeit provisionally.

However, their policy did not succeed since distribution remained a crucial problem. In this field it was necessary to come to terms with the American circuits firmly settled in Europe. Some American companies, impressed by the success of the European New Waves, were ready to back independent production, but before new relationships were established with the USA, the studio system collapsed. Since the middle of the 1950s the majors which had produced at low cost in Europe, particularly in Britain, had too many movies in stock. As audiences were declining, partly under the influence of television, these firms decided to shoot serials for the TV networks and to reduce their film production to exceptional, expensive movies, domestically made. American cinema could no longer be equated with Hollywood; the myth which had filled the mid-century film-buffs with enthusiasm and exasperation was over.

Instead of making films in Europe, the Americans acquired considerable shares and sometimes a majority interest in European companies so that the budget for production and distribution was managed by them. By the beginning of the 1970s European production was entirely reorganized with the building of huge firms of international size. European companies and banks also decided to invest in American productions, which resulted in the shooting of movies so cosmopolitan that it was impossible to assign them to any particular country and in the making of typically American films such as *The Deerhunter* (USA, 1978), more than half-financed by European capital, or *Paris, Texas* (1984), co-produced by Germany and France, shot by the German director Wim Wenders and a German crew. The watershed of the 1960s was not merely a change of generation or a new trend in cinematic aesthetic. It happened at a time when the western film-market was turned upside down since Hollywood and the European cinemas were facing the same catastrophic decline in cinema-attendance.

THE LONELINESS OF THE CINEMA-GOER

The amplitude of the crisis was immediately detected by the managers who understood that cinema was not going through one of its cyclical successions of disaster and hope but was on the way to terminal decline.[14] As early as 1958 Penelope Houston emphasized in *Sight and Sound* the fact that the audiences of the day were not just the audiences of 1946–50 on a reduced scale but represented something totally unprecedented.[15] Her perspicacity might be explained by the sudden and drastic character of the decline in Britain. When she was trying to explain to her readers what was happening, the British picture-houses had already lost 56 per cent of their customers since the peak year 1946, and there had been no temporary reversal in this decrease; the rate had been permanently, consistently orientated downwards. *Sight and Sound* could easily forecast a slow, continuous fading away. The unquestionable success of the Angry Young Men did not change the trend; the losses were as heavy the year *Saturday Night and Sunday Morning* was a terrific hit as they had been previously and would be later. By 1970 cinema was already a rather unimportant form of entertainment and, during the 1980s, with a yearly average of 60 million seats sold, it was totally marginalized.

If the evolution was slower and slightly different on the continent the failure of the newcomers was as obvious there as it had been in Britain. The German picture-houses which had lost half of their patrons between the peak year 1956 and 1964 lost three quarters of their remaining customers at the time of the revival and finished, in the 1980s, at the level of their British counterparts. The decade of the New Wave witnessed the departure of half of the French viewers. On the other hand, Italy, which had no 'new cinema', resisted until the mid-1970s. Then, within a decade, she lost three quarters of her public. At the end of the 1980s, for the four countries, the total attendance was well under 400 million tickets a year (less than two visits for every inhabitant). Of course, more or less similar figures did not have the same meaning in the four countries. In 1990 France maintained one quarter of her peak year 1947. There, a slow decline resulted in the maintenance of a relatively impressive number of spectators. Italy was close to France, but in the peninsula this level, which was only one eighth of the 1957 maximum, indicated a sudden estrangement of a public which had been exceptionally loyal for thirty years and then had suddenly deserted the picture-houses.

The economic structures of the market do not fully account for the changes which occurred during the second half of the century. It is true that the reaction of the distributors was especially drastic and probably extremely damaging in Britain. Right at the outset of the crisis the two major exhibition chains decided to close some of their cinemas. In 1990, with 1,300 screens concentrated in Greater London and in the main urban areas, Britain had the smallest network in Europe. Financially, the loss in attendance was compensated for by an increase in prices: in 1990 the ticket, in constant prices, cost five times what it cost two decades before. Television channels, which showed up to 1,600 films yearly, and video-players are often charged with having undermined the cinema-going habit. Nevertheless, it must be added that 70 per cent of the population had no material possibility of ever seeing a film in a picture-house, that the tickets were much too expensive for the unemployed and that the ownership of video-players was higher among the remaining cinema-goers (who were rather well-off people) than among the other inhabitants. In Germany and France exhibitors converted their cinemas into multiple-screen theatres with small, cosy, acoustically well-equipped rooms. Cinema complexes were also built in the growing suburbs. In both countries the number of screens decreased, but more slowly than the number of spectators. As for Italy she had more screens in 1975 than in 1950. There, it was only when audiences dropped substantially that many picture-houses closed and that prices rose. Once more a parallel between the four countries is revealing inasmuch as it prevents us from overrating the impact of companies' policy. The restrictive attitude adopted in Britain accelerated the decline but the clever response of the German exhibitors was not rewarding. It was possible to slow down the decline but not to prevent it since people were less and less willing to spend their time off in cinemas.

While cinema was the definitive art of 1950 it was a negligible social activity by 1990. Is it then sensible to follow its fate throughout the three decades of its decline? I think it is, for reasons which will be revealed in the last chapter of this book. Limited though it was, film consumption was one of the cultural practices of the years 1960–90 and in this respect it deserves some attention. Cultural practices can never be studied in isolation, and this is especially true with cinema which has always been linked to the other arts, photography, theatre and so on. During the years under consideration strong relationships were established between cinema and television. Technicians, actors and directors began to move slowly towards the TV studios so that what had been experimented with by film-makers in the 1960s became some of the staple components of the 1990s television programmes.

Cinema was in crisis but it survived, with drastically fewer clients, thanks to various supports. The States, which had for a long time provided official help, continued to contribute one quarter of the budgets. Co-productions were organized between three or more countries so that financial backing was obtained from several national institutions. Yet, given the narrowness of the market, traditional sources of capital do not explain why Europe, during the 1980s, still produced a yearly average of 350 films, two thirds of which would be commercial failures. Other factors have to be considered here. The most obvious one was the intervention of the television networks. What Britain did with Channel 4 occurred, with slight variations, in the other countries where TV participated in the financing of films. In addition to the fact that they needed good fictions to balance the dramas and soaps which were the main part of their programmes the television companies desired to maintain small crews of technicians trained outside the routines of the studio: backing elaborate films offered a constructive solution to this problem. Another source of money came from private sponsors – car factories or tobacco firms – which advertised by having their names printed in the credits of a few movies. What must be understood is that cinema, which was no longer a popular form of entertainment (maybe *because* it was not popular) had become a legitimate activity, an art. Sponsoring a film was as rewarding as giving millions to restore Romanesque paintings or to erect a statue in a square. Although they did not attract huge crowds, the films made between 1960 and 1990 still have something to tell us about their epoch and the societies which produced them. The two first aspects of the survival of cinema – film consumption and the links with television – will be studied in this chapter while Chapter 6 will focus on the fictional world depicted by the movies.

Who visited the picture-houses throughout our three decades? Making generalizations about the public of the mid-century would be unfair since the audience composition varied socially, but after 1970 the rarification of attendance and the standardization of jobs in advanced countries made it possible to delineate a few, well-defined categories of spectators. Where attendance is concerned the 1960s were again a watershed. There was then a big divide between two different kinds of viewers – the 'popular' public of the mid-century which vanished and another public, yet to be defined here, which declined slowly but remained socially unchanged.

In 1950 going to a picture-house was a collective recreation. Families, which were the core of the regular spectators, attended at least one projection every week. Three decades later the average spectator was a lonely person who would occasionally visit a cinema with friends but who would generally decide individually when, how and for what purpose a film had to be seen. After the war audiences were equally divided into three groups, 15–24, 25–50 and over 50 years. In 1990, for the same age groups, the proportions were respectively 55, 20 and 25 per cent. In the wake of the family audiences those over 60 deserted. The few of them who remained interested had an extremely particular practice. They went seldom to the movies (six times a year) but they carefully prepared their visits by talking with friends and reading the comments in the papers. Limited though it was, theirs was probably the most motivated form of participation. A good quarter of the spectators were between 25 and 60. For them money was a decisive factor, and it is among them that the successive increases in ticket prices resulted most immediately in desertion. Cultural motives were also determinant for this group. Adult workers, even with comfortable wages, stopped attending the picture-houses in the mid-1950s; the closure of the suburban cinemas and the improvement of the urban ones had devastating effects on people who felt that they could no longer enter places which were too luxurious and located in streets they were not used to visiting. As could be observed in industrial districts, this was not a question of distance (many workers had cars) but of social status and self-image.

In cities, a broad distinction has to be established between the members of the managerial and professional middle class and the clerks. The former were regular visitors (once a month) when they were in their thirties but gave up progressively as they got older, wheras the latter avoided that kind of expense when they were 30 (with kids to bring up) and, around 50, began to go to the movies. The difference of behaviour is easily understandable. Most managers had university degrees and, as will be explained anon, students formed the bulk of the public. These people who could afford expensive tickets did not modify their habits when they got married and had children but they saw the films on their own, each of the spouses taking it in turn to look after the kids. After a decade or two managers stopped going to the cinema but their children, who were now teenagers, took over. On the other hand, 50-year-old clerks rid of their family obligations and getting better salaries could at last satisfy a desire previously restrained. Roughly speaking, the 30-year-old public was managerial/professional and was characterized by a regular attendance from 18 to 40 whereas the 50-year-old one the clerks – made its visits between the ages of 50 and 70.

The crucial knot was the 15-to-24 age group. Every member

of this cohort went to the movies at least once a year and, on average, once a month. Of course, these figures must be carefully scrutinized. A good half of the young people were occasional viewers (less than ten times a year) whereas the others were regular spectators (up to once a week). Employment and family income were the basic determinants, but cultural habits were also of great significance. For those born into lower-middle-class families, visiting the picture-houses, even if they could afford it, was a superfluous, almost immoral expense. They restrained their desire which would be fulfilled much later when they were about to retire. On the other hand, those born into working-class families where there was no habit of visiting cinemas and no opinion on the matter would unexpectedly attend a series of film-shows but would never become regular spectators. This is of great interest inasmuch as it provides us with a glance on the social conditioning of cultural practices. For the exhibitors the only important circle was the group of secondary-school pupils and students. Generally when they were under 20, these people went to the movies in groups whereas later they preferred going as couples. For them, attending cinemas was a ritual, a way of displaying a social status which provided more leisure time than that permitted to clerks and shop-assistants. Movies were a good topic for casual conversations, an excuse for endless arguments.

They were also a part of the specific subculture of universities. Films did not appeal to students by chance, since movies were strongly influenced by the change in taste and fashions which occurred after the middle of the century. Visual images at that time were given a pre-eminent position in social life; magazines were better illustrated, advertisements were more imaginative and, on a purely individual level, as cameras and colour film were offered at reasonable prices, photography spread quickly. Enquiries carried out in about 1960 proved that the conception of photographic images was changing. People tended to despise traditional objects (home, family), to care more about the aesthetic quality of their pictures (framing, sharpness), to consider photography as an art and themselves as artists in photography. In the 1950s most film magazines, in the manner of *Sight and Sound*, had been keen on giving their readers precise information and accurate criticism on the newly released films and on their value. A few reviews, *Bianco e nero* in Italy, the French *Cahiers du Cinéma*, the German *Filmkritik* fought hard for what they maintained to be *the* good cinema – in fact, a revised version of neorealism defined not as a set of movies but as an attempt to unveil the ambiguity of 'real' human life.[16] In the 1960s reality was forgotten in favour of aesthetic. At the same time, film criticism began to become increasingly sophisticated. Besides the cheap weeklies filled with stars' stories, glossy magazines expounded at length on film analysis. The 1960s (again) were marked by what could be called the semio-structuralist offensive which stemmed from the overwhelming influence of linguistics in all fields of scientific research. If cinema was a language (and theoreticians had defined it as such for a long time) it could be studied like a language and divided into codes corresponding to all the elements involved. Later, in the 1970s, the limits of pure description, systematic though it was, led to concern about the economy of films in the light of marxism and to a scrutinization of the spectators' involvement from a psychoanalytical point of view. *Screen*, launched in 1959, was the best exponent of these successive approaches which were also developed in *Cahiers du Cinéma* throughout a whole decade and in feminist reviews such as the German *Frauen und Film*. The articles printed in these magazines aimed to define how spectators are positioned by the stream of pictures and sounds; they were extremely elaborate and could only be understood by students or academics. Instead of merely enjoying movies, enlightened spectators who were generally fond of aesthetics and of psychoanalysis tried to develop a critical view and to expose, in their endless debates on cinema, justified evaluations. To put it differently, cinema was then the preserve of a learned, highly specialized culture.[17]

The cinematic public was thus clearly delimited. There was a large circle of cultivated people who liked 'intelligent' films and a group of ageing or elderly people who demanded entertainment of good quality. The former appreciated *auteurs* - Godard in the 1970s, Wenders in the 1980s – and constituted the core of the public interested in abstract movies aimed at small audiences. Thanks to the latter, comedies (*Educating Rita*, 1984) or nostalgic evocations (*Chariots of Fire*, 1981) met with success. Despite the permanence of these groups of spectators it was impossible to define a production policy since, in the four countries, throughout the whole period, the American cinema played a leading role and constantly attracted about one half of the spectators. American films upset the market. A few of them were ritually top money-makers and attracted up to one fifth of the attendance, the remaining four fifths being divided between a wide range of half-successful, half-unprofitable movies. The reasons for some American productions smashing box-office records were unpredictable. In series such as *Rocky*, *Rambo* or *Star Wars* some items would reach a top position, others would make little money. An erratic public composed of irregular spectators (that is to say, people who don't go very often to the pictures) would run to see only one film – not necessarily heading for great success – and creating thus a fashion, they would draw in their wake audiences amounting sometimes to over 10 million people in one country.

Historians interested in cultural activities stress the necessity of evaluating fiction films as evidence of social change in the light of their context of exhibition, and this sounds reasonable for the mid-century. *Open City* was more representative of its epoch because of the enthusiastic response of the spectators than because of its content. But for the period which followed the 1960s watershed things were not as simple. The biggest hits of these years say little if anything about the contemporary world. What could be inferred from the commercial triumph of *Rambo II* or *Rocky IV*? On the other hand, films which were modestly appreciated dealt uninhibitedly with crucial issues of the time and, nowadays, can help us to understand the period in which they were made. The relationship of cinema to society had changed drastically. The Americans and a few European producers focused on the box-office, while other cinematographers cared more about the problems and significance of making films. This was, to a large extent, an aftermath of the 1960s challenge to Hollywood. Financially the USA had won, but the very conception of movies, of their potentialities, of their impact on viewers, had been disrupted so that we must now try to define what kind of film style was inaugurated then.

TWO OR THREE THINGS WE KNOW ABOUT THEM

Modify a few boards in the railway station of *Brief Encounter* and viewers will be convinced that the story takes place in Germany or in Norway or in the USA. After the war the film was admired because it was timeless and featured an 'eternal' situation – happiness versus duty. The events were reconstructed through the subjective vision of a central character, a sensitive, perceptive woman, and avoided superfluous details (there were only a few glimpses of Johnson's family, enough to guess it would impede her from leaving, but no more) and established firmly a relationship between causes and effects. In short, a serious narration which provided food for thought.

It would be hard to disguise *A Taste of Honey* as a German film; there are too many shots which would have to be changed. The fact that it is located in England does not matter since the story is not especially 'English', but there is a consistency in the numerous pictures taken outdoors or in public places which create a specific atmosphere. (Not a realistic climate since the film is not a documentary, not even marginally.) Spectators are given images borrowed from actual England which, all together, create a fictional but coherent world. And there is nobody to tell viewers the story, no eye to reflect it. No psychological motivations are attributed to Tushingham; the public observes her but is not asked to 'understand'.

A Taste of Honey was not an audacious film but it was outside the norms of the classical cinema. David Bordwell defines two alternatives[18] to classical narration; first, the art-film which uses classical style but does not comply with its rules and adapts them to its own purposes and then the parametric film which is 'style-centred'. It is hard to establish a clear distinction between the two models which can be simultaneously effective in the movies. I would rather say that there are two trends of non-classical cinema which are not opposed to each other and which often co-exist. On the one hand, there is the work of narration which consists in narrating something while emphasizing at the same time the limitations and inconsistencies of any narration. What do films tell? Is not the delimitation of a 'story' an illusion or an artefact? *A Taste of Honey* is a story, but what of? It would be risky to offer a precise answer. On the other hand, there is an attempt to play with the materials of expression, to experiment with their flexibility and their resistance to delivering a precise significance. It is the interplay between these possibilities which give rise to what has been called 'modernity' in films – modernity as opposed to the 'classicism' of Hollywood.

Modern films did not eliminate the fictional protagonists. It was even this basic point which differentiated them from experimental movies made of series of abstract or at least ill-identifiable shapes. Living people were photographed for modern films, and since their images were edited with and alongside other pictures, they were inserted in the fanciful universe of movies. Behind them the horizon was not closed by the walls of a studio. The modern films were open onto the streets and much more interested in the contemporary world than their classical counterparts. Generally they were not overtly political inasmuch as they did not try to defend a cause, but they often included current events to such an extent that foreign spectators or people who saw them ten years after their release missed a great many allusions. For instance, roughly in the middle of *Yesterday Girl* the girl, Anita G., who is having dealings with the law, wants to contact a Fritz Bauer who, in 1965, was a prominent German jurist and champion of prosecuted individuals. Who could still grasp the hint and interpret it in 1975? And in Resnais's *Muriel* (F., 1963) the consequences of such conflicts as the Second World War, the Algerian war and the recourse to torture by the French army, lie at the background without ever being openly discussed. Similarly Bertolucci's *Before the Revolution* (I., 1964) constantly alludes, in an indirect way, to the rites, internal clashes and difficulties of the Italian communist party. This was a manner of emphasizing the limitations of the screen: there was a huge un-filmed world outside the cinemas; the pictures had been taken, literally extracted, drawn out of the actual universe which, out there, remained unchanged.

The new films focused on the uncertainty of any form of representation. Who was Anita G.? *Yesterday Girl* does not answer this but offers its viewers bits of information. Right from the beginning inconsistent interpretations are suggested. The German title, *Abschied von gestern*, that is to say 'departing from yesterday', seems to contrast past and present. Anita who has left East Germany might be starting life afresh. But immediately after the credits a caption tells us that 'there is no gap between us and yesterday, just a changed situation'. Anita is in another country: is there a real difference? Yesterday is imbricated constantly with today in the editing process, and the two Germanys are partly confused. Throughout the movie a judge, a social worker and a professor try to make the girl say whether she was influenced by the war and the twelve years she lived in East Germany. They say they want to help her and yet she does not give them any coherent clue. Nevertheless, she must have memories; the depiction of her present problems is interrupted by shots in which she looks much younger. Reminiscences? Or elements gathered by the film to complement the vague details collected by the well-intentioned inquirers? Every now and then the film attempts to reorder its material. Captions are displayed that define the objective of the subsequent scenes: 'she would like to mend her ways' and in reality she tries to fit into West Germany. But what do these captions point out? What is the purpose of the opinions expressed by other characters that accompany and underline some sequences? Are they meant to explain simultaneously what is being shown? Are they external accounts of behaviour, Anita's, which in fact has no coherence? There are, however, chronological markers in the film. Although they do not follow the passing of the years, it is possible to assign them to Anita's life before the outset of the film or after its beginning. It is also easy to isolate moments or events such as Anita's affair with her boss, her visit to a Jewish cemetery and her attempts to study at the university. However, these elements do not delineate a portrait of the young lady. This failed biography has nothing to do with what was achieved in *Citizen Kane* (USA, 1941). In his movie Orson Welles paralleled the contradictory testimonies of five witnesses, leading thus to a clear conclusion: we cannot account for the life of a man. In this respect *Citizen Kane* was a classical film, centred around a character and ending with an explicit statement. Unlike Welles (whom they admired) the 'new wavers' neither focused on a dominant topic nor aggregated disseminated elements around an implicit assumption. They refused to make a drastic choice and indulged in diversions which were fragments of other possible films. We see much more than is needed in the telling of Anita's story; of the judge who questions the girl, of her boss and his wife, of the student who is Anita's passing boyfriend. What is interesting is that these aborted or uncompleted secondary plots are not isolated items; they all overlap with each other, not in offering a linear reading but, on the contrary, in making the centre, the objective of the film, shift constantly and therefore in displacing the attention of the spectator. Many elements are altered or modified by doublings. Anita is in jail at the outset and at the end; she has affairs with two comparable married men, she steals several times, she is in touch with two social workers. The general principle of reiterating situations suspends any attempt towards a direct interpretation. In the affair with the boss, there is Anita, there is the particular story of the man with his wife and there is also a prelude to the affair to come. By multiplying the points of view, by precluding any simple reading and by dissolving any item (picture, sound, factual information, situations) into other items, the film proposes the bases of a story and at the same time contests them. Speaking of Antonioni, Millicent Marcus formulates an opinion which could be extended to many cinematographers of the 1960s: 'Cinema is vision in process and such a process is always an interrogative one that denies prefabricated significance and opens itself up to continual inquiry by cinematic means.'[19]

Spectators of the post-war period were provided with ready-made objects which filled two hours of show. Two decades later, viewers (who were not the same people) were alternately offered and refused the same gratification – another kind of pleasure arising from the displacement of expectations successively fulfilled and frustrated. *Yesterday Girl* wavers between two contradictory prospects – continuity and discontinuity, causation and arbitrariness. Just after the credits have been projected, the story begins. A young lady is reading while eating. Cut. She is now trying to find a convenient seat in a café in order to watch the room comfortably. Cut. A judge is questioning her. Three aspects of her personality? But then we understand she will be in jail for some time. The sequence with the judge seems to have settled something which could be understood as the present time of the film. So what was the status of the initial scenes? They are alien to the plot and it is up to the spectator either to forget them, to accept them as

Yesterday Girl (G.): How to settle in an ever-changing world?

separate bits of an unfinished portrait, to integrate them into a supposed continuity or to find many other solutions.

It must be admitted that spectators had to be fully active when looking at the new films. The public had not been passive before this period, but its participation was of another kind: given her education and sense of guilt, was there any chance for Celia Johnson to choose love in place of duty? This was a moral query in which aesthetics were only marginally involved. The new movies required that viewers built a text on the basis of the unstable data they were presented with. But the looseness of the plot made a great deal of room for other species of pleasure or surprise. Strong consistency, such as is realized in classical works, precludes diversion. Once this became weak or even lacking, patterns which would have been lost previously could now be observed. Let us try another exploration of Godard's *Pierrot le fou*. Summarizing the script would be misleading and useless. Suffice to say that Ferdinand, having met by chance one of his former girlfriends, Marianne, leaves his family, drives southward with the girl and settles on a small island.

Pierrot le fou (F.): Don't trust anything – neither the notes nor the story

The audience is shown some aspects of the French country-side, French villages, the French Riviera, but these pictures are displayed lazily as if they were the pages of a tourist brochure. There is often no contrast or complementarity between the frames, whose junction seems to be made at random. The abstract just provided does not do justice to the film since it is restricted to the story of Ferdinand and Marianne, whereas in fact the fiction is constantly interrupted by images which slow down the rhythm of the story. Some of these images are perfectly external to the plot. For example, at the outset we see two women playing tennis; we will not see them again and nobody will play tennis in the rest of the movie. Other pictures are mere repetitions of what has already been screened. Ferdinand and Marianne, having decided to leave Paris, are getting into a car; now they are in Marianne's flat again, they go down, they get into the car. Finally, there are a lot of flash shots – posters, drawings, paintings, advertisements, comics – introduced in the middle of many scenes. We have already noted the effort made by the new cinematographers to remind the audience they were looking at an artificial work and not at life, but there was more to it than this: an attempt was made to

162

enlarge the film and make the spectator's mind slip from the story to developments which were not included in the plot but which could have been developed as well as the central story. Instead of preventing viewers from trying various readings, which would have been achieved by focusing their attention on the details directly linked to the plot, *Pierrot le fou* seldom induced the audience to concentrate upon an object or an action. Spectators were allowed to let their attention linger on small details, and the film helped them to follow the story in a casual way by suggesting that the story could be different, that there were many manners of going out of a building, that any scene could be understood as a part of either a love story, or a gangster film, or a comic-strip and so on.

Another kind of spectatorial pleasure was exploited here. There was an incitement simply to enjoy pictures and sounds – their quality, their beauty, their unusualness, sometimes their uncanniness. The trip towards the south is framed by hold-ups (the characters say they need money) in two petrol stations. It is a parody of a gangster film, and this is emphasized by a purposeless, but bright and very funny, arson of a car. Before they chance to steal another car Marianne and Ferdinand walk here and there through three different landscapes. They do not talk, the sound-track is filled first by noises and then by music. The function of these sequences is not clear at all, but we are allowed enough time to observe the scenery and to note unexpected modifications in the protagonists' clothes. (Marianne is first seen in a swim-suit, later, under a heavy summer sun, she wears a jacket and a jumper. At times they have their luggage with them, at other times they do not.) The same sort of long-lasting interruption is introduced on the island. Some spectators will think that this is an attempt to suggest the duration of idle days. But even in this case, even if for many viewers these sequences are not simply casual images of sunny landscapes, the 'plot' is forgotten and we are faced with a poetical conjuring up of vacation days. The film is not a documentary about holidays in southern France. Neither is it the story of people who want to live together. However, there are two characters around whom the sequences are organized. If these people do nothing or very little they nevertheless orientate and attract the objective of the movie-camera. Look at

Ferdinand walking, in long distance, along the beach. As the camera pans to follow him it films the sky, the sea, a small hill. Then it goes closer to catch the meeting of the protagonists. Later it takes them in wide-angle. Two silhouettes, the colour of their clothes, the light of July and the nice, slow motion of the camera as it unveils a great many details without ever losing the couple, suggest a feeling more akin to the vision of photographers or painters than to the tension created by the unfolding of a fiction.

Indeed, the quest for beautiful landscapes was part of a wider research into the plastic arts and representation in general. The depiction of Anita G.'s stay in jail is interrupted by illustrations taken from a children's album. There is nobody to leaf through the book which has no part in the plot and which is too out-of-date to have been read by Anita when she was young. Drawings such as these are another means of visualizing a story, and Kluge parallels them with the film (moving images) as he will later parallel the film itself with stills or, as in his second movie, *Artists at the Top of the Big Top – Disoriented* (G., 1967), contrast newsreels and fiction. The cross-questioning on the nature of likeness and simulation which has been underlined above is supplemented here by a purely sensitive impression: these unexpected items are charming, stimulating or challenging. If such things are cleverly displayed in a movie they can even initiate something else, a non-narrative (although still fictional) segment of film. For instance, to return to Godard's film, Ferdinand and Marianne have spent the night in the girl's flat and are observed at dawn. Marianne is captured first, in semi close-up, wearing a blue dressing-gown. Cut. A girl painted by Renoir. Cut. Marianne is now in a white room whose walls are decorated with drawings and magazine and newspapers cuttings. While Ferdinand's voice calls her 'Marianne Renoir' she picks up a red pan. Godard has implanted into his film two series of visual impressions which will play an active part up to the end. The first is composed of colours – red, white, blue – which signify both the French flag and the American one as well as blood, emptiness and death. When the lovers twice leave Marianne's flat she is wearing a blue jacket and they jump into a red car. But it would be tedious for us to pursue here this three-colour pattern until the final shot of Ferdinand's suicide, painted in blue. Let us just say that it is up to the spectators to follow it and attempt to make sense of it if they want to. The second series is more artistic but just as arbitrary as the first. Paintings are inserted seemingly at random throughout the film. Sometimes they are on a wall, sometimes they suggest a similarity (Marianne could be a Renoir – although she does not look like any of the women he portrayed), but more often there is no obvious reason for them to appear. It is the pleasure of quotation, the amusement of deceiving the spectator and a wink at learned audiences: 'Can you identify this one? and that one?'[20]

Even a direct address to the public is included in the film. In the red car, Marianne and Ferdinand are filmed from behind. Ferdinand turns round while driving, looks at the public and says: 'Look, laughing is all she ever thinks about.' Marianne who sees nobody is surprised: 'Who are you talking to?' Ferdinand: 'To the spectator.' In contrast to the conventions of classicism the viewers here are not supposed to watch as if they were behind a window since the film has been made for them and would not exist without them. The new cinematographers wanted to stress the evidence of their work and to impose the idea that movies were their own products. After the credits and the initial caption of *Yesterday Girl* we are presented with Anita, in semi close-up, looking outside the limits of the screen as someone is laughing. She turns her head towards the audience, glances in our direction, then begins to read as she eats. 'Normally' the shot should not start before she is reading but Kluge seems to have edited the whole take, including the bits of film in which his actress was distracted by the crew, in order to encourage reflection on the importance of choice in film-making: 'What you see is not what has been filmed but what has been selected.' The rules of classical cinema are violated, and in this way spectators are forced to concern themselves with cinematic practices rather than with plot-content.

If it were necessary to summarize what the new cinema was aiming at we could say that it shifted the focus from the narrative to the telling of this narrative or from the message to the images. Movies were still fictions, but their inconclusiveness, their fabrication were emphasized and audiences were invited to find their pleasure elsewhere – in the diversion from story to story or in a free progression along the lines suggested by the variations in shape, colour, sound, motion and framing.

Even when they were awarded international prizes, the new films met with a weak response from the general public; they were accused of being provocatively elitist, and many of them were flops. In Britain during the 1960s the leading genres were, in order of preference, domestic comedies, romantic comedies, musicals and sex dramas. In Germany and France none of the new films was among the ten top money-makers. During the first years the clash with tradition and the challenge to Hollywood were too strong for people to accept them but even after two or three decades when the scandal had faded away, the impact of these innovations on the standard European product was limited. Take a success of the mid-1980s such as *Educating Rita*; spectators appreciated immensely the classicism of a narration which centred itself on a single character, a working-class woman, and which led inexorably to her emancipation thanks to a modern Pygmalion, the Open University and the major English poets.

Is this to say that the New Waves were unimportant experiments? Not in the least. Their weight was considerable but it lay in other fields – in the realm of television, advertising and American colossals, which were now the leading ones. I do not say that the new films exerted a direct influence but that they were part of an upheaval in taste and aesthetic judgement which took place throughout the 1970s and 1980s. When TV sets were rare people gathered around them and were just intent on watching. Once every household had its own set, attention slackened and spectators learned to skip from channel to channel. Programmes were thus reshaped to provide viewers, against the background of a dominant topic, with enough secondary themes to allow them to take a glance at the screen, enjoy a few images and quit. Dispersed attention and capacity to make details prevail over generalities, which had been fostered by the new cinema, became a daily practice on television. During the same decades television advertising, which had been initially uninventive and mostly verbal, learned to play with surprise, contrast and casual association. Short stories, or more often a series of uncoordinated pictures, led to a slogan (buy this or that) which had little to do with the images just presented. By stressing the visual quality of pictures, by separating and even opposing sounds and images, by contrasting message and content, the new films had initiated a style which was practically unacceptable in the 1960s but which became trite shortly afterwards. As for the American movies the most spectacular of them – those which would mobilize millions of spectators – broke with classical cinema. Consider *Rocky III*, a big hit of the early 1980s. It has absolutely no story. Rocky will have to confront an implacable, savage adversary, but an initial sequence preceding the credits tells us that he will win: the end is unveiled before the beginning. Presenting no surprise and no risk, the film will unfold quick, highly contrasted, colourful images against a roaring, heavily stressed sound-track. America had not seen many of the new European films which were sometimes projected by film societies but were never circulated by the big circuits. However, American film-makers were well aware of what was happening beyond the Atlantic, and producers were keen on getting young Europeans to work for them. The European challenge to Hollywood was tested, swallowed and turned into another form of shooting. Later Europe was hit in return when she adapted her television programmes to American standards. Indirectly, the lessons of the New Waves had reached a large public, but only at a time when the new cinema no longer existed.

Cultural history has rhythms of its own. In this field things change slowly, and it is often impossible to tell when the fashion of a certain time becomes out-moded. The classical cinema was well alive for about a half-century and it survived in various forms long after it had been debased by other patterns. Is it possible to speak of events here? And, first of all, what is an event in cultural terms? I would answer that it is any substantial modification occurring over a short, well-defined period of time. Cultural events are therefore rare, and it is all the more striking to see that 'something' happened in the 1960s. We should now try to discuss the extension and significance of this transformation.

In most European countries newcomers fought to get an audience, but their attempt at modifying the rules of the cinematic business did not result in a break with the existing system of production. Fiction, understood as the depiction of characters who are the pretext around which pictures and

The Eclipse (I.):

sounds are arranged, was not questioned. If a few innovators aimed to promote another, more sophisticated style, the majority of the young cinematographers went on telling stories dealing with families, love-affairs and individual concerns. They focused more on contemporary situations, recruited lively, exciting actors and insisted on making pictures technically as good as those of Hollywood; this was not an event, only a diversion.

If we want to measure the impact and limits of what was occurring then we had better take a look at Italy, which has not been mentioned frequently in this chapter since she did not follow the same road as the others. There were a few fierce innovators such as Bertolucci in the peninsula, but there was also an extensive series of movies which merely prolonged what had been successful for many years – comedies, family dramas, stories of separated lovers and abandoned children. Nevertheless, between these contrasted solutions, film-makers who were not newcomers modified their own practice. There was no necessity for them to bring in social issues since neorealism had already introduced them into the cinema. Before the Angry English, Antonioni and Fellini, to take but two examples, had featured disadvantaged young people trying to make their way in society. Broadly speaking, the main novelties of the 1960s were, on the one hand, that the

A couple and nothing else

continuity of narration was made less rigid and, on the other hand, that films tended to present themselves as artificial creations rather than as windows opened onto reality. Both tendencies can be easily delineated in Italian films. Fellini's *8½* (1963) is a fiction with a main protagonist. Nevertheless, the film persistently shifts from this man's daily life to his dreams, memories, expectations and fantasies. Marcello Mastroianni plays the part of a director who is unable to start his new film but who has a terrific imagination which provides him with much better pictures than those he would be able to shoot. The story-line is not very consistent, being mostly a succession of moments containing literary and classical dialogues, against which elaborate and sometimes disturbing pictures are combined with recurring music and a wide range of sounds. We have evoked earlier the tenuous story which is the pretext for Antonioni's *Eclipse*. At a particular moment, the two lovers part. We enter a street with the lady, we see what she sees, but so much visual data is introduced that we forget which character to observe. Then we find ourselves in another district; we watch passers-by, children, trees. Here is a lady who, from behind, looks like the protagonist but when we catch sight of her face it is not her. In fact, we have lost the characters and yet the film goes on, as if to tell us that this is cinema and we should not care about imaginary protagonists.

These new trends adopted by a few people were not rejected by the Italian public. It is true that Antonioni and Fellini were already known by 1960 and that Bertolucci's first movies were less disorientating than those he made in the 1970s. However, the cautious strategy of the Italians does not explain why their films, instead of being merely appreciated by restricted circles, met with an enthusiastic response among the general viewing public. The answer cannot be found in their style which was no less innovative but it can be found in their audience which continued to be interested in all sorts of movies while spectators were disappearing everywhere else. We are not used to looking at culture in terms of consumption, and yet it is this radical shift which precisely may be seen as an event; within a few years the commercial status of films, their value as goods, changed. We have examined in Chapter 3 the social origins of that modification, and I would like now to focus on its consequences.

For two or three decades the Europeans had regularly attended picture-houses and, throughout the same period, also listened to the radio so that they had become familiar with narrative patterns based on dialogues and linear, continuous stories. When they deserted the cinemas because their way of life and the structure of their budget was being transformed, radio and later television provided them with the form of entertainment they liked most. As has been noted previously television was sometimes (as in Germany) a prominent factor in the decline of the cinema, but more often television audiences grew up after the picture-houses had been left half empty. Throughout the 1950s and 1960s the television was a mere extension of the radio – a kind of radio with pictures – and it took it a long time before it settled the relationship between music, sounds and images in new ways. The watershed of 1960 was of little importance for most spectators who experienced more exciting changes in their lives, but it was an event for all those working in film; the Americans reorganized their production on the basis of a shrinking market and the Europeans turned towards new formulas. Yet the innovations were not simply provoked by the desire to maintain an audience; they extended to Italy where there was no emergency, as well as to the less fortunate countries. Everywhere the effort to renovate the inheritance of Hollywood and the existence of conflict between the generations were involved in the stylistic transformations. However, the results were fairly different. The Italians, still being movie-buffs, accepted novelties which repelled the other spectators. If there was, initially, no direct connection between the decrease in attendance and the new experiments, the massive desertion entailed unexpected effects for the innovators whose films were seen as elitist and useless. Other periods, and especially the 1920s, had witnessed a split between 'avant-garde' movies and mass products, but later Hollywood had considerably reduced the gap. After 1960 the interest in films declined while difficult movies gave back to the cinema its reputation as an art. There is little doubt about the inventiveness of the 1960s generation, but it was the social evolution which was the event and which modified decisively the behaviour of the European public.

6

A TIME FOR REVISIONS

In the 1980s several European films featured the death of cinema. Sometimes a picture-house which had entertained an enthusiastic community for many years was shown as progressively deserted and finally obliged to close. In other cases a group of movie-buffs sadly recollected the wonderful 1960s, a period when life could be centred on the cult of 'great' movies. This wistful vision was characteristic of a decade which witnessed the end of separated, often opposed, national traditions in Europe and which was therefore keen on revisiting the past. Yet cinema was not really decaying. Films were financed by banks or industrial firms more often than by studios; they were sold to television networks or dealers in video-cassettes rather than to distributors and they were viewed on small screens rather than in cinemas, but the number of movies regularly issued and offered to the public was almost as great as it had been during the glorious period of the mid-century. The nostalgic films of the decade were also typical of their period inasmuch as they focused on a few people minutely observed in their daily activities. The cinema of the 1980s was akin to television; it provided television channels with prestigious, well-made products and at the same time it was deeply influenced by the practices of television companies which enquired into the life of various social strata and offered the result daily to their audiences. Caught between their desire to return to the past and the necessity of looking around them film-makers were also attracted, in two contradictory ways, by the sophisticated, highly intellectual legacy of the New Waves and by the more direct, much simpler style adopted by television. Films may no longer have been shot to be shown in picture-houses but, economically as well as artistically, they were still important enough to furnish social scientists with relevant information about the tastes and the main concerns of the period.

TELEVISION, CINEMA, HISTORY

Cinema was still in its infancy when it discovered 'History' and then established a long-lasting involvement with the representation of the past. During the 'classical' era historical films were seldom top money-makers but neither were they disasters and they were in distribution for many more years than most of the other movies since spectators knew exactly what they could expect: the depiction of an unfamiliar period on the one hand, combined with good, involving stories on the other. Cinema contributed in reinforcing the various national traditions, in celebrating their great men and in strengthening the somehow stereotyped division of the past into 'periods' such as the Ancient World, Medieval Times and so on. The percentage of history films (about one sixth of the production) remained the same after 1960, and the title of the movies continued either to evoke an atmosphere – the charm and flavour of older times – or to focus on important people. *Amarcord* (I., 1973) – in other words 'I remember' – synthesizes perfectly the spirit of the first kind which recalled the late Victorian era, the splendour of the dying colonial empires, the hopes and fears of the inter-war period or the reconstruction of Europe. The second type of history film included such figures as *Stavisky* (F., 1974), *Our Hitler, a Film from Germany* (G., 1977), *Gandhi* (1982) and *Rosa Luxemburg* (G., 1987). History films continued to be advertised in the same, traditional way with an emphasis on costumes and heroes and yet they offered not only another vision but even another conception of the discourse on the past. It is this shift that we should now analyse, and the causes and effects of which we should try to explain.

Television was the most obvious factor in the evolution. Deciding whether a film is 'historical' is simple, but the definition does not apply so easily to television. Documentaries dealing with contemporary situations or describing political contests in our time often refer to the past in order to explain the present. Television combines various epochs by inserting as examples or illustrations bits of newsreels, engravings, or testimonies of witnesses. And there is even more to it than that. Radio and television beget television; their archives are a valuable, constantly renewed and inexhaustible source of future programmes. *Heimat*, a television serial (G., 1984), which attempted to review the evolution of Germany throughout the twentieth century as it was experienced by a country family, does not open with the first days of the First World War but with the beginning of broadcasting. One of the characters who has just been demobilized in 1919 becomes a radio amateur and by exchanging messages with other amateurs widens the horizon of the village. The successive episodes of the serial integrate aspects of the development and influence of the audiovisual media. Where history is concerned spectators' expectations are therefore fairly different in a picture-house and in front of their television set. The cultural background against which they enjoy a historical movie is their previous knowledge which will be confirmed and improved whereas television offers them incursions into their own life by reusing documents they have already seen five or ten years earlier. Cinematic history looks a bit like school history, televisual history has the flavour of an ever-present memory.

Classical history films were artefacts which attempted to re-enact, to recreate, dead events. The scenery had to be accurate and to conform to the models already offered by pictures or engravings. Laurence Olivier's adaptations of Shakespeare were praised not only for the quality of the performance but also because the director had managed to find colours, lines, framings and clothes which reminded his audience of medieval manuscripts. Visconti's *Senso* (1953) enthused its viewers all over Europe since it imitated, deliberately, the Italian painters of the mid-nineteenth century with their vast horizons, their skies ending in the sea and their sunny mornings. Actors recited elaborate texts which were lectures on history and encapsulated what was considered the 'spirit' of an epoch. Cinematic history was simultaneously close to its model and artificial, possible and fallacious. Julian Barnes, taking the case of concentration camps, has humorously explained why actors prevent audiences from fully accepting or being taken in by what they were shown:

The eye – ignorant or informed – is always drawn to these pyjamaed extras. Their heads may be shaven, their shoulders hunched, all nail varnish removed, yet still they throb with vigour. As we watch them queue on screen for a bowl of gruel into which the camp guard contemptuously spits, we imagine them offscreen gorging themselves at the catering van.[1]

Televised history parted very early from its cinematic counterpart in at least three ways. The cameraman who filmed an event as it happened took what he could see, which was extremely limited, his lenses being obstructed by passers-by. His movements, however careful he was, had repercussions on the screen, so that his pictures looked rough and imprecise. It was therefore necessary to compensate for their bad quality and to link them by means of a commentary. The function of the journalist or of the specialists who explained the story was fundamental. Their voices told how things had happened; it was the truth. As they wanted to avoid monotony and as they often lacked visual material they asked witnesses: 'what did you think of that event, how did you interpret it?'. But a great many viewers had also lived through the same event or had heard of it at the time; they felt deeply involved and reacted against or in favour of the talking heads who reminded them of their own past. Television history lacked the righteousness, the certainty, the simplicity and evidence of cinematic history; it was not artistically organized and was as uncertain and imprecise as the look everybody takes at the contemporary world.

Contrary to traditional history films, which often began with a scholar opening an old book and saying 'This is what I have found in the archives and I am going to disclose the whole truth on the topic', the films made after 1960 were frequently presented as enquiries which were still in progress. The past career of Stavisky (a swindler whose bankruptcy had a dramatic impact on French political life between the wars) was reconstructed thanks to questions raised by the police or by some of his friends. Important moments of Gandhi's life were reported by a journalist who could only take a partial, incomplete glance at the events. The main character of *The Ploughman's Lunch* (1983) was a BBC commentator who tried to

175

reinterpret British foreign policy not in the light of archives but in accordance with Britain's present situation. The possibility of different versions of the same event (already mentioned among the innovations of the New Waves) was reversed onto history which was no longer pictured as a pre-existing reality that films should copy but as something painfully, contradictorily inferred from partial testimonies. Replacing historians by journalists was not a mere trick. In fact, the origins of what was said and its credibility were different; an attempt to establish truth (if this is ever possible . . .) lost its importance in comparison with immediacy, which was what television offered its public.

Written reports made after an event has occurred can expand on its origins and circumstances whereas visual documents of the same event are more alive but less explanatory since they originate in the middle of the incident and at no distance from it. Even when films were shot during a riot, a car-crash or a murder attempt it is extremely hard to tell how things happened just by looking at the pictures. Television has accustomed the public to simultaneously listening to a limpid talk and watching chaotic, ill-ordered shots. A history film could easily make its viewers apprehend, visually, how Gandhi organized the march to the sea or in what circumstances he was killed or why his funeral turned out badly. An aerial view of the site, a glimpse at the protagonists, a few well-chosen details are just what is needed for that task, but it is the sort of exposition television cannot provide when it tries to show what is happening; in the 1970s shots of that kind became outdated, since they appeared too abstract, too deprived of the immediacy television supplies. In Richard Attenborough's *Gandhi* the dramatic moments were emphasized by the rapidity and seeming incoherence of the editing. Here we are in the middle of a crowd, the importance of which we appreciate only because of its roars. A young man half-makes a gesture of protest, a policeman runs into him. Quick close-ups of faces, of the policeman, of frightened women, of witnesses backing away, of the young man. A uniformed arm crosses the screen – striking whom? The shots become shorter and shorter, mixing up horses, bodies, limbs, faces – and the dust which blurs everything. If television had been there it is probably what it would have presented its audience with.

What *Gandhi* and with it all the screened biographies

mentioned above were questioning was the ability of the historical discourse to account for the continuity of time as it is experienced in daily life. Movie-cameras only catch limited moments – sometimes important and sometimes not – which are, at any rate, separated bits of an uninterrupted flow but which are likely to become significant, 'historical', only because they have been conserved on film. It is the document which, very often, gives an episode its relevance. Instead of telling the whole life story of the Mahatma, *Gandhi* reconstructed a few precise, well-known circumstances which have for a long time been the main components of a general, widely diffused knowledge about India. *Rosa Luxemburg* was almost entirely organized according to the succession and content of Rosa's letters since it is on this limited basis that we have access to her life. *Our Hitler* went even further. There are a great many pieces of evidence to document this period, but how is it possible to order them? Historians are able to explain Hitler's career and the rise of Nazism, but in 1978 Hitler was more than a historical figure, he was 'theirs', a cumbersome item belonging to all the Germans, passed over in silence and yet present everywhere in papers, in records, in libraries, in discussions. There were hundreds of Hitlers – the private man, the leader, the chancellor, the warrior – and there were many periods in his relationship with Germany. *Our Hitler* manipulated the material television would also have exploited – newsreels, photos, radio transmissions – and it submitted it to the rules of television. The entire film was conceived as a patchwork, a collection of partially inconsistent pieces of information in which the trivial disclosures of Hitler's valet were given as much space as the Führer's speeches. Hitler was at times himself or rather his photographic or cinematic representation, and at times an actor in the various clothes which a tyrant or a ridiculous, very bad actor could have worn. As the film lasts about eight hours it was divided, in picture-houses, into two shows. Nobody was able to follow all of it attentively, and spectators were meant to watch it with the same alternating attention they paid to television. Pauses were even managed with the intervention of puppets, or the comings and goings of a small girl who might be the public itself looking for its way through a heap of ill-assorted elements. There was something purely experimental in this film, but it shared with the other biographies its indifference towards chronology and its contempt for global, comprehensive explanations. People saw more of Stavisky's private life and petty larcenies (he was able to steal his girlfriends' belongings) than of the gigantic swindles in which MPs and journalists were compromised. Stavisky's peaceful, hedonistic activities were interrupted by sequences devoted to the arrival and short stay of Trotsky in France. These two separated universes were so far away from each other that the film did not try to contrast or parallel them. They existed in the same years, the 1930s, but so many events occurred then that attempting to evoke them all would be preposterous. So the film contents itself with mentioning a few of them. While *Stavisky* and *Gandhi* renounced an explanation of the fate and actions of a man and merely represented some points in his life, *Rosa Luxemburg* tried to follow a leading strand. Rosa used to write when she was in jail but she was imprisoned so often that one jail could readily call forth another jail and then another one. From the guardhouse where she was held in 1916 and where the film began, a jump was made backwards to her first time in jail in 1906. At that time she was forced to endure the ritual of execution cancelled at the last minute. Death/life: the ordeal was a good pretext to look at her childhood and education. The film wavered from one period to another – the letters with their strong emotional appeal being the only stable references, the pivots of the narration.

Here television was again the model. 'Oral history' – in other words, history in interviews – was adopted early as the commonest trick of broadcasting since it costs little and sounds alive, spontaneous. The history evoked by witnesses is everybody's history, a compound of minute individual reminiscences and more general facts. As Robert Rosenstone has noted, this kind of documentary

> bows to a double tyranny of the necessary image and perpetual movement. Woe be to those elements of history which can neither be illustrated nor quickly summarized . . . . This kind of work must not be mistaken for critical history, and cannot be judged by the standards of written history. It is a visual sort of history, history of hommage. The strength of this sort of work is not analysis or theory,

Rosa Luxemburg (G.): A story told in jail

not the combining of details into a powerful, logical argument, but the evocation of emotion, the etching of individual character, the magic ability of verbal and visual memory to bring an earlier world and earlier selves into the present.[2]

Spectators quickly became accustomed to a simple, often touching and involving vision of the past. The person who was telling their experiences looked like them, was one of them and consequently made them potential candidates for future confidences on their own lives. Film-makers adhered to this fashion which liberated them from the tedious task of transcribing into pictures or words the complexity of historical events. Rosa Luxemburg was thus depicted primarily as a woman, then as a militant and never as one of the most important marxist theoreticians of the early part of the century. Rooted in a scrupulous study of the letters and written documents, the film was perfectly accurate in its presentation of the main character but was allusive on important aspects of the context such as German social democracy, its parliamentary situation and its impact on the working class. Rosa remained first and foremost a private individual. On leaving her first jail, she was seen going to her brother's house, taking her niece to her bedroom, singing her to sleep. Her two lovers, her best friend Louise Kautsky, her cat were some of the leading protagonists, she talked with the first man about love, children and family, she visited the Italian lakes with Louise. She was not interviewed directly by an imaginary reporter, as was the case in other historical movies,[3] but the film aimed to reconstruct her internal vision and to recreate her feelings or impressions. The sequences in jail were edited abruptly with shots taken from different angles and in various scales, as if the days spent there were a mere addition of fragmented moments. When she was free, longer, more elaborate shots exposed uninterrupted actions. During the first visit to Louise in Berlin the colours were extremely sophisticated. The ladies wore dresses whose whiteness was accentuated by Louise's pink collar and Rosa's black belt; they moved slowly, making it clear that they enjoyed fully the pleasure of being together. The two meals taken at Louise's with the leaders of the Social Democrats, despite the harshness of the political debate, were filmed with the softness characteristic of delightful hours, whereas the rupture with Kautsky (Louisa's husband and Rosa's old friend) were limited to a deliberately clumsily framed and rather quick shot.

THE RETURN OF THE REPRESSED

In the 1970s the European cinemas, prompted by television, which was quickly gaining an audience, adopted a new presentation of history which relied on people's recollections or beliefs; it combined various documents and sources, did not concern itself with continuity and no longer tried to offer a global, all-encompassing account of events. Is this to say that cinema copied television? There was certainly a standard European pattern of cinematic history which can be traced in the different countries, but cinema was also differentiated from its rival. Televised history depended mostly on talking heads – on their attractiveness and capacity to convince. It was authoritative and peremptory inasmuch as the immediate presence of the voice signified direct, unquestionable truth. Cinematic history had much more variety; it could say rather complex things by playing on the complementary relationship between words and pictures. During a meeting featured in the film, Rosa Luxemburg accused the German government of preparing for war. Immediately after her speech the film showed her in a court. The public prosecutor had finished his statement and Rosa was about to speak. No words were necessary; the contrast between the initial shot and the following ones was strong enough to explain that she was being prosecuted. In replying to the prosecutor Rosa addressed the court, not the spectators; the speech was a plea, it was unequivocally presented as Rosa's personal account of the facts. Cinematic history was thus less assertive than its television counterpart and managed more space for doubt or reflection. Cinema often made use of heterogeneity – contrasting two inconsistent stories in *Stavisky*, assembling disparate constituents in *Our Hitler*, interweaving private affairs and public concerns in *Rosa Luxemburg*. The intersection of different periods was especially effective. Flashbacks can be prosaic devices in films, and historical movies avoided them before 1960. After that date they became more and more frequent since, in opposition to the common conception of causality, it was often a recent event which, retrospectively, gave meaning to a previous episode. This was the case, for instance, with Stavisky's first arrest which took on another significance eight years later when the swindler was at the peak of his success, or with Rosa Luxemburg's first love affair in Poland which looked differently when it was inserted in the middle of her fight for an international union of workers. Interestingly cinema, which had for a long time accepted the linear, continuous discourse previously developed in history books, began to question the methodology of historians and to contest the ability of scholars to reconstruct the actual sense of past events. Television provoked noticeable changes in the field, but cinema was able to go farther and to offer an original, often provocative, version of history.

If they were comparable from a stylistic point of view the European historical films told disparate and contrasting stories. When dealing with social issues film-makers tended to treat the same problems, but where history was concerned national pride resisted such contamination. The themes themselves were borrowed from local traditions, and few cinematographers attempted to cope with the past of a country other than their own. Inside these strictly geographical limits various inflections, various accents, were given to the representation of former times; the four countries displayed their respective production along a curve, one extremity of which was occupied by British nostalgia, the other by German self-criticism.

Longing for 'these days we have lost' had been a commonplace of cinema since its beginning. *Chariots of Fire* (1981) or *Maurice* (1987) prolonged a long tradition of pictures which softened the potential harshness of social, racial and sexual prejudices by idealizing the good old times. If the characters had to suffer, nevertheless recourse to faded colours, outmoded clothes, fanciful furniture, social rites and a harmonious musical accompaniment was enough to give their fate the flavour of a happy period. Nevertheless, beside sentimental remembrance, nostalgia had another, rather surprising aspect, when it was the regret for an avowedly distasteful period. The Italians took a glance, half-ironic, half-fascinated, at fascism. It is true that the father of the main character in *Amarcord* was administered castor oil by the Black Shirts, but after all he was an old bore; and fascism, with its masquerades, its street demonstrations, its Mussolini portrayed in flowers, seemed more childish than harmful. France focused more on a very disheartening epoch, the Nazi occupation. While confessing that people starved and that Jews and resistants were threatened by the police, the films could not help depicting the mysterious spell of the period. In a context of fear and persecution the most trite stories (an actress who cheats on her absent husband with a young actor in *The Last Metro*, 1980) were given a hint of morbidity which made them more thrilling than ordinary melodrama. Critics coined the expression 'retro-epic' to label a retro-gradation in time which allowed film-makers to lure their spectators by embellishing a dull past. Love was more exciting when the Gestapo was hanging around.

Britain indulged in the fashion but she added to wistfulness an even stranger touch. Trapped beneath a grey sky, drowned in rain or smog, her cinematic characters did not have romantic affairs. *Wish You Were Here* (1987) was emblematic of this dreary and yet captivated look at a mean past. It was first of all a reconstitution of the Golden Age of movies with all its rituals.[4] The gags – for instance, the boy called to by a girl who turns his head and falls from his bike or the dog which chews a french letter – were borrowed from black-and-white films.

Linda, the central character, went to the movies with her first boyfriend and imitated the stars to such an extent that while he was pawing her her fears and desires were expressed by the heroine of the film which was on at the time. Her second lover was a projectionist and she lived with him in the attic of the picture-house. After having described her failure, the film ended with a dream in which she imagined her triumph as it would have been represented in a happy-ending movie. Against this background the plot developed a double nostalgia. As a fictional protagonist Linda looked back with longing to the war because at that time she had had her mother (who died shortly after her father's return) to herself. At the same time the camera was looking with fondness at the setting, a reconstitution of 1950s England, in which the actress, Emily Lloyd, was being filmed. Yet the story was pitiful, and there was nothing to give Linda's part any exciting or at least involving aspect. Reminiscent of *Family Life*, which was indirectly quoted by similar frames or situations, *Wish You Were Here* did not accuse the family or the medical system, as was the case with the other film. There they were, these 1950s, desolate, squalid and yet appealing. With the exception of Germany the European cinema yearned for the first half of the century when nations were still nations, when Englishness or Italianness were supposed to have had their full meaning. Life was not always pleasant but it was spent in a familiar cultural environment. If bemoaning over past periods is common to all epochs the peculiarity of the 1970s and 1980s was that a decaying cinema, confronted by a television mostly interested in present, urgent problems, undertook the mourning but achieved it in an equivocal, half-despising, half-grieving way. Cinema, possibly because it had lost its influence and was being marginalized, was an exceptional yardstick by which to measure the reluctance of the Europeans when they entered Europe.

Idealizing the German past would have been difficult. After two decades of quasi-silence Germany looked again at Nazism, and films began to present the direct effects or pervasive influence of Hitlerism and to depict the ruin brought about by war. We have noted that *Our Hitler* emphasized the invisible presence of the Führer in 1978. Almost simultaneously Fassbinder's *Marriage of Maria Braun* and *Lola* focused on the continuity of German history. In Coburg, the town where Lola lived during the 'economic miracle', rebuilding was not finished yet. As for Maria Braun her fate was followed from the days of the Allied bombings over Berlin to the late 1970s. Both films dwelt on the actuality and permanence of war threats: pacifists demonstrated in the streets of Coburg and broadcast talks on rearmament poured through Maria's flat. The recourse to radio (a typical trick of the period, as has been said) had an important function in the movies. It created a feeling of reality: the Stockholm soccer cup or Chancellor Adenauer's speeches had actually been heard on radio and they were unquestionable chronological landmarks. However, their status in the films was ambiguous. In the middle of *Lola* the girl is given a lift by a high-ranking civil servant whom she fancies. Before they part she warns him against the corrupt politicians of the town. Their dialogue – half-serious, half-flirtatious – is scrappy and every time they keep silent a radio intrudes. Broadcasting can thus be interpreted either as an unbearable nuisance which encroaches upon the most intimate moments, as a giver of information on the historical context or as an expansion on Lola's distrust of politicians. All the historical clues are ambiguous and can be interpreted in contradictory ways. Take the presentation of the pacifists. Undoubtedly the films are hostile to war but their vision of pacifism is equivocal. Chancellor Adenauer is heard twice in *The Marriage of Maria Braun*; the first time, he speaks against the rearmament of West Germany, which he endorses in his second talk. If the pacifists of Coburg are mocked by stupid middle-class people they also get the support of the worst swindler in town and their leader walks out as soon as he is offered a good job. However, the movies did not aim to develop the banal idea that there are several truths because Fassbinder was mostly interested in providing a multidimensional version of history. Various layers of events were set down throughout the narration, and many of them resurfaced later at different moments of the story. The hidden presence of the past was symbolized in *The Marriage of Maria Braun* by Maria's husband, Hermann, who alternately was forgotten or had his part to play in the plot. At the outset of the movie unquestionable evidence proves that Hermann, who left for the front line the day after he married Maria, has been killed. Yet he comes back; but the film, under the pretext of a melodramatic murder, conceals him again. He will reappear every now and then and will eventually die with Maria. While he is away the lady leads her own life with two other men she does not want to marry. Marital fidelity? It is possible,[5] although she does not display much fondness every time Hermann re-emerges. As James Franklin says, the components of the film 'function not only as elements of naturalistic setting but as metaphors'.[6] The emblematic character of these elements manifests itself in the fate of Maria herself. Using her skill and sex-appeal she gets the help of a GI, later of a French businessman, and becomes wealthy. This allegory of Germany evolving from her reconstruction to membership of the EEC would be prosaic if it were not modified by the cyclical, ill-motivated recurrence of other characters or objects. I have stressed in Chapter 5 Maria's periodic visits to her ruined family house and I have just noted the importance of radio broadcasting. I could consider the intermittent appearances of a doctor, an accountant or Maria's mother or the reappearance of various objects. Unlike the ruins which point out the long-lasting effects of the war, or radio which stands in for politics, most characters or objects do not personify any defined fact and are mere resurgences of the past.

The German historical films must be studied in the light of the controversies which broke out over Germany in the 1960s. Georges G. Iggers has explained how, after a general consensus to avoid any re-examination of the Nazi period had become apparent after two decades, a new generation – those born after 1945 – denounced the inadequacy of the classic history. The condemnation involved 'not only disillusionment with the German political past but also doubt regarding the cultural value and relevance of history in a modern techno-logical society'.[7] The debate was not purely academic, since the public felt deeply concerned. In Germany, between 1974 and 1982, there were only eight domestic films out of the ninety top money-makers but five of them dealt with Nazism and its aftermath. If *The Marriage of Maria Braun* was not among the top ten it ranked twelfth in 1979, which was more than decent for a difficult movie. Cinematographers played their part in the discussions. They contributed to deepening the scepticism regarding the relevance of a linear and prevalently political account of the past and emphasized the continuing influence of Hitlerism. However, they were not historians and their movies were addressed less to scholars than to the community of film-makers. It is necessary to see their works in the context of European film production and in this respect the most striking fact is the influence of the New Waves.

Let us contrast two films which were successful both domestically and abroad – *Chariots of Fire* and *The Marriage of Maria Braun*. Alexander Walker notes rightly that the former 'is not the story of a rivalry: its two heroes do not run *against* each other, they run *for* their ideals'.[8] He could go farther: the film deliberately escapes any risk of conflict. Not only does it create minute problems (is it fair for an amateur to pay a coach? Are Christians allowed to run on a Sunday?) which are easily solved but it has recourse to all the available devices – music, colours, camera-motions, framing – in order to confer a perfect smoothness on the narration. Stylistically the film is on the other side of the world from modernism. On the other hand, *The Marriage of Maria Braun* takes advantage of the legacy of the New Waves to establish contradiction as the core of the movie. Conflicts do not concern opposed fictional characters but are created by the discrepancy between a continuous story – Maria's progress towards wealth – and the intrusion of seemingly ill-mastered elements of the narrative. Contrasting British nostalgia with German criticism is correct but superficial. Two visions of history were in competition. The first conceived of the past as a continuously and peacefully unfolding process and mourned for that lost time. The second asserted that beneath a seemingly coherent evolution the world is doomed to variability and unevenness and that the most dreadful periods of the past are those which have the most lasting effects. Freud called the brutal, irrepressible irruption into con-sciousness of unacceptable feelings or recorded memories buried deep in the unconscious the 'return of the repressed'. The notion, formulated at a time when Freud was applying psychoanalytic findings to anthropology,[9] is simple enough to be exported from metapsychology into sociology. Television, with its carefully controlled evocation of individual destinies, did not facilitate such 'return' and it was therefore cinema which liberated the hidden past and unveiled two different kinds of repression. In Germany, Nazism resurfaced violently.

Inasmuch as it had been concealed by the dominant discourse, its return induced film-makers to disqualify any form of history. In the other countries, and especially in Britain, history was used to display the fears provoked by the imminent decline of national traditions. There the discourse on the past was mostly a disguise for more urgent concerns, and the methodology of history was not directly attacked. In this respect cinema helps us to evaluate how distant from each other the Europeans were on the eve of federalization.

FROM FIGURAL NETWORKS . . .

The Marriage of Maria Braun reminds us of something we have already observed when studying Godard and his participation in the New Wave. *Pierrot le fou* was studded with elements such as colours, drawings or paintings, which were not related to the plot but which could be linked together because they shared some similarities. Godard used them to suggest that many combinations, many texts dealing with various aspects of art, were to be found in a film. Fassbinder did not isolate clusters of images which could be read either separately or jointly. What he did was to make all the components interlock in Maria's story and create another text behind the story of his character. The films of the 1970s, be they historical or not, were penetrated by these elements of signification which acquired force because they found echoes in the course of the movie. I suggest we call 'figural networks' the patterns that spectators are likely to constitute by bringing together the various components which are dispersed throughout a film but which are stylistically akin to each other. Many of these fragments have a function in the story but once they have been extracted from the continuity of the plot to be related to other fragments they stop conveying a significance. They become 'figures' – that is to say, pictures or sounds which catch viewers' attention because their external appearance allows them to be referred to other fragments. Together, these components constitute a partially autonomous whole, a 'network' based on formal properties, not on the logic of the plot. In *The Marriage of Maria Braun* the ruined house when it was seen for the first time was assigned to 1945. When it came back for the third time viewers could also interpret it as a sign of the permanence of war (and its origins, Nazism) in the 1970s. Of course, not all spectators were sensitive to figural networks and many of them were content with following Maria Braun's progression from poverty to affluence. However, those who detected the figures behind the story practised a more active reading which contrasted individual destiny and collective evolution.

All this may sound a bit abstract and, given the importance of figural networks in a great many movies of these decades, I think we had better start with a case-study. I shall focus on *Stavisky* because it is a history film which has already been examined from another, more classical, point of view. After an initial sequence dedicated to Trotsky the second sequence of the film introduces us to Stavisky. He settles with a friend and his secretary in the lobby of the luxurious hotel where he lives and begins to talk with the other men. The shots are classically ordered and present us sometimes with the group, sometimes with one of the interlocutors. Suddenly, while the friend is reading loudly from a paper about the persecution of the Jews in Nazi Germany, we are offered a close-up of a splendid diamond pendant. Later we shall understand that Stavisky, who is not interested in what his friend is reading, has spotted the pendant on the neck of a lady but at any rate he cannot inspect it as closely as the spectators do. By focusing on the jewel, the film tells us that this is a relevant item. For the plot? Yes, to a large extent since the swindler succeeds in purloining it and gives it to his wife. But the same pendant and many other jewels intervene throughout the movie. If they prove that Stavisky is able to cheat a harmless lady as well as on a famous jeweller they point also to other, less obvious things. In the film some diamonds are genuine, some are fake and none of those who sell or buy them is perfectly honest. Glittering and beautiful though they are, diamonds convey with them a suspicion of fraud and forgery. They are also closely associated with ready money. Stavisky and his fellows do not stop speaking of money, but it is an abstraction, a pretext for endless discussions. If cash is seldom seen it is related to jewels when it appears. Genuine or fake diamonds circulate; they are bought and given to women as symbols of true love or love that is bought. At the same time, women are regularly associated with money – or rather to discussions on money. Immediately after he has spotted the pendant, Stavisky questions his secretary about cheques he has to sign. Later, while they are making love, the lady with the pendant tells him about her financial problems. I do not need to prolong the list – the fact is that women trigger off debates on money.

In the course of the film Stavisky is in touch with three women – the lady with the pendant, his wife Arlette and a young German Jewess, Erna. We have seen that the lady is introduced into the narration while Stavisky's friend is commenting on Nazi persecutions. Erna tells Stavisky she has been obliged to leave Germany. As for Arlette, she is insistently associated with three colours – black, white and red – the colours of the imperial and then Nazi flag. Stavisky does not listen to his friend or Erna and although he is extremely sensitive to Arlette's elegance he never notes the colours she is fond of. The first appearance of the lady with the pendant, which has dragged in its wake money, jewels and Nazism, is also underlined by a profusion of flowers. Discreetly summoned by Stavisky, bellboys come and surround the lady with bouquets. Later the same will be done with Arlette. Of course, the symbolism of women/flowers is so trite that the significance of flowers must not be overrated. Nevertheless, let us look at Arlette while she is between her bouquets. She is lying on her bed asleep and there are bunches all around. It is as if she were dead – and retrospectively the bouquets which enclosed the lady, parting her from the rest of the lobby, acquire a funereal significance. There is Nazism, there is death and to boot there is the red which intrudes where Arlette is – the red wine she spills on the white tablecloth, the red flowers she is given, her blood. Interestingly, Arlette is almost silent. She is young, slim, beautiful, she is a perfect woman of fashion framed by the camera as if she were a model; her whole body is an image of happiness but the three times she has a few lines she only speaks of death. However, the film does not tell spectators: 'Women are easily bribed' or 'Women are dangerous', it avoids that kind of trivial generality. Arlette or Erna never ask for money, and if Arlette is insistently linked with death; Erna, who has escaped Nazism and is keen to earn her living, calls to mind hope and life. It is therefore impossible to define the network, let alone to give it a title.

To a large extent, *Stavisky* is a classical biography told from the point of view of the main character. Once upon a time there was a charming fellow who was able to fool wealthy people and make them entrust him with managing their capital. As long as he continued to borrow more money he led a sumptuous life. But the day he was asked to reimburse he was lost and he did not realize very clearly that bankers, politicians and managers were imperilled by his swindles. It is a banal story which has been filmed many times, but spectators do not dislike being shown a fresh version of an everlasting plot. The film was made a bit intriguing by the lack of temporal sequence of the narrative, the continuity of events often being broken by the intrusion of events which had taken place earlier or would happen after Stavisky's death; but, in the 1970s, viewers had got used to the partial reversibility of cinematic time. Spectators were offered a psychological portrait. The historical context was reduced to very little – a few hints at Nazism, the strange, seemingly irrelevant sequences on Trotsky and short references to the French political situation. Everything was focused on Stavisky, and even details (he liked to look magnificent, covered women with flowers but he stole jewels like a vulgar thief) were likely to confer a moral significance.

What neither gave access to the fiction nor was assignable to Stavisky's personality was the convergence of regularly associated independent components – in other words, the figural networks which were neither heavy nor insistent and which looked more like an imprecise horizon, a vague, blurred background. Actually, this network was a counterpart to the obvious story – a non-historical allusion to the situation of France in the mid-1930s, to her political divisions, to her moral decay, to the incapacity of her leaders. Threats were impending upon peace and democracy, but what is perceptible with hindsight was not clear at all at the time. The discretion of the film in this direction was possibly a reflection on 'context' in a historical situation. It might also be useless to try and interpret the figural network in this way since it was basically a non-discursive creation, a play on shapes, colours, words and objects related to each other by proximity or similarity. What was typical of many films made in the 1970s was an opposition between a linear temporality producing a story and a timeless process of repetition which generated nothing and merely interwove visual and aural fragments. The figures of the network were sometimes borrowed from an external cluster of cultural or historical data, as was the case with paintings in *Pierrot le fou* or marks made by the war in *The Marriage of Maria Braun*. In other cases they were created by the film itself. In Antonioni's *The Passenger* (F.-I., 1975) screens were interposed throughout the movie. At times they were white walls or ill-defined surfaces on which protagonists appeared as if they had been brought about by the whiteness, by the fact that there must be a form on a white screen. At times they were fountains, fences, bushes which prevented one from seeing distinctly what was happening behind. As the film dealt with a former reporter who was constantly capturing images or noises, the floating screens which could alternatively reveal or conceal something were conflicting with the attempt to record everything recordable.

Networks were all the more present and effective where the story was more loosely built up. With *The Marriage of Maria Braun* it is easy to integrate most figures into the life of Maria, but this reduction no longer works when films overtly deny viewers a continuous narrative. Wenders' *Anxiety of the Goalie at the Penalty-kick* (G., 1971) begins with the destruction of its title and of the plot which it seems to introduce. Exactly two minutes and forty seconds after the credits the goalie, Ernst Bloch, who is never anxious, misses the penalty-kick and is free to roam about for the rest of the movie. He then does various things – he walks, buys several items, visits friends, travels, makes love. He even kills an usherette. However, none of these facts becomes an event since they are not related to each other, except by repetition, and seem to happen at random. Even the murder is a trifle which does not give way to a detective story. Since he has strangled the girl only just after meeting her and sleeping with her, who would suspect Bloch? If the film, from time to time, reminds us of a thriller it is because it is shot like a thriller with night scuffles, dreadful blows and corpses; but these are empty signs which alert the public to the fact that although it is seeing a film which conforms to certain conventions of film-making the signs themselves cannot be ascribed to a plot. If evidence of a crime is to hand nobody will realize it. After a journey Bloch settles in a country hotel. One morning the maid gives him a paper on which his identikit portrait is printed, and her comment is that the murderer has surely changed his external appearance. The following day while reading in the paper that the murderer has lost American coins in the victim's room the maid tells Bloch she has found American coins under his bed. She is not concerned about the coincidence and neither is Bloch. Clues convey no meaning but there are many of them and, again, they are linked by synchronism, similarity or displacement. Long before committing the murder Bloch compulsively looks for papers, switches on juke-boxes, goes to the pictures and plays with American small change. Speaking of these coins, Peter Brunette rightly notes that the film 'plays up the motif'.[10] He should specify that the four above-mentioned motives 'provide an unifying structuring device' and that these figures associate Bloch with other protagonists, notably with the women. All the girls are fond of movies and music, interested in papers and money. The usherette is not a character – merely a passing silhouette. But nevertheless we are informed that she met her former lover in a cinema, that she likes records and that she has dreamt of a dress made of American banknotes. Immediately before she is strangled she reads a paper and promises Bloch she will bring him another one. The network, strongly constituted, frames the whole film but it would be hopeless to try to interpret it since Bloch has no fictional personality and is simply what we see him do on the screen. The movie is thus a chain of signs; the most surprising aspect of it being probably the constancy and cleverness with which it brings in and interweaves its figures. There is no progression (for instance from the murder to the arrest), the same tokens appear repeatedly but in changing contexts. The figural network does not inform viewers about the protagonists and it does not help to solve an enigma; its many elements are offered as basic components of successive, variable bindings.

The Anxiety of the Goalie at the Penalty-kick and other works akin to it confronted spectators with a radical alternative to the classical cinema. In the 1970s enthusiastic critics wrote that this was a decisive shift, the end of the privilege granted to writing – that is to say, to linear, continuous reading. Truly some of the movies made during this decade were extraordinarily provocative, and the fact that they did not meet with a 'popular' response (at least quantitatively) does not prove anything. To a large extent they were close to the modes of filming and editing which television was establishing in the same period. Before coming to the relationship between figural networks and televisual patterns I would like to scrutinize what was, in many films, an inheritance of the New Waves. Even the most radical movies of the 1970s were centred on an actor, a famous name (Jack Nicholson in *The Passenger*, Hanna Schygulla in *The Marriage of Maria Braun*) or a less well-known personality. Actors were all given a pseudonym and elements of a possible biography. They were also firmly inserted inside the cinematic background. Settings were often presented as artificial constructions, flat surfaces deprived of any depth. There were for instance the recurring white screens of *The Passenger* or the movie-like pictures in *The Anxiety of the Goalie at the Penalty-kick*, but protagonists moved inside their two-dimensional frames as they would have done on a stage and there was no attempt to create fanciful or irrelevant surroundings. The novelty was that characters were not presented as fictional subjects – supposed consciousnesses capable of thinking and reflecting the world for the public. They were empty forms created by the camera and aimed only at giving spectators a feeling of continuity during the time of the show. While actors/characters were treated like signs it was the film and the film only (not the eye and brain of a protagonist) which ordered the succession of the pictures. In the middle of *The Passenger* the main character, Locke, is observing a wedding in a German church. Unexpectedly, we see him setting fire to leaves and branches in his London garden and his wife telling him this is dangerous. Then the wife is watching the garden which is now empty. Finally, we are taken back to the church where branches and leaves are lying on the floor. It is not Locke who, seeing the branches, remembers his garden; it is the film which arbitrarily brings us to London, which compares the past (Locke at home) to the present (Locke absent) and which explains how, via the branches, it has jumped from Germany to Britain. In movies of that kind characters were images, moving images. At times they were dramatized by a lethal thread which was useful to lead the protagonists to their end and therefore to conclude the films with a climax. Protagonists happened also to be totally de-dramatized. In *The Anxiety of the Goalie at the Penalty-kick* death was no more than a word. It was caused by chance (the usherette having wound a ribbon round her neck, Bloch merely pulled the ends) – and a bloody stupid chance when a boy was killed by a pumpkin. Non-dramatic films had no logical ending. After 101 minutes of film Bloch went back to a football-match and that was all. Death was an exciting device or it was mocked but it was not what characters and, with them, the audience feared since protagonists were denied any kind of psychology. Around the empty human forms figures gathered, shifted, reunited. If the permanence of the characters and the recourse to traditional devices helped to keep spectators watching, cinematic action consisted mostly in a constant modification and reordering of the figural networks.

. . . TO SOCIAL ISSUES

Inasmuch as the adjective 'formal' applies to art-works which do not convey a message it must be admitted that many of these films flirted with formalism. We have noted that the use of figures was effective to criticize a common, rather prosaic way of treating history. Figures were also elements regularly introduced in television advertisements; very often ill-defined forms crossed the screen and united to create a car or a bottle of beer. Of course, it can be argued that advertisements are short while feature-films last up to three hours, and it is not here that the most significant links between television and films are to be detected. For practical reasons (lack of time, bad lighting, unsuitable locations) television shots conform to a few, very simple patterns and are centred on recurrent objects or scenes. When television tried to deal seriously with social issues it was faced with the poverty of its pictures. But what were people used to seeing or to caring about in the 1970s? Was the restricted universe of Bloch (papers, music, movies, money) so absurd, so different from spectators' main pre-occupations?

Confronted by a rapidly progressing television, cinema could, in the 1970s, either follow its own way and indulge in fantasy or challenge its rival by showing interest in people's daily concerns. Less frequent though it was, the second solution deserves our attention for the light it throws on European societies. I have chosen to focus on the depiction of foreign immigration. There were not many films on the theme, but even with a limited sample we can observe significant variations regarding both the content and the conception of them. In the early 1970s cinematic immigrants came from west Mediterranean countries – North Africa, Spain, Italy – and fiction was considered the best way of describing their problems. Simultaneously (1973) a German movie, *Ali: Fear Eats the Soul* showed why it was difficult for alien workers to find a place in western societies while an Italian film, *Bread and Chocolate*, explained how Italians were exploited and then expelled from the richest countries. The titles were symmetrical; the Italian Nino who wanted to find a job in Switzerland was reduced to eating bread and chocolate; the Moroccan Ali earned more money but had his stomach eaten by stress (by an ulcer). Despite the difficulties Nino preferred vague hopes and intermittent work to abject poverty in Italy and Ali was too much transformed by his German years to contemplate a return to North Africa. Both films emphasized the moral, psychological and even sentimental aspects of the situation. Once he had married his German mistress Ali was caught between the invisible, creeping hostility ot the neighbourhood and the unconscious but efficient pressure of Emi who, being a German, was undoubtedly considered superior to her husband. For his part, Nino had to fight the Swiss who were always ready to make him and his fellow immigrants sweat; their misery is not permitted any kind of pity. He had an affair with a Greek lady – a difficult relationship, on account of their different habits and traditions. The films had an impact on domestic audiences and exported well. They were praised because they treated a controversial, almost forbidden topic, but it must be admitted that they stuck to classical patterns and that they relied heavily on the performance of good actors who were the focus, the individual consciousnesses through which impressions and feelings were communicated to spectators. The movies also exploited intriguing or disgusting situations, as was the case in the sequence in *Bread and Chocolate* where Nino encountered immigrants who, having lived for so long in a hen-house, behaved like hens. Here the distance from television was at its maximum since the films emphasized dramatization and avoided any similarity with documentaries.

The mirror theory accounts quite well for the cinematic variations on immigration. In the 1970s when the capitalist world was in full expansion immigrants had reason to contemplate possible integration and cinematographers could criticize the selfishness of affluent Europe. A decade later the picture was fairly different. There were only 8 million non-Europeans in the EEC (out of a total of 320 millions) but they were mostly concentrated in Germany (5 per cent of the population), France (4 per cent) and Britain (3 per cent). The contrast between Germany and Britain was noticeable. In the former, Asians were, as the title of a German film read, *Ganz unten* (d. G. Wallraff, 1986), that is to say 'At the very bottom' of society. They did not understand the language, entered illegally, had no family or friends, got irregular, ill-paid jobs, settled in industrial districts and worked for the biggest firms, which benefited from their strength without caring about their lives. In Britain immigrants often came from former colonies, spoke English and were aware of local traditions. They were helped by relatives previously established in the UK, gathered mostly around London and found jobs in the service sector.

Ganz unten was a sober, lucid depiction of the state of things. The first section showed miserable Turks queuing for hours during the night, in front of factories, hopelessly waiting for vacancies, getting the worst situations, suffering cold and humidity and leaving work to shelter in jerry-built houses. The second section followed a kind of recruiter, Vogel, who was looking for six Turks ready to accept an extremely dangerous task, the cleaning of a nuclear power-station. The movie can be fruitfully contrasted with the less dramatic but much more sophisticated production of Stephen Frears, *My Beautiful Laundrette* (1985). While focusing on a Pakistani family the film tried to illuminate the complicated relationship existing between the immigrants and the British. Racial prejudices, strong on both sides, were distorted and even partially mitigated by social contrasts. In the film the rich Nasser has two nephews, Selim and Omar. The former wants to reach the top of the ladder as soon as possible. He wears expensive clothes, has a luxurious car, an expensive house and he hates trouble-makers, the seditious, beggars and hippies. He would run them down with pleasure, especially when they are British. To get the huge amount of money he needs he has no means other than drug-selling. Despite his longing for integration and his affluence, he is therefore terribly vulnerable. Nasser, who prefers a safer way of progressing, exploits other, less perilous deficiencies of British society such as the lack of housing or the inadequacy of services in suburban areas. He buys derelict tenements or old launderettes; he lets the former to poor people – English or immigrants – and refurbishes the latter to attract those who have no washing-machine at home. There is nothing illegal in Nasser's speculations, but he has to control his tenants and to protect his shops against vandalism. In short, he needs a private police. Omar, who accepts his uncle's cautious strategy, recruits a former skinhead, Johnny. The alliance of Nasser–Johnny and its opposition to Selim is, from a sociological point of view, the most clever aspect of the film. Johnny, who used to demonstrate for the expulsion of immigrants because he had no job, eventually understands that given his lack of education and social background he will never be offered a decent salary even if Asians are swept out. The only thing he owns is his Britishness and he sells it to Nasser. He becomes a bodyguard and the lover of Omar who manages one of the launderettes. The commercial side of sexual intercourse, usually linked to heterosexuality (a poor, handsome immigrant marries a girl and her dowry), is reversed towards homosexuality. Johnny now has a roof and a social status, and Nasser's tenants are obliged to pay.

Neither *Ganz unten* nor *My Beautiful Laundrette* was a totally reliable depiction of immigrants' problems but they reflected brilliantly two contrasting situations.[11] They can be labelled 'images' with reference to the meaning we have given to the word. However, it would be wrong to analyse them as purely factual accounts of the condition of aliens in Europe. They are also films, audiovisual artefacts, and their cinematic treatment is as important as their content. When he decided to investigate the condition of Turkish workers, Günther Wallraff, an already well-known journalist, interviewed a few of these men and then disguised himself as a Turk to film their daily life with a hidden video-camera.[12] Speaking hesitantly, combining broken German and Turkish, the talking heads provided moments typical of documentary. Their interventions were separated by ill-related shots which were either glimpses of exhausted, resigned workers or glances at locations, at tools or objects, at Germans as they could be seen by immigrants. The daily horizon of the Turks, confined to employment bureaux, workshops, dormitories and infirmaries, was so narrow that the same items and the same surroundings appeared repeatedly. Objects or places did not evoke an atmosphere, as is often the case in a film. They formed, rather, a figural network in which the workers seemed to be trapped. The sound-track, filled with noises or bits of unfinished sentences, did not contribute to link the shots, and its disparity prompted spectators to concentrate on the pictures to try to unify them in order to escape a disturbing cacophony. The film was not presented as the Turkish version of Germany, and viewers had to infer from recurring figures what the life of people at the 'bottom' was. *Ganz unten* was a compromise between direct observation caught at random and ordinary, television-like interviews. It was even more of a compromise in that testimonies and figures were not enough to complete a feature-length film. This was one of the reasons why Wallraff shot the half-fictional, half-realistic second section. Vogel was actually a seller of manpower whom the cinematographer persuaded that finding six Turkish volunteers would be a good bargain. Disguised this time as a chauffeur, Wallraff made his 'boss' play his own part in a hopeless quest. The point was that the search itself was a fiction but that in order to make spectators admit the credibility of a man like Vogel being ready to sweat immigrants the film had to confess its fraud: since Vogel had been taken in, the audience could accept the absurd story it was shown. In depicting the exploitation of the Turks Wallraff did not depart from the style many German film-makers had developed in the 1970s. His fiction was light, deprived of psychology; it was not organized around the eye or the consciousness of an actor, and recurring but not numerous figures constructed a changing network. Despite the talking heads the film was not a television production. If it conveyed powerfully the idea that immigrants were rejected by Germany this resulted as much from the distance created between the screen and the spectator as from the very content of the pictures.

On the other hand Frears did not try to escape classical standards. Adopting a traditional pattern repeatedly used by nineteenth-century novelists, he told the story of a beginning in adulthood. Omar, who was not the most important character, was the focus of the film. He was introduced immediately after the credits; viewers discovered his world through his eyes, met Nasser, Selim and Johnny thanks to him. It was his experience which unveiled the ambitions and strategy of the others. To complete the information the film-maker added another protagonist who had no significant part in the plot – Omar's father, whose comments and questions emphasized what really mattered. If the shooting was technically perfect it was mostly an illustration or an extension of the subject, and it was thanks to the dialogue that the respective positions of the characters and the phases of the story were explained. The permanence of the same young man around whom other people gathered, the family and sentimental relationships he was given, made Omar and his universe look very close, almost intimate to viewers. Change the actors and their names, and the same narrative could take place in a German or an English context. It was the narration which suggested that Pakistanis were able to integrate in Britain.

Wallraff addressed spectators' feelings, whereas Frears explained. Both were obviously influenced by the actual position of immigrants in their respective countries and, at the same time, conformed to the cinematic styles currently used around them. It was the conjunction of information, derived from the example of television, and of cinematic work which, in the best cases, gave the movies of the 1980s their originality and contrasted them with their counterparts of the 1970s. If the latter played on individual situations and dramas, the former emphasized more collective problems. By dealing with social issues in the wake of television, film-makers found a road between imitation and independence of their rival.

A WOMAN IS A WOMAN

There was another field in which the productions of the two decades under consideration were relatively different. In 1973 women who did not play a prominent part in the plot had a symbolic function: they were the limit beyond which immigrants were not allowed to trespass. Nino (in *Bread and Chocolate*), who was episodically the playboy of a rich lady, knew that women were ready to exploit him as much as men were and would never help him to find a job. He quickly gave up the idea of living with one of them. Conversely, it was because he broke the rule that Ali (in *Ali: Fears Eats the Soul*), who otherwise would have been tolerated, was confronted with insuperable difficulties and was finally 'eaten' from inside. 'Do not touch white ladies', films seemed to tell their public. In the mid-1980s women ceased to represent the reserved part of Europe. The Turks who necessarily had contacts with women, be it only with prostitutes, were confined by Wallraff in a male circle. As for the three women of *My Beautiful Laundrette* they were all the property of Nasser – being respectively his wife, his mistress and his daughter. They admitted he owned them as he owned garages or launderettes. Again, it was the relationship between men which was the driving force behind the story.[13]

Social standards do not evolve so quickly that what had been relevant in 1973 became obsolete less than fifteen years later. The only noticeable modification was a more tolerant attitude towards homosexuality which, still treated cautiously in the 1970s, was the theme of a great many European movies in the 1980s. But homosexuality had no room in *Ganz unten* and was rather marginal in *My Beautiful Laundrette*. Actually, it was the imaginary world of the film-makers, their way of representing their characters, of filming them, of organizing their relationship on the screen, which changed. The difference cannot be understood without a quick look at the cinematic vision of women. Few people were interested in this topic before about 1975, and everybody considered that women were simply fictional characters congruent with social models. But feminism, which had strengthened during the initial years of the decade, highlighted the problem. As has been noted in Chapter 5, semiology and psychoanalysis were then losing their attractiveness in the realm of film criticism. Feminism, backed by the publication of magazines and books, by conferences, even by films, became a new theoretical framework inside which movies were discussed and criticized. It has been argued throughout this volume that critical writings have constantly influenced discourse on film and contributed to the shaping of viewers' tastes. In this respect feminism strongly affected the understanding of film production.

How did men who had dominated the film business since its origins construct the feminine? The answer put forward by

Laura Mulvey in 1975 was the beginning of long, passionate debates:

> The presence of women is an indispensable element of spectacle in normal narrative film . . . Traditionally the woman displayed has functioned on two levels: as erotic object for the characters within the screen story, and as erotic object for the spectator within the audience . . . An active/passive division of labour has similarly controlled narrative structure . . . The man controls the film fantasy and also emerges as the representative of power . . . His power as he controls events coincides with the active power of the erotic look, both giving a satisfying sense of omnipotence.[14]

In other words, for a long time cinema had reproduced a pre-constituted pattern of sexual roles according to which women merely wait for men to act and to come and pick them up. It had also set up a spectatorial phantasm produced by the male gazes – that of the actors as well as the spectator – focusing on the female body. These statements are best illustrated by Godard's *A Woman is a Woman* (1961). The female character of the film 'is a woman' because she is unpredictable, whimsical, unreliable and extremely pretty. She has wishes but she counts on men to fulfil them. Godard was of course making fun of himself and of his public when he indulged in such a stereotype. However, his caricatured portrait was filmed in a manner which made the actress an object for converging looks. The two male characters walked around her, glanced at her, talked of her. Contemplated by the camera and by the actors, she was offered to the audience but she was denied any self-achievement except thanks to an intervention by her male counterparts. While mocking a convention, Godard exemplified a well-established structure of sex differences.

The tritest convention related to women's social activities. Audiovisual fictions have generally represented more 'ladies of leisure' than working women as they have also focused on middle- or upper-class men rather than on proletarians, but the privilege of men as initiators of the action was never a peculiarity of film; it existed in literature and in the theatre, and it was even challenged sooner in cinema than in the other fields. Once more it was during the 1960s that significant modifications appeared. Remember *The Eclipse* and *Pierrot le fou* – two films already mentioned in the book. Contrary to what had previously been the rule, the female characters of these movies had as important a part as their male partners. To both of them independence was life. Vittoria, the main protagonist of the former, had a profession, a flat, friends. She was able to live on her own and did not long for a continuous relationship with a man. Marianne's activities in *Pierrot le fou* were more problematic, but nevertheless while she was with her lover she was able to earn more money than he was. She also made it perfectly clear that her affair with Ferdinand was temporary. Many films could be taken as illustrations of the sexual, moral and economic liberation of western women during that decade. Were they consonant with social evolution? Measuring emancipation is, of course, an impossible task and we must be content with speaking of material independence. Let us consider the case of Vittoria who, in the film, seems to be well integrated into Roman society. In the Italy of the 1960s there were only twenty-eight women in a hundred workers, and very few of them were professionals. Is it then preferable to say that films anticipated a transformation which would occur one or two decades later? In the 1960s women formed 26 per cent of the working population in Rome. Two decades later the figure amounted to 28 per cent: the difference was insignificant. Moreover, a large majority of women lived in their parents' house with their family, and 70 per cent of married women stayed at home to look after the children. Vittoria and Marianne were out of the ordinary. In their depiction of liberated women films took for granted, from 1960 onwards, a sexual equality that was far from being established at the time.

Cinema has always created images which are only partially connected to the contemporary state of things and simultaneously it has permanently modified or distorted it. It is, of course, worth noticing that in the 1960s it delineated an ideal model of female protagonist which was acceptable to audiences and which contributed to the success of several films, but feminists emphasized less the social status of women than the use of the male gaze to create the female anatomy and then to contemplate it. It must be remembered that in audiovisual productions eyes communicate expressions and also suggest that one of the protagonists is observing what is happening in the world of the film. In the classical cinema things were often supposed to be perceived by an individual, autonomous consciousness. A protagonist took a look at an object which was then presented in close-up, and spectators generally inferred from this succession that they were watching 'with' the character. Feminists who focused on the dominant cinema, Hollywood's, rightly noted that men were the only ones who did the gazing. What was unquestionable where American movies were concerned was not as clear in Europe, even in the middle of the century. *Brief Encounter* is entirely constructed around Celia Johnson's eye: she discovers her partner when he arrives, she spots him in the middle of the crowd and gives substance to him. Viewers are prompted to observe him as she does. When he falls into a pond they see him through the actress's eyes as muddy, awkward, ashamed, and they are tempted to start laughing with her. Giving female protagonists an investigating gaze and vesting them with an active subjectivity was frequent in European films, but Johnson's example points to the difference between the sexes: women's glance was never desiring but was rather motherly and protective. Cinematic gazes were thus divided into two big categories assigned to pre-determined sexual roles. To what extent was this typification symptomatic of cinema? The stereotypes of distinct frames of mind – of male voyeurism and of the feminine body offered as an object for viewing – pre-existed cinema. They can be traced throughout the nineteenth century, especially in its last decades which witnessed a burst of publicity in papers, magazines and leaflets and on placards, posters and postcards. Dressed or half-naked, the female anatomy was used extensively to advertise anything from soaps to bicycles, from shopping in department stores to travelling in the Alps. The fascination with the female body, of which cinema is but a limited aspect, is a symptom. Of what? Of a patriarchal ideology which subdued women to men and reduced the former to the state of objects for the pleasure of the latter? Why is it, then, that the anatomy of the dominated element which had been carefully hidden until the middle of the nineteenth century was exhibited and denuded once pictures began to advertise widely for the interests of cheap consumption? Feminists cleverly emphasized the coincidence between the Freudian discourse on female sexuality and the birth of cinema, but that is not enough and many other aspects of capitalist, industrial countries at the turn of the last century should be taken into account. While such an enquiry is carried out it is necessary to bear in mind the critical approach of feminism but to remember that cinema was merely one of the various fields in which voyeurism flourished.

If cinema was deeply rooted in an antecedent tradition of sexual opposition it used it and developed it in its own manner. Superficially it can be said that cinema, being financed by men who wanted to make money, conveyed the accepted idea that men had to decide and women to obey and in doing so it aimed to satisfy viewers' wishes. But, in the 1960s, the cinematic relationship between genders changed rapidly. Female characters were depicted as practically and morally equal to men; some of them fooled their partners not only by dominating them sexually, which had happened previously, but by overtaking their economic or intellectual skills. Women were also less exposed to the undressing glance of men. While acquiring, on the screens, a social status and an ability to decide, while being no longer confined to 'feminine' functions, women were still denied longing glances of their own, as if, in films, they had to be mothers or professionals, housewives or businesswomen, but never desiring beings. The modifications which occurred in the last third of the twentieth century suppressed secondary aspects of sexual representation (incapacity of women to direct action, fascination for the female body) and revealed a deeper prejudice, a capacity denied to women by fiction. The new aesthetic standards typical of the period have to be taken into account in understanding what was being manifested in films. Roughly speaking, supposed psychology and fictional continuity faded while figural compositions expanded. Given the looseness of the plots which could not structure the narratives, cinematographers had to look for other, well-accepted oppositions likely to sustain ill-defined characters and circumstances. Sexual division which was easily represented was a convenient, simple solution. We have noted how, in *Stavisky*, women stand for 'the other' – not the opposite, the dark, the dangerous, but merely the different. Sexuality, in *The Anxiety of the Goalie at the Penalty-kick*, is deprived of any kind of exhibitionism. Bloch and his girlfriends seem to feel unconcerned when they look at each other, and the latter find as many men as Bloch finds women. The body and sex matter less in the film than the figural correspondences and contrasts which develop between the main character and the female protagonists. It is true that the films of the 1970s and 1980s exposed naked people and love-making in a cruder (or a less hypocritical) way than had been done before. At the same time, since current, trite psychology was eliminated, concern about love or sexual intercourse lost the significance it had before, and even in the most traditional comedies or dramas the constitution of a couple (heterosexual or homosexual) was no longer considered a fitting ending. However, sexual division remained a powerful marker, a visual discriminant which spectators caught and interpreted instantly. Women on screen were represented as non-men rather than as sexual beings. Beyond obvious physical disparities whose importance diminished in audiovisual representations, cinema manifested another polarity which survived the (relative) levelling of status and which was, in fact, a contrast between two different natures. But, again, films were mere symptoms of a profound cultural preconception.

The European cinema witnessed noticeable stylistic innovations in the 1960s and tried to adapt to them during the following decades. I have emphasized various transformations in this chapter, but their practical importance must not be overrated. If they affected deeply the conception of films they had little impact on exhibition since American products continued to dominate the market and were followed, at the box-office, by the most classical, not to say the most conformist, European movies. Cinematographers had also to face the challenge of television which was progressively draining their potential customers. Some of them borrowed from television, others stuck to established cinematic patterns but none of them was in a position to retain vanishing audiences. The paradox of cinema was that it continued to exist despite insufficient attendance. Britain, for instance, produced 480 films in the 1980s against 680 in the 1950s but, meanwhile, the audience had decreased by 93 per cent. Like the performing arts, which are seldom popular enough to survive without external help, cinema became a protected species, sponsored by patrons, protected by the state and financed by television networks. Not surprisingly, the countries in which spectatorship had declined most – Britain and Germany – made drastic aesthetic choices, whereas France and Italy which kept a reasonable number of cinema-goers were more cautious. Britain opted for tradition. What was called the 'revival' of the British cinema was a combination of linear plots, touching feelings and technical perfection. On the other hand, Germany, less demanding on achievement, explored fully the potential of figural processes. The adoption of contrasting models was not simply a question of style; it was also consequent on two different forms of representation. It is here that films reveal best what they are – artefacts which neither mirror nor ignore actual problems. Europe, in the last quarter of the century, had to deal with vigorous conflicts which did not seriously threaten her stability. Images which condense and simplify were central for the expression of contemporary stress and uneasiness. Confronted by disruptive tendencies, Britain reacted by indulging in nostalgia. She promoted (effectively, since this kind of film was highly successful) a vision of the past which was not necessarily idealized but which was depicted as something lost for ever. Germany did not linger on her history but dealt, in a dynamic way, with the problematic relationship between her past and her present. In both countries cinema grasped urgent issues (housing, urbanization, immigration) or clamorous matters (status of women) but, because of their distinct, almost opposed, aesthetic options, it treated them differently, stressing alternately integration and disintegration, which were two drastic manners of dealing with the questions. There was certainly an incongruity between the claims expressed at political meetings, street demonstrations or in the papers and in their cinematic depiction because cultural expression and social concerns do not coincide. Nevertheless, it is in images that most people's awareness of their situation originates, and that is the reason why images, distorted though they are, are significant documents for historians.

CONCLUSION:
MOVING PICTURES:
CONCEPTION/CONSUMPTION

In introducing this book I deliberately avoided justifying its chronological boundaries. Their historical significance is obvious. The volume opens on the eve of the last European war and closes when Europe is about to become a federation, but for cinema these dates are of no importance. Taken as a cultural whole or considered in relation to their respective countries of origin, European films did not go through any change in 1940 or in 1990. Sure enough, there were considerable modifications in their development, but this happened in the 1960s at a time when, from a political point of view, Europe was very peaceful. I could have told my readers right at the beginning that they would be confronted with a discrepancy in chronology. I did not do so because it is problematical to question historical delimitations which, being considered evident by historians and by the general public, are directly imported into film studies. Many works have already stressed the impact of the Second World War, of decolonization or of May 1968 on film production. It is certainly true that politics are sometimes echoed in movies: there were films on resistance, on the nuclear threat, on the Cold War and on the rivalry between west and east. But while these series deserve to be scrutinized for the information they provide on public opinion and reaction, they are extremely limited in number and are exceptions among the dominant production which scarcely concerned itself with current events.

This book aimed to deal with cinema as a source and reserve of images, as a means by which spectators actively engage in a conception/construction of the universe and in doing so find further insight into it. Politics plays a rather marginal part in this continuing discovery of the world. I wanted to compare and contrast four European societies involved in an important shift from competition to collaboration in one of their modes of entertainment and one of their sources of collective knowledge. The first conclusion which can be drawn from this enquiry is that no simple, direct connection exists between political evolution and the tastes of the public. Cinema has rhythms of its own, it changes over long periods and it is necessary to take into account at least half a century in order to detect a relevant modification in this field. Even fifty years are not sufficient to determine precisely all the most noticeable transformations: for example, the American preponderance, firmly settled between the two world wars, was still indisputable at the end of the century. In this volume Hollywood's influence has been merely a part of the background, another aspect of the consumption of movies, which had to be borne in mind constantly but which was not discussed for itself. Nevertheless, the USA was one of the main actors in the whole story. Long before 1939 Hollywood had imposed its aesthetic patterns – namely, a style of narrative, a conception of lighting, a way of using stars; it had also monopolized vital sectors of distribution, sometimes even of exhibition, in Europe. The Europeans had recourse to various expedients to contain this American invasion but they failed except on one point: European production was not destroyed but remained, at least quantitatively, at a level comparable to the American one. Politicians and film-makers continued to lament the decay of the European studios, but their complaints were hypocritical. As long as the market was totally open, the USA won easily since its products were the best; only protectionism – in other words, a political decision – could have saved the European producers and directors in the face of demands by European viewers who wanted to have more of Hollywood.

It would therefore be useful to evaluate the impact of American images on European audiences since a good half of the movies exhibited in Europe were American. Europe had been accustomed for a long time to American films which depicted another universe, a different society, so how effectively did films advertise the American way of life, American goods or American domestic and foreign policy? Unfortunately, we have practically no evidence on the topic. Opinion polls were held every now and then but they were so unsophisticated, while the rules on which they were based changed so often, that we cannot arrive at any sensible inference by studying them. Even if we had suitable material I doubt whether we would learn much more. The fact remains that, despite their popularity and unquestionable technical superiority, when European audiences receded drastically, Hollywood's productions were deserted to the same extent as those of Europe. Spectators may have liked American movies but they were not addicted to them and could easily shift to other forms of entertainment.

Economists might say that the circulation of films was 'rigid' – that is to say, was not strictly related to what was on offer. Audiences regularly saw the same proportions of items of various national origins and were not affected by the quantity of movies with which they were presented. Attendance, which was already large before the war, increased after 1940 despite the shortage of new productions. Conversely, the decline which occurred in the 1950s and 1960s cannot be correlated to any restriction in the making of films. I am led to an assumption which may sound a bit odd but which is worth noticing: film production and film consumption are two partially independent variables. I have devoted much space in this volume to the flow of cinema-goers and I have compared the practices of four countries which, roughly speaking, followed the same trend throughout the five decades under consideration but which, during these fifty years, showed rather different behaviour. I have stressed some possible, partial explanations but I am convinced that we are not in a position to account for the causes of the evolution. It is obvious that by 1970 television and other kinds of social pleasure had replaced cinema all over Europe, but neither television, nor sport, nor touring was likely to have taken over from cinema at the time it began to decline. To a certain extent, the recession of cinema created a gap which was filled by other entertainments. As for film production, it changed after the crisis had begun and was a response to it. Far from provoking a fall in audiences, production and exhibition of films were often clumsy adaptations to that fall.

The joy of visiting a picture-house, which was not merely for

Cinema Splendor (I., 1989): The European cinema dreaming of its past splendour

the pleasure of watching a movie, was a significant social fact by the middle of the century. Historians who have always emphasized the function of theatrical performances in ancient Greece, of stadium games in Rome, or religious mysteries in medieval times cannot ignore the forms and modes of social gatherings in the twentieth century. There were big mobs in Nuremberg for the Nazi parades, in Moscow for the Communist party celebrations, in London for the coronations and royal weddings, but statistically, the crowds which haunted cinemas were immensely more important, and far from gathering just from time to time they queued assiduously in front of the ticket-offices. Social scientists are themselves spectators, and it is difficult for them to distinguish their scientific enquiries from their behaviour as members of a collective group of consumers. Nevertheless, this is a preliminary step to any study of cultural practices in the contemporary world. In the middle of the century members of the European working and middle classes were accustomed to spending some four hours of their weekly spare time in picture-houses, which meant that they had to economize on both their time and money in order to do so along with their families. This was a massive phenomenon which, at the same time, was experienced in fairly different manners all over the four countries.

Trying to understand and analyse practices as independent factors does not mean that the objects themselves, the movies, are uninteresting. My only reservation in this field is related to the liberty of the public, since by 1950 few spectators had any chance to choose what they would like to see in cinemas. Box-offices tell us little about the real 'tastes' of film audiences, and as we have insufficient information on viewer reactions we are left in comparative ignorance about what they enjoyed and what they disliked. However, the fact remains that throughout the half-century considered here Europe produced about 18,000 movies and that this huge amount of stories – all these faces, bodies, landscapes, sites and buildings miniaturized on film, easily available thanks to video – have something to tell us.

I feel a bit sceptical regarding the scientific value of the 'mirror' theory. Not that it is wrong: on the contrary, it is obvious that movies 'reflect' aspects of the society which has produced them. I have often chosen, as a starting-point, films which confirm this idea. Although they were artefacts made in studios, *It Always Rains on Sunday* and *Brief Encounter* inform us accurately about the look, the external appearance, the clothes and habits of London East End workers or suburban middle-class people, and in the same way some of the transformations which occurred in the 1960s are perfectly mirrored in *A Taste of Honey* or *Blow-up*. But I wonder whether what can be learned from films in this respect is worth looking at them for. Other sources, especially photographs, are as informative and require less time or effort. It could even be held that to a large extent films escape their period. I opened this book with the cinematic depiction of war in the 1930s, since the European cinema, if it had reflected the concerns of its contemporaries, should have explored the theme extensively. It is worth noting that war novels, reminiscences, histories of the first conflict never fell out of popularity between the wars, whereas cinema only reluctantly coped with the topic. Historians who would only rely on films would be mistaken and would believe that people did not care much about a future conflict, whereas all the other sources – newspapers, radio transmissions, mass-observation records and literature – prove that the Europeans were constantly anxious about the coming war.

Various reasons account for the inaccuracy of films. I have tried to explain how the context of production influenced the making of movies dealing with the war. Censorship, money, politics were involved, but a much more important factor was the permanent relationship and inter-communication between film-makers. Studios have always been a limited universe, a small cluster of people who react upon each other and who look more at each other than at the outer world. Cinemato-graphers constantly bear in mind the productions of their colleagues/competitors and they stick to the fashions of their clan. Cinema is not society-proof but it filtrates and modifies what is observed in the street according to the modes of cinematic circles. This bias, this distorted version of an otherwise existing state of affairs, has been examined in all the chapters of this volume, and I find it necessary to synthesize it here.

Let us begin with an example. In a great many films of the 1960s cars play a fundamental part, to such an extent that they are almost protagonists or, at least, objects which the characters constantly care for. Lovers go to their first rendez-vous by car and start flirting by comparing their respective qualities. At parties: people do not speak of anything except means of travel. Cars are exchanged, borrowed, lent, used, stolen, even sunk in water – which seems to declare that private transport was basic to contemporary life. What was the exact relationship between those images and the context within which the films were made? A quick answer might be that films were a mere reflection of what was happening then: in Italy the number of driving licences doubled during the first half of the 1960s. But comparisons oblige us to go beyond the obvious concordances. Images of cars are identical in all the European films of the 1960s. However, the transport revolution took place much earlier, in the early 1950s in Britain and France. In 1965, France, with one vehicle for every seven inhabitants, came immediately after the USA, but it took Italy fifteen years to reach the same level. Private transport was slow to submerge Europe and quick to triumph on the screens. Cinema had a timing of its own, a studio-timing partially independent from the social evolution. There was of course an unwitting imitation of Hollywood. Car chases, car crashes, cars sunk in the sea were a reflection of American pictures rather than an observation of current European practices. Private transport, which was unequally developed in Europe, was on a level in films, and this was all the more predictable in view of the fact that directors, actors and technicians were shifting from one country to another and playing comparable parts everywhere with the same clothes, the same cars and against the same backgrounds.

Admittedly, in the 1960s, cars were actual items that people used daily. But historians do not need recourse to films to evaluate the importance of this means of transport in that period. It is not the direct representation of cars – their shape, colour or comfort – which interests us since professional leaflets or magazines are much more revealing on these topics. What cannot be inferred from literature is the function of cars in people's self-definition. We guess that independently from their practical utilization vehicles appeal to the imagination and allow women or men to experiment with self-assessment and luxury, but how is it possible to gauge these subjective, fantastic valuations? It is here, precisely, that films have something to disclose to us. They introduce us not into daily life but into the realm of accepted, unquestioned images; they are like extended advertisements whose slogans might have been: 'cars are fun', 'cars: the best way of beginning an affair' or 'cars give you freedom'. Inserted into fictions – that is to say, experimental, artificial situations – means of transport were placed in opposition to other objects, other tastes or habits so that we can test them comparatively. Films say little about the performance of the automobile and a great deal about those who fancied them.

Cars are not the most significant products of the twentieth century. I have taken them as an example in this Conclusion because I wanted to explain as simply as possible what I have in mind here. In this book I have treated three cases which seem much more far-reaching. I began with resistance since I needed a theme with historical as well as political echoes and a theme which could have been common to the four countries.

Cinema has not deserted history during the period considered here but it has created (or contributed to creating) no 'founding myth' comparable, for instance, to the American Civil War. The resistance to Nazism with its popular, democratic background and the real dramas it involved could have been considered a perfect founding ordeal for the new Europe. Few resistance films were big hits. The memory of the secret war was evoked in politically orientated movies, but resistance remained a marginal subject for the European cinema. What has been observed about the First World War in the 1930s was still true after 1945. Rare film-makers exploited the topic and illustrated resistance with reference to other films which they tried to imitate or to criticize, but there was a large gap between their attempts and the dominant attitude of producers or viewers. Resistance was selected for this book because of its obvious significance, and the conclusions I have drawn about it are easily generalized. The European cinema reluctantly dealt with controversial questions. It is true that terrorism, drug addiction, speculation in housing were analysed in depth by some cinematographers. Francesco Rosi was especially sharp and precise in filming the eviction of poor people from central Naples where constructors expected high profits, the dirty bargains surrounding the fight for independence in Sicily and the links between international terrorism and political parties. It is no wonder that this is the first time I have mentioned his name in this volume, for Rosi was rather exceptional. His films were courageous, intelligent pamphlets, and no political historian will miss their message. But there is no room for them in a work which focuses on the average films diffused to Europeans. Political tensions and conflicts were widespread in Europe during the second half of the twentieth century but had little impact on cinema.

Social issues were sometimes tackled, especially when television had already popularized them. However, if immigration was the central motif of several movies in the 1980s, was it because the Europeans were wondering whether poor, untrained foreigners would adapt to an industrial environment? Or because coloured people speaking unfamiliar languages were modifying the landscape? Unlike documentaries, fiction films did not describe the condition of the immigrants but played with the uncanny, the unexpected, thus stressing the new features, the new 'visibility' introduced by the strangers. For it is in this field, in the realm of images, that cinema tells us something regarding the common vision of the world around us. Apart from resistance I have focused on two main themes – cities and women. Urbanization spread all over Europe after the war, but films provide only deceptive information about this big transfer of population. What can be grasped from them is rather a series of ideas, a vision of what a town is, a depiction of its essence and being. Over the half-century explored here cinematic towns, initially pictured like geo-metrical figures, as circles with a centre and a circumference, lost their well-defined shape and became unlimited areas or conglomerations of dwelling places. The mutations in the social and legal status of women were seemingly more truly reflected in movies, since actresses were given the leading part in a few films. Fictionally, they were entrusted with responsibilities and behaved sexually as freely as men. Social scientists have been tempted to evaluate to what extent films were ahead of their time or true to life, but how is it possible to calculate the degree of independence of a person or a group and then to refer it to a fictional depiction? Therefore, rather than comparing filmed ladies with actual ladies I have suggested that cinema itself could be a measure – an imprecise, ambiguous one, which is still better than nothing. If, formally, cinematic women were freer from male authority in the 1980s than in the 1940s, the fictional and visual treatment of women maintained a strict division between genders and a predominantly masculine point of view. Cinematic heroines did not coincide with their social appearance.

Films were part of social change insofar as they integrated the deepest mutations which affected the behaviour of people, but even if this is undeniable it would be hazardous to connect directly social modifications with filmed images. Take one of the limited but amazing conclusions which can be inferred from the study of resistance. The movies depicting the secret war of World War Two which were generally intended to denounce the horrors of the Nazi occupation contributed in making images of violence more acceptable on screen and to widen in that direction the sphere of the visible. Cinematic cities and cinematic women wore an aspect in the 1980s which, while obviously not alien to their actual form and presence, was a long way from being a reproduction of what could be perceived in the outside world. The images of women and of towns were not clear; they were a bit faded, faltering and contradictory, and it is this uncertainty which makes them worth while for historians since it questions the deductions that could be derived from other documents while adding to these sources the life and emotional appeal pertaining to moving images.

The theoreticians who began thinking over the nature of cinema at the very outset of the twentieth century baptized it as a language. This was an uneasy word which has been a pretext for useless arguments ever since. Another expression would have been preferable, but it is too late – cinema is for ever a language. Languages are necessary to communicate and to manifest feelings. In the classical movies emphasis was put on the first aspect – that it to say, on the transmission of unequivocal messages rather than on the expression of feelings. As spectators could be confused by the quantity of information conveyed by the pictures and the sound-track everything was calculated to channel and direct their attention. Instead of competing with each other the various materials were used to stress the most important points and make the viewers perceive them. Later, television adopted the same method which was never totally forsaken in cinema. However, another, statistically less important tradition in cinema had been exploring for a long time the second aspect of language mentioned above. Having been relegated to the underground from the end of the 1920s to the end of the 1960s, it resurfaced in the last third of the century. The contrasts between the two modes must not be overrated since on both sides films told stories, had main characters and led from an initial to a final situation. The difference (and again this was not a rule – many productions did not depart from the previous fashion) was that continuity and irreversibility were no longer considered the most important aspects of a movie. Instead of assigning to every element a defined function cinematographers preserved its potentiality of having various significations. Similarity, contrast and complementarity could allow a spectator to associate colour, motif, motion or music in a meaningful way, thus enabling them to follow several leading strands, some purely fictional, others more figural. According to their taste and inclination, viewers focused on the plot or cared more about shapes and sounds bound to each other by formal properties or even tried to apprehend both and to make a multidimensional journey throughout the movie.

Film-analysts and a few cinematographers assumed, then, that this was a new, freer textual activity, more poetical and less intent on delivering a message. We do not need to discuss aesthetic opinions in a book dealing with the social functions of films. Suffice to say that the looseness of narrative and spatial continuity, the explosion of conflict inside the shots or between shots, the reversibility created by the deviating chains of figures point to another treatment of cinematic language akin to the role sounds and pictures play in social life. Surrounded by luminous advertisements, giant posters, signs moving with the lorries on which they were painted, by graffiti, by music or the noise of juke-boxes, transistors and loud-speakers, people experienced what it was to be overwhelmed by visual and aural images. Cinema provided them with the same combinations but it ordered and distributed them according to regularities which did not exist in the street and public locations. Here, cinema was simultaneously close to and far away from television. Television firmly maintained the tradition of a coherent, continuous stream of information. It even reinforced it by giving spoken commentaries the precedence over pictures. But audiences which consumed television programmes at home in the midst of their ordinary problems were mostly uninvolved, part-time listeners. Their reception was often casual and consisted as much in impressions hastily grasped from quick, irregular glances at the screen as in long-lasting scrutiny of what was shown and explained. Cinema also played on spectators' selective receptiveness but it did not let their thoughts stray at random and it guided them by organizing and pointing to a limited cluster of possible readings. Television has often been compared to a flow of signals which people encounter casually and for irregular, generally short, periods. By contrast, cinema remained a language – that is to say, an ordered choice of signs which were likely to convey messages or impressions because relations had been constructed between them. After 1960 telling a story seemed less relevant than suggesting or provoking emotions, but cinema was not modified in its basic principle, which is a calculated combination of moving pictures and sounds.

Stylistically, differences between countries were therefore limited in the course of the half-century. Movie fabrication was too small an industrial sector to allow much diversity. During the 'Golden Age' Europe stuck to Hollywood's standards and modified them only marginally so that a kind of narrative which has been recurrently mentioned in the book became a permanent feature of the western vision of the world. So it is not in this area that an answer can be found to one of the questions which opened this volume: what does cinema tell us regarding the contrasts between European nations?

In two other fields, consumption and contents, particularities are more readily perceptible. We have noted a shift all over Europe during the 1960s from family to individual attendance. Other, more demarcating, aspects of film consuming can be stressed. Frequenting the picture-houses was considered a 'popular' entertainment in Britain and Italy. This does not mean that highbrows despised it but that cinema was regarded as a cheap, democratic amusement. Its sudden decline in Britain and its exceptional strength in the peninsula were partially linked to the manner in which spectators conceived of it. In both countries it was expected to cost little, so that English people felt angry when prices went up and were deterred from going even before they could buy television sets, whereas low prices kept alive the Italian notion of film as an inexpensive pleasure. France and Italy shared a common 'literary' apprehension of movies since in both countries film criticism and specialized magazines influenced strongly not the actual practice (French people were far less interested in pictures than were other Europeans) but the idea of cinema and of the way it ought to be enjoyed. On the other hand, in Germany, at least during the decade when audiences were considerable, films which were either low-quality domestic productions or American imports were treated scathingly by intellectuals or opinion-leaders. Attendance reached at that time the same high level in Germany as in Italy, but whereas cinema looked legitimate in the latter, it seemed childish and a bit shameful in the former. Later, viewers' expectations were evened out by television, but during the central years of the century, 1940–60, the notion of what liking films meant revealed the cultural habits and criteria of valuation in the four countries.

One would expect that contents would be directly influenced by the traditions and situation of the nation which produced the films. Before 1939 Germany, which was getting ready for war, did not hesitate to represent various aspects of the previous conflict, whereas Britain and France reluctantly dealt with such an unpleasant past. From 1945 onwards there were no reasons for Germany to depict the resistance to Nazism, but Britain could easily ponder over the extent and limits of her own resistance. But things are not that simple. Emphasizing the links between politics and cinematic themes does not help to explain why fascist Italy systematically avoided the Great War or why the four countries which were not very keen on featuring resistance all offered (for there were a few German films on the topic) the same vision of the secret war. National customs and prejudices demarcate acceptable from unacceptable issues, which resulted, for instance, in the possibility for the British to evoke the IRA and the impossibility for the French to picture the Algerian war. Silence is always revealing, and historians can list the topics which are not, or are seldom, treated in movies, but when a topic is avoided there is no material on it and therefore no comparison. It is when films have been made that a parallel has a meaning, and then it is less the matter itself than the screening of it which is stimulating. Imagine a batch of resistants trying to fool the Germans. Starting from that idea, you can make a thriller, a drama or a documentary. Or, to take another case studied in this book, European comedies contrast less in their gags, often borrowed from Hollywood, than in their style. The four European cinemas were diverse, although they depicted the same social strata (mostly the middle classes), the same situations and the same social configurations (family life under all its aspects). There was a basic uniformity, a kind of international or rather western sphere of cinematically tolerable issues, and there was on the side of film-makers an extreme permeability to reciprocal influences. The movies were not similar and yet there was a relation, a consonance between them. The wonder is that spectators reacted disparately. Although the market was open, supply and demand were never correlated. This gap is, of course, typical of cultural industries which do not satisfy primary needs, but it is rare to observe such considerable discrepancy with regard to objects as relatively homogeneous as films, and it is this interval which was worth examining in relation to European cinemas.

NOTES

INTRODUCTION: IMAGES IN SOCIETIES

1 'Social Change in 1960s Europe: Four Feature Films', in XVIth International Congress of Historical Sciences, *Reports*, vol. 1 (Stuttgart, 1985) p. 229.
2 In S. Harding and M. B. Hintikka (eds), *Discovering Reality* (Dordrecht, 1983).
3 Feminist film criticism has greatly contributed to clarification of the question of gender representation and sexual differences in cinema. The issue will be examined in Chapter 6.
4 *A Mirror for England. British Movies from Austerity to Affluence* (London, 1970).
5 Madison, 1985.
6 'Social Change in 1960's Europe: Four Feature Films', p. 226.
7 *Keywords. A Vocabulary of Culture and Science* (London, 1974) p. 9.
8 *Narration in the Fiction Film*, p. 157.
9 'Social Change in 1960s Europe: Four Feature Films', p. 220.
10 South Brunswick, New York, London, 1975.
11 Oxford, 1986.

1 THE COMING WAR

1 Dieter Langewiesche, 'Politik–Gesellschaft–Kultur. Zur Problematik von Arbeiterkultur und kulturellen Arbeiterorganisationen in Deutschland nach dem I. Weltkrieg', *Archiv für Sozialgeschichte* 22 (1982) 359–402; Modris Ekstein, 'War, Memory and Politics: The Fate of the Film *All Quiet on the Western Front*', *Central European Review* (March 1980) 60–81; Andrew Kelly, '*All Quiet on the Western Front*: "Brutal Cutting, Stupid Censors and Bigoted Politicos" (1930–84)', *Historical Journal of Film, Radio and Television* 9/2 (1989) 135–50.
2 The film was of course banned in fascist Italy and in Germany after 1933. On the American war film see J. Spears, 'World War I on the Screen', *Films in Review* 17 (1966) 274–92 and 347–65; T. J. Lyons, 'Hollywood and World War I', *Journal of Popular Film* 1 (1972)

15–30; Ivan Butler, *The War Film* (Crambury, NJ, 1974), and M. Isenberg, *War on Film* (London, 1981).

3 Distributed in the USA as *Comrades of 1918*.

4 For the sources of the table see Bibliography (first section), Guides and Catalogues.

5 These films were not co-productions: there was a national producer for every version but charges (locations, clothes, extras) were jointly paid for by the different companies.

6 Title of the American version: *The Doomed Battalion*.

7 Despite their differences it is worth comparing James Whale's *Journey's End* to *King and Country*. In the first picture Captain Stanhope is sick of having his men uselessly killed but he never wonders why it is like that. When a subaltern is about to have a breakdown for the same reasons he is keen to make him change his mind and go back to the front line. Personal boredom and critical analysis of the orders are totally separated.

8 Jeffrey Richards identifies (*The Ages of the Dream Palace: Cinema and Society in Britain, 1930–1939* (Henley, 1984), pp. 279–85) a handful of films that explore the theme of pacifism, but it is always in the context of a futuristic setting with no connection with the Great War.

9 'The British Board of Film Censors and Content Control in the 1930s: Foreign Affairs', *Historical Journal of Film, Radio and Television* 2/1 (1982) 46–8. The attitude of the German Foreign Office, of the Censorship Office and of the Film Office of the German Institute for Education which was charged with determining the 'educational' value of films is analysed by Garth Montgomery, ' "Realistic" War Films in Weimar Germany: Entertainment as Education', *Historical Journal of Film, Radio and Television*, 9/2 (1989) 115.

10 The main character is a bastard who has never been acknowledged by his father. Once he has sacrificed his life to help the Navy capture a German ship, his father changes his mind. A hero is fit to be the son of a naval officer.

11 'The British Post-bellum Cinema: A Survey of the Films Relating to World War II Made in Britain between 1945 and 1960', *Historical Journal of Film, Radio and Television* 8/1 (1988) 40.

12 The question of adaptation, seen from the point of view of spectators, has not been fully explored up to now. For a first insight see Joachim Paech, *Literatur und Film* (Stuttgart, 1988). An excellent series of case-studies is to be found in A. Horton and J. Magretta (eds), *Modern European Film-makers and the Art of Adaptation* (New York, 1981). For statistics on literary influences in films see Brian McFarlane, 'A Literary Cinema' in Charles Barr (ed.), *All Our Yesterdays* (London, 1986), p. 126.

13 This is the reason why the film, deeply concerned though it is with the aftermath of war, is not included in the synoptic table.

14 In the USA, *Hell on Earth*.

15 In 'The British Board of Film Censors and Content Control in the 1930s' Jeffrey Richards shows that the British Board of Film

Censors, kept on the alert by the Foreign Office, was keen to ban 'subjects which are calculated to wound the susceptibilities of foreign people'. How was it possible to scrutinize the origins of the war without speaking of France and Germany's foreign policy?

16 Julian Symons, *Bloody Murder: From the Detective Story to the Crime Novel. A History* (London, 1974), p. 234.

17 Compare this with *Grand Illusion*, in which a French POW hides in a German farm where he behaves willingly as if he were a German farmer. Later the German lady behaves as if she were French and helps the man to return to the French lines. This mixing up of opposed values was unthinkable in a German movie.

18 A long paper on the film published in the daily of the German Communist Party, *Die rote Fahne* (27 May 1930), reads:

> Although it tends to explain, the film is weak and unbalanced from an ideological as well as from a formal point of view. Avoiding drawing any conclusion regarding the necessity to fight imperialism it is no more than a pacifist jumble . . . Still some aspects of war are depicted in a courageous, realistic way, without sentimentalism and with an efficiency which reminds us of the Russian films.

Siegfried Kracauer says exactly the same thing in *From Cagliari to Hitler. A Psychological History of the German Film* (Princeton, 1947). For the response to the film in Germany see Montgomery, ' "Realistic" War Films', pp. 121–4.

19 In Chapter 11 of *Narration in the Fiction Film* (Madison, 1985), esp. pp. 241 ff., David Bordwell examines what he calls 'Historical–materialist narration', which developed in Soviet Russia in the 1920s. As he explains, films of this kind gave judgements on the facts they exposed; they adopted an omniscient point of view in order to give spectators all the necessary information. Unlike 'classical' films they did not withhold any clue; this was done to avoid the kind of suspense which prevents viewers from thinking straight. Not surprisingly *Niemandsland*, which was made by a socialist director, might be labelled 'historical–materialist', but the same could be said of *Stosstrupp 1917* which is a Nazi film. In fact, as Bordwell points out, it is the relation a film cultivates with its public which defines it as well as its narration. In 1934 Germany, spectators could not see *Stosstrupp 1917* as a 'materialist' film.

20 I mention one exception, *Paix sur le Rhin* (F., 1938), an attempt to show how Germans and French could establish peace on the Rhine which, despite (or because of) its pacifism, was a failure.

21 Jeffrey Richards and Anthony Aldgate, *Best of British, Cinema and Society, 1930–1970* (Oxford, 1983), p. 43.

2 RESISTANCE

1 And also possibly because this was a way of resisting American influence. Throughout Chapter 1 of his *Ealing Studios* (London, 1977) Charles Barr emphasizes the intention of Ealing people to free the British cinema from Hollywood. *Went the Day Well?*, on which we shall expand later, was made at Ealing, where three other resistance films were shot after the war.

2 David Stafford, *Britain and European Resistance, 1940–1945* (Toronto, 1980), p. 56.

3 M.R.D. Foot, *SOE in France* (London, 1968) p. 505.

4 'Cinema e resistenza negli anni 70', in E. Chamoux (ed.), *Cinema, storia, resistenza* (Milan, 1987) 30. Other quotations are analysed by Millicent Marcus in *Italian Film in the Light of Neorealism* (Princeton, 1986), pp. 365–70.

5 G. Warner, 'Italy and the Powers', in G. Woolf (ed.), *The Rebirth of Italy, 1943–1949* (London, 1972).

6 *The Sun Rises Again*; *Achtung, banditi*.

7 I. F. Clarke, *Voices Prophesying War, 1763–1984* (London, 1966).

8 Anthony Aldgate and Jeffrey Richards, *Britain Can Take It* (Oxford, 1986), pp. 115–37.

9 David A. T. Stafford, 'Spies and Gentlemen: The Birth of the British Spy Novel', *Victorian Studies* 24/4 (1981) 489.

10 Jeffrey Richards, 'Wartime Cinema Audiences and the Class System', *Historical Journal of Film, Radio and Television* 7/2 (1987) 129.

11 Discussion in Aldgate, *Britain Can Take It*, pp. 132–3.

12 Thomas Elsaesser, 'Screen Violence: Emotional Structure and Ideological Function in *A Clockwork Orange*' in C. W. E. Bigsby (ed.), *Approaches to Popular Culture* (London, 1976), p. 171.

13 *Shuttlecock* (London, 1981), p. 49.

14 The film was not a success, but interestingly it was criticized for not being sympathetic enough to the Irish cause (Michael A. Anderegg, *David Lean* (Boston, 1984), p. 136). A good many films dealing with Ireland were shot in the 1980s. Apart from *Ascendancy* (1981) which, starting from a time when 'the Troubles' had resurfaced, went back to 1921, they were often deprived of political perspectives. Violence was present but mostly as a dramatic background. See Brian McIlroy, *World Cinema, 4: Ireland* (London, 1987) and K. Rockett, L. Gibbons and J. Hill, *Cinema and Ireland* (London, 1988).

15 The film was made in the worst possible conditions. Begun in 1957 in 16 mm, it was not finished for lack of funds. A new shooting started in 1963, in 35 mm, the already-available footage being transferred onto 35 mm. In 1957 there was still one resistance film made every year in Britain, but not in 1964 when the film was, released. See K. Brownlow, *How It Happened Here* (London, 1968).

16 The exception was a German film, *Long is the Road* (1948), which tells how a Polish Jew whose parents have been taken to a concentration camp joins the partisans.

17 Margaret Dickinson and Sarah Street, *Cinema and State. The Film Industry and the British Government, 1927–84* (London, 1985), pp. 187 ff.
18 A question well explored by W. von Bredow, 'Filmpropaganda für Wehrbereitschaft. Kriegsfilme in der Bundesrepublik', in W. von Bredow and R. Zurek (eds), *Film und Gesellschaft in Deutschland* (Hamburg, 1975), pp. 322–3. See also G. Donaldson, 'War Themes in Austro-German Cinema Today', *Films and Filming* 2/9 (1956) 8.
19 Popular Memory Group, 'Popular Memory; Theory, Politics, Method' in *Making Histories. Studies in History-Writing and Politics* (Minneapolis, 1982), pp. 205–7.

3 A GOLDEN AGE

1 An arguable case, which will not be discussed here since there is a vast literature on the subject. Hollywood made the best profits of its history in 1946, but within the two following years takings fell below the level of 1942. Did the producers know their prosperity would not last? As early as 1944 they began to prompt the government to support the film industry on the foreign markets and especially in Europe. See D. B. Jones, 'Hollywood's International Relations', *Quarterly of Film, Radio and Television* 11/3 (1957) 362.
2 G. C. Peck, *Bedfordshire Cinemas* (Luton, 1981); L. Bern, *Cinema in Portsmouth* (Portsmouth, 1975); C. Anderson, *A City and its Cinemas* (Bristol, 1983); J. Garnier, *Histoire des salles de spectacle orléanaises* (Orleans, 1966). L. Halliwell's memoirs, *Seats in All Parts: Half a Lifetime at the Movies* (London, 1985), describes vividly the life of a cinema manager after the war.
3 J. P. Mayer, *British Cinemas and Their Audiences. Sociological Studies* (London, 1948).
4 'The Cultural Industry. Enlightenment as Mass Deception', in *Dialectic of Enlightenment* (New York, 1944; repr. New York, 1972). The book is extraordinarily pessimistic in its description of what it calls 'a cultural chaos': 'Culture now impresses the same stamp on everything; films, radio and magazines make up a system which is uniform as a whole and in every part.'
5 'Female Identity and Italian Cinema of the 1950s', in G. Bruno and M. Nadotti (eds), *Off Screen. Women and Film in Italy* (London, New York, 1988), p. 125.
6 In G. Gori (ed.), *Rimini* (Rimini, Paris, 1989), pp. 62–3.
7 An evolution well analysed by Asa Briggs, *The History of Broadcasting in the United Kingom*, vol. 1 (Oxford, 1961), pp. 47–51 and vol. 2 (Oxford, 1979), pp. 239 ff. For complete figures see the report 'Cinema Going in London and the Provinces', published in the *Board of Trade Journal* 169/19 (1955), p. 1106.
8 For an economic analysis of the crisis in Britain see Spraos's excellent book, *The Decline of the Cinema. An Economist's Report* (London, 1962), which parallels the variations in the standard of

living with the decline of audiences.

9 Figures in the yearly *Filmstatistische Taschenbücher* (Wiesbaden, since 1950), A. Kutter, *Die wirtschaftliche Entwicklung der deutschen Filmtheater nach 1945* (Biberach am Riss, 1972), K. Sigl, W. Schneider and I. Tornow, *Jede Menge Kohle? Kunst und Kommerz auf dem deutschen Filmmarkt der Nachkriegszeit* (Munich, 1986) and M. Loiperdinger, 'Amerikanisieirung im Kino? Hollywood und das westdeutsche Publikum der fünfziger Jahre', *Theater Zeitschrift* 28 (1989) 50 ff.

10 Figures in Centre National du Cinéma, *Etude de marché du cinéma français* (Paris, 1954).

11 Statistics in L. Quaglietti, *Storia economico-politica del cinema italiano, 1945–1960* (Rome, 1980).

12 I am endebted to Giuliana Muscio for the details given here on *Hollywood*.

13 Willi Höfig's *Der deutsche Heimatfilm, 1947–1960* (Stuttgart, 1970) is a distinguished book which combines content analysis and computerization and establishes close connections between the various themes, characters and periods staged in the series. The lack of sophistication of these films entitles the author to use methods which could hardly be used with other, more complicated films.

14 There is a good introduction to the subject in A. Apra and C. Carabba, *Neorealismo d'appendice. Per un dibattito sul cinema popolare: il caso Matarazzo* (Florence, 1976).

15 John Ellis, 'Made in Ealing', *Screen* 16 (1975) 107. See also Charles Barr, *Ealing Studios* (London, 1977), and G. C. Perry; *Forever Ealing: A Celebration of the Great British Film Studio* (London, 1981).

16 The film was criticized for its ambiguity: it is very critical of NCOs but at the end discipline is easily restored by a 'good' commanding officer. On the three *08/15* films see J. Hauschild, 'Auf welche Weise wird marschiert? Zur den *08/15* Filmen von Paul May', in H. Puknus (ed.), *Hans Helmut Kirst. Der Autor uns sein Werk* (Munich, 1979), p. 138.

4 THE BLURRED IMAGE OF CITIES

1 Naples is a slightly different case. Film-studios were active there from the beginning of the twentieth century but produced only films in local dialect. As soon as a company wanted to make movies for the national market it moved to Rome.

2 J. Belmans, *La Ville dans le cinéma, de Frits Lang à Alain Resnais* (Brussels, 1977); A. Abruzzese, M. L. Buovolo, A. Pisanti, S. Masi, *Spettacolo e Metropoli* (Naples, 1981); W. Uricchio, 'The City Reviewed: Berlin's Image', *Film and History* 18/1 (1988) 16.

3 There are countless works on the topic. The best to my mind is Millicent Marcus's *Italian Film in the Light of Neorealism* (Princeton, 1986), especially for the study of the roots of neorealism (3–29). See also Roy Armes, *Patterns of Realism* (Brunswick, New York, 1971),

M. Liehm, *Passion and Defiance. Film in Italy from 1942 to the Present* (Berkeley, Los Angeles, London, 1984), pp. 103 ff. and the books mentioned in the bibliography.

4 Millicent Marcus has a different vision of De Sica's Rome which is, for her, an uncoordinated, broken-up cinematic town. Yet she agrees that as soon as Ricci and his son begin exploring the city on their own Rome 'becomes a setting worthy of Ariosto, where hidden secrets and dangers seem to lurk around every corner' (*Italian Film*, pp. 72–4).

5 Antonioni's cinematic description of cities deserves a long analysis which cannot be conducted here. An introduction to the topic is to be found in Ned Rifkin's *Antonioni's Visual Language* (Ann Arbor, 1977), pp. 23 ff.

6 'Room at the Top, Saturday Night and Sunday Morning and the Cultural Revolution in Britain', *Journal of Contemporary History* 19/1 (1984) 135.

7 D. Albrecht, *Designing Dreams, Modern Architecture in the Movies* (London, 1987).

8 For a closer study of the two faces of Paris see Dudley Andrews (ed.) *Breathless* (Rutgers, 1987).

9 I. Cameron and R. Wood, *Antonioni* (London, New York, 1971), pp. 125–6.

10 This is also suggested by the French title, *Deux ou trois choses que je sais d'elle*, which is purposely ambiguous. Viewers think first that *elle* is the female character, Juliette, as is expressed in the English title. But they realize soon that *elle* could be a suburb of Paris. Both *elles*, lady and town, are protagonists. For a thorough analysis of the film see Alfred Gruzetti's *Two or Three Things I Know about Her. Analysis of a Film by Godard* (Cambridge, Mass., London, 1981).

11 'Reading the illegible', in H. J. Dyos and M. Wolff (eds), *The Victorian Cities: Images and Realities* (London, 1973).

5 CHALLENGING HOLLYWOOD

1 Fellini exemplifies perfectly the ambiguity of the cinematic European towns which are simultaneously rich, varied places and constantly changing chaos. A good introduction to the question is in Stuart Rosenthal, *The Cinema of Federico Fellini* (New York, London, 1975), pp. 49 ff.

2 'Narrative Space', in *Questions of Cinema* (London, 1981).

3 The strength of tradition and the impact of the American model are analysed by H. P. Kocheurath, 'Kontinuität im deutschen Film', in W. von Bredow and R. Zurek (eds), *Film und Gesellschaft in Deutschland* (Hamburg, 1975), pp. 287 ff.; by Margot Schmidt, 'Solange du da bist'. Restauration und Regression im bundesdeutschen Spielfilm der Nachkriegszeit und der fünfziger Jahre', *Theater Zeitschrift* 28 (1989) 61 ff.; and, for Britain, by A. Walker *Hollywood, England. The British Film Industry in the Sixties* (London, 1974), pp. 127 ff.

4 While it was still in progress the new trend was already being analysed by Ulrich Gregor and Ennio Patalas, *Geschichte des modernen Filmes* (Güterslah, 1968), p. 296.

5 'Primary Identification and the Historical Subject: Fassbinder and Germany', *Cine-Tracts* 11 (1980) 45.

6 'British Feature Directors. An Index', *Sight and Sound* 17/5 (1958) 289 ff.

7 *Hollywood, England* (London, 1986), p. 45. For a highly critical evaluation see John Hill, 'Working-class, Realism and Sexual Relations: Some Theses on the British "New Wave"', in J. Curran and V. Porter (eds), *British Cinema History* (London, 1983), pp. 303ff. and J. Hill, *Sex, Class and Realism: British Cinema, 1956–1963* (London, 1986).

8 Rainer Landowski, *Die Filme von Alexander Kluge* (Hildesheim, 1980), documents the Oberhausen manifesto, the elaboration of which was deeply influenced by Kluge.

9 While he was at Oxford, Anderson edited with Gavin Lambert a quarterly, *Sequence*, which played its part in the development of the cinematic culture evoked in Chapter 3.

10 There were two periods in the German new cinema, the 1960s and the 1970s. During the former, most directors had university training while, during the latter, younger people like Fassbinder or Wenders started work straight away in theatres or studios without going first to a university.

11 'Female Identity and Italian Cinema of the 1950s' in G. Bruno and M. Nadotti (eds), *Off Screen. Women and Film in Italy* (London, New York, 1988), pp. 121–2. In *Beauty in History* (London, 1988) Arthur Marwick notes that, until the middle of the century, 'big breasts were highly respected but preferably allied to an air of innocent wholesomeness' (p. 346) while 'in the 1960s beauty was universally praised and sought after; it had achieved a kind of parity with wealth and status' (p. 343). In 1966 actress Claudia Cardinale could say: 'You used to look only at the bosom. Now you look at the legs, the body, the whole girl.'

12 *Hollywood, England*, pp. 265 and 86.

13 *Best of British. Cinema and Society, 1930–1970* (Oxford, 1983), p. 131.

14 On film production and film audiences after 1960 see R. Bonnell, *Le Cinéma exploité* (Paris, 1978); K. Sigl, W. Schneider and I. Tornow, *Jede Menge Kohle? Kunst und Kommerz auf dem deutschen Filmmarkt der Nachkriegszeit* (Munich, 1986); D. Docherty, D. Morrisson and M. Tracey, *The Last Picture Show? Britain's Changing Film Audiences* (London, 1987); M. Livolsi (ed.), *Schermi e ombre. Gli Italiani e il cinema nel dopoguerra* (Rome, 1988).

15 'Time of Crisis', *Sight and Sound* 27/4 (1958) 168.

16 On film criticism see Dudley Andrew, *André Bazin* (New York, 1978); David Rodowick, 'The Political Avant-Garde. Modernism and Epistemology in Post-68 Film Theory', *Iris* 1/2 (1983) 47 ff.; Janet Staiger, 'The Politics of Film Canons', *Cinema Journal* 24/3 (1985) 4 ff.

17 Docherty, Morrisson and Tracey, *The Last Picture Show?*, draw the same conclusions from statistics and opinion polls, and comment humorously: 'There is clearly something about an arts- or social science-based education which leads to the perception of cinema as an art-form . . . The specialist film audience is media rich: they are theatre-goers, art gallery habitués, discomaniacs and clubbers' (pp. 55 and 57).

18 In fact Bordwell speaks of four alternatives. One of them, the 'historical–materialist' one, mentioned in Chapter 1, note 19, above, applies only to the inter-war cinema. Godard is a fourth category, but for our enquiry on film as a cultural product this category is negligible. For the two alternatives mentioned here see *Narration in the Fiction Film* (Madison, 1985), pp. 230 and 287.

19 *Italian Cinema in the Light of Neorealism* (Princeton, 1986), pp. 190–1.

20 Perceptive analysis of this insertion of paintings into films is found in Jean-Louis Leutrat, *Kaleidoscope* (Lyons, 1988), pp. 81 ff. and Jacques Aumont, *L'Oeil interminable* (Paris, 1989), pp. 223 ff.

6 A TIME FOR REVISIONS

1 *A History of the World in 10½ Chapters* (London, 1989), p. 136.

2 'History, Memory, Documentary', *Cineaste* 17/1 (1989), 14.

3 In such movies as *Culloden* (1974) or *The New World* (I., 1982) people living in the eighteenth century were interviewed by reporters and answered as if they were in front of a television camera.

4 It is worth noticing that the film initially conceived for television was eventually released in cinemas.

5 This is Thomas Elsaesser's interpretation. According to him it is for Hermann that Maria 'does what she does but only on condition that his place remains empty – reduced to the sign where someone once was. Absence turns her object-choice into an infatuation which becomes an alienated self-image' ('Primary Identification and the Historical Subject: Fassbinder and Germany', *Cine-Tracts* 11 (1980), 49). Important films are susceptible of various, often inconsistent, readings – psychological as well as sociological.

6 *New German Cinema. From Oberhausen through the 1970s* (Boston, 1986), p. 138.

7 *New Directions in European Historiography* (Middletown, 1983), p. 108. See also G. G. Iggers, *The German Conception of History* (Middletown, 1968), G. Heydemann, *Geschichtswissenschaft im geteilten Deutschland* (Frankfurt, 1985) and W. Weidenfeld (ed.), *Geschichtbewusstsein des Deutschen* (Cologne, 1987).

8 *National Heroes. British Cinema in the Seventies and Eighties* (London, 1986), p. 173.

9 The notion was developed in *Moses and Monotheism* (1939).

10 'Filming Words', in A. S. Horton and J. Magretta (eds), *Modern European Film-makers and the Art of Adaptation* (New York, 1981), p. 201.

11 No French film on immigration went as far as the movies examined

here. The most popular production, *Black Mic-mac* (1987) could be compared to *Whisky Galore*: immigrants easily fool the French. By laughing at themselves Frenchmen got rid of the question.

12 Video tapes were then transferred onto 35 mm.

13 Nasser's daughter tells his mistress she does not like women who live on men. 'What do you live on?' the mistress replies, and there is no answer since all women live thanks to men. Nasser, who is aware of Omar's sexual drives, nevertheless wants him to marry his daughter, since his nephew is the son he longed for.

14 'Visual Pleasure and Narrative Cinema', *Screen* 16/3 (1975) 10–12.

SELECT BIBLIOGRAPHY

GUIDES AND CATALOGUES

Brüne, K., *Das komplette Angebot in Kino und Fernsehen seit 1945* (Sreinbeck, 1987).

—— *Catalogo Bolaffi del cinema italiano* (Turin, since 1973).

Chirat, R., *Catalogue des films français de long métrage. Films sonores de fiction, 1929–1939* (Brussels, 1975).

—— *Catalogue des films français de long métrage. Films de fiction, 1940–1950* (Luxemburg, 1981).

Gifford, D., *British Film Catalogue* (Newton Abbot, 1973; many subsequent reprints).

Helt, R. C. and Helt, M. E., *West German Cinema since 1945: A Reference Handbook* (London, 1987).

Hilmar, H. and Schobert, W. (eds), *Zwischen Gestern und Morgen. Westdeutscher Nachkriegsfilm, 1946–1962* (Frankfurt, 1989).

Magill, F. M. (ed.) *Survey of Cinema* (Englewood Cliffs):

—— *English Language Films*, 1st series, 4 vols (1980).

—— *English Language Films*, 2nd series, 6 vols (1981).

—— *Foreign Language Films*, 8 vols (1985).

—— *Cinema Annual* (since 1982).

Nash, J. R. and Ross, S. R. (eds), *The Motion Picture Guide, 1927–1984*, 12 vols (Chicago, 1984–7).

Sabria, J. C. and Busca, J. P. (eds), *L'Index du film français, 1944–1984* (Paris, 1985).

Savio, F., *Ma l'amore no. Realismo, formalismo, propaganda e telefoni bianchi nel cinema italiano di regime* (Milan, 1975).

GENERAL

Abruzzese, A., Buovolo, M. L., Pisanti, A. and Masi, S., *Spettacolo e metropoli* (Naples, 1981).

Albrecht, D., *Designing, Dreams, Modern Architecture in the Movies* (London, 1987).

Allen, R. C. and Gomery, D., *Film History. Theory and Practice* (New York, 1985).

Andrew, D., *The Major Film Theories* (New York, 1976).

Armes, R., *Film and Reality. An Historical Survey* (Harmondsworth, 1974).

Atkins, T., *Sexuality in the Movies* (London, 1975).

Austin, B. A., *The Film Audience. An International Bibliography with Annotations and an Essay* (Metuchen, NJ, 1983).

Belmans, J., *La Ville dans le cinéma, de Fritz Lang à Alain Resnais* (Brussels, 1977).

Berger, A., *Television in Society* (London, 1986).

Bordwell, D., *Narration in the Fiction Film* (Madison, 1985).

Cohen, S. and Young, J. (eds), *The Manufacture of News* (London, 1973).

De Bernardi, A. (ed.), *La Cinepresa e la storia* (Milan, 1985).

De Lauretis, T., *Alice Doesn't: Feminism, Semiotics, Cinema* (Bloomington, 1984).

De Lauretis, T. and Heath, S. (eds), *The Cinematic Apparatus* (New York, 1980).

Degand, C., *Le Cinéma, cette industrie* (Paris, 1972).

Ellis, J., *Visible Fictions: Cinema, Television, Video* (London, 1982).

Estermann, A., *Die Verfilmung der literarischen Werke* (Bonn, 1965).

Fero, M., *Cinema and History* (Berkeley, 1989).

Gregor, U. and Patalas, E., *Geschichte des modernen Films* (Güterslah, 1968).

Heath, S. C., *Questions of Cinema* (London, 1981).

Huaco, G., *The Sociology of Film Art* (New York, London, 1965).

Hurd, G., *National Fictions: World War II on Films and Television* (London, 1984).

Jarvie, I. C., *Towards a Sociology of the Cinema* (London, 1970).

Jowett, G. and Linton, J. M., *Movies as Mass Communication* (Beverly Hills, 1980).

Manvell, R., *A Seat at the Cinema* (London, 1951)

—— *The Film and the Public* (London, 1955).

Marwick, A., *Class: Image and Reality in Britain, France and the USA since 1930* (London, 1981).

Nichols, B., *Movies and Methods: An Anthology* (Berkeley, 1976).

Pegg, M., *Broadcasting and Society* (London, 1983).

Peterson, R. A. (ed.), *The Production of Culture* (Beverly Hills, London, 1976).

Prawer, S., *Caligari's Children. The Film as Tale of Terror* (Oxford, 1980).

Silverman, K., *The Subject of Semiotics* (New York, 1983).

Smith, P. (ed.), *The Historian and Film* (Cambridge, 1976).

Spraos, J., *The Decline of the Cinema. An Economist's Report* (London, 1962).

Thomas, S. (ed.), *Film/Culture: Explorations of the Cinema in its Social Context* (Metuchen, NJ, 1982).

Throsby, C. D. and Withers G. A., *The Economics of the Performing Arts* (Melbourne and New York, 1979).

Tudor, A., *Image and Influence* (London, 1975).

Wagner, G., *The Novel and the Cinema* (Cranbury, 1975).

Ward, K., *Mass Communication and the Modern World* (Basingstoke, 1989).

Wollen, P. (ed.), *Sociology and Semiology: Working Papers on the Cinema* (London, 1971).

EUROPEAN CINEMA

Armes, R., *The Ambiguous Image. Narrative Style in Modern European Cinema* (London, 1976).

Der Film in Europa (Baden, 1953).

The Film in Six European Countries (London, 1950).

Frayling, C., *Spaghetti Westerns. Cowboys and Europeans from Karl May to Sergio Leone* (London, 1981).

Giannelli, E., *Cinema europeo* (Rome, 1953).

Guback, T. H., *The International Film Industry: Western Europe and America since 1945* (Bloomington, 1969).

—— 'Cultural Identity and Film in the European Economic Community', *Cinema Journal* 14 (1974) 2–39.

Harvey, S., *May 68 and Film Culture* (London, 1978).

Hewitt, N. (ed.), *The Culture of Reconstruction. European Literature, Thought and Film, 1945–1950* (London, 1989).

Horton, A. S. and Magretta, J. (eds), *Modern European Film-makers and the Art of Adaptation* (New York, 1981).

Manvell, R., *New Cinema in Europe* (London, New York, 1966).

Marwick, A. and Sorlin, P., 'Social Change in 1960's Europe: Four Feature Films', (in XVIth International Congress of Historical Sciences, *Reports*, vol. I, (Stuttgart, 1985) 214–39.

Monaco, P., *Modern European Culture and Consciousness* (Albany, 1983).

Monterde, J. E., Riambau, E. and Torreiro, E., *Los nuevos cines europeos, 1955–1970* (Madrid, 1987).

Quinn, J., *The Film and Television as an Aspect of European Culture* (Leyden, 1968).

Britain

Aldgate, A. and Richards, J., *Britain Can Take It: the British Cinema in the Second World War* (Oxford, 1986).

Allsop, K., *Angry Decade* (London, 1958).

Armes, R., *A Critical History of British Cinema* (London, 1978).

Aspinall, S. and Murphy, S. (eds), *Gainsborough Melodrama* (London, 1983).

Auty, M., and Roddick, N., (eds), *British Cinema Now* (London, 1985).

Barr, C., *Ealing Studios* (London, 1977).

—— (ed.), *All Our Yesterdays: 90 Years of British Cinema* (London, 1986).

Betts, E., *The Film Business. A History of British Cinema* (London, 1986).

Bogdanov, V. and Skidelsky, E. (eds), *The Age of Affluence, 1951–1964* (London, 1970).

'British Feature Directors: An Index', *Sight and Sound*, 27/6 (1958) 289–98.

Browning, H. E., Browning, A. A. and Sorrell, A. A., 'Cinemas and Cinema-going in Great Britain', *Journal of the Royal Statistical Society*, Series A, 117 (1954) 133–74.

Butler, I., *Cinema in Britain: An Illustrated Survey* (South Brunswick, 1973). 'Cinema Going in London and the Provinces', *Board of Trade Journal*, 169/19 (1955) 1106–32.

Coultass, C., 'British Feature Films and the Second World War', *Journal of Contemporary History*, 19/1 (1984) 7–16.

Curran, J. and Porter, V. (eds), *British Cinema History* (London, 1983).

Docherty, D., Morrisson, D. and Tracey, M., *The Last Picture Show? Britain's Changing Film Audiences* (London, 1987).

Durgnat, R., *A Mirror for England. British Movies from Austerity to Affluence* (London, 1970).

Edson, B., 'Commercial Film Distribution and Exhibition in the United Kingdom', *Screen* 21/3 (1980) 36–42.

Ellis, J., 'Made in Ealing', *Screen* 16 (1975) 78–121.

Falk, O., *The Golden Gong: Fifty Years of the Rank Organisation* (London, 1987).

Feather, J., *A History of British Publishing* (London, New York, Sydney, 1988).

Gillett, J., 'State of the Studios', *Sight and Sound*, 33/2 (1964) 55–9.

Guback, T. H., 'American Interests in the British Film Industry', *Quarterly Review of Economics and Business*, 7/2 (1967) 7–22.

Hill, J., *Sex, Class and Realism: British Cinema, 1956–63* (London, 1986).

Houston, P., 'Time of Crisis', *Sight and Sound*, 27/4 (1959) 166.

Jarvie, I. C., 'Media and Manners: Film and Society in Some Current British Films', *Film Quarterly*, 22/3 (1969) 11.

Johnson, I., 'We Are All Right, Jack', *Films and Filming* 8/12 (1962) 44–51.

Kael, P., 'Britain: Commitment and the Strait-Jacket', *Film Quarterly*, 25/1 (1961) 4.

Lovell, A. and Hillier, J., *Studies in Documentary* (London, 1972).

Low, R., *The History of the British Film*, vol. III, *Film-making in 1930s Britain* (London, 1985).

Malassinet, A., *Société et cinéma. Les Années 1960 en Grande Bretagne* (Paris, 1979).

Mann, P. H., *Book Publishing, Book Selling and Book Reading* (London, 1979).

Manvell, R., *New Cinema in Britain* (London, 1969).

Martan, P. J., *The Cinema and Social Scene: Some Changes as Reflected in the British Cinema of the Times (1958–1968)* (doct. dissertation, Los Angeles, 1969).

Marwick, A., 'Print, Pictures and Sounds: The Second World War and the British Experience', *Daedalus* (1982) 135–55.

—— 'Room at the Top, Saturday Night and Sunday Morning and the Cultural Revolution in Britain', *Journal of Contemporary History* 19/1 (1984) 127–52.

Mayer, J. P., *British Cinemas and Their Audiences. Sociological Studies* (London, 1948).

Morley, D., *The Nationwide Audience* (London, 1980).

Moss, R. F., *The Films of Carol Reed* (Basingstoke, 1987).

Murphy, R., *Realism and Tinsel. Cinema and Society in Britain, 1939–1948* (London, 1989).

Park, J., *Learning to Dream: The New British Cinema* (London, 1984).

Perry, G. C., *The Great British Picture Show. From the 90s to the 70s.* (New York, 1974).

—— *Movies for the Mansion: A History of Pinewood Studios* (London, 1976).

—— *Forever Ealing: A Celebration of the Great British Film Studio* (London, 1981).

—— *The Great British Picture Show* (London, 1985).

Pirie, D., *Heritage of Horror. The English Gothic Cinema* (London, 1973).

Porter, V., *On Cinema* (London, 1985).

Richards, J. and Aldgate, A., *Best of British. Cinema and Society, 1930–1970* (Oxford, 1983).

Ritchie, H., *Success Stories: Literature and the Media in England, 1950–1959* (London, 1988).

Robertson, J. C., *The Hidden Cinema: British Film Censorship in Action, 1913–1972* (London, 1989).

Rockett, K., Gibbons, L. and Hill, J., *Cinema and Ireland* (London, 1988).

Stead, P., *Film and the Working Class* (London, 1989).

Sussex, E., *Lindsay Anderson* (London, 1969).

Swann, P., *The Hollywood Feature Film in Postwar Britain* (London, Sydney, 1987).

Taylor, J. R., *Masterworks of the British Cinema* (London, 1974).

—— *Directors and Directions* (London, 1975).

Taylor, J. T., *Anger and After* (Baltimore, 1963).

Taylor, P. M. (ed.), *Britain and the Cinema in the Second World War* (London, 1988).

Tunstall, J., *The Media in Britain* (London, 1983).

Walker, A., *Hollywood, England. The British Film Industry in the Sixties* (London, 1986).

—— *National Heroes. British Cinema in the Seventies and Eighties* (London, 1986).

Walker, J., *The Once and Future Film: British Cinema in the 70s and 80s* (London, 1985).

Warren, P., *Elstree. The British Hollywood* (London, 1983).

Wood, L., *British Films, 1971–1981* (London, 1983).

France

Andrew, D., *André Bazin* (New York, 1978).

Armes, R., *The Cinema of Alain Resnais* (London, 1968).

—— *French Cinema* (London, 1985).

Bonnell, R., *Le Cinéma exploité* (Paris, 1978).

Buss, R., *The French through their Films* (London, New York, 1988).

Cameron, I. (ed.), *Second Wave* (New York, 1970).

—— *The Films of Robert Bresson* (New York, 1970).

Clouzot, C., *Le Cinéma français depuis la Nouvelle Vague* (Paris, 1972).

Dumazedier, J., 'Loisir cinématographique et culture populaire', *Diogène* 31 (1960) 113–24.

Durand, J., *Le Cinéma et son public* (Paris, 1958).

Durgnat, R., 'The Decade: France – A Mirror for Marianne', *Films and Filming* 9/2 (1968) 48.

—— *Nouvelle Vague: The First Decade* (Loughton, 1963).

Forbes, J., *French Cinema since 1968* (London, 1988).

Giannetti, L. D., *Godard and Others: Essays in Film Form* (Rutherford, NJ, 1975).

Graham, P., *The New Wave: Critical Landmarks* (New York, 1968).

Grignaffini, G., *La pelle e l'anima. Intorno alla Nouvelle Vague* (Florence, 1984).

Hayward, S. and Vincendeau, G. (eds), *French Film: Texts and Contexts* (London, 1990).

Jeancolas, J. P., *Le Cinéma des français: La Ve République, 1958–1978* (Paris, 1979).

—— *Quinze ans d'années trente: Le Cinéma des français, 1929–1944* (Paris, 1983).

Leglise, P., *Histoire de la politique du cinéma français*, 2 vols (Paris, 1970, 1977).

Monaco, J., *The New Wave* (New York, 1976).

Morin, E., 'Recherches sur le public cinématographique', *Revue Internationale de Filmologie* 12 (1953) 3–72.

Petri, G., *The Cinema of François Truffaut* (New York, 1970).

Pivasset, J., *Essai sur la signification politique du cinéma. L'Exemple français de la Libération aux événements de mai 1969* (Paris, 1971).

Reif, T., *Innovators of the French Cinema* (Ottawa, 1965).

Roux, J. and Thevenet, R., *Industrie et commerce du film en France* (Paris, 1979).

Russel, S., *Semiotics and Lighting: A Study of Six Modern French Cameramen* (Michigan, 1986).

Sabria, J. C., *Cinéma français. Les Années cinquante* (Paris, 1988).

Taylor, J. R., *Cinema Eye, Cinema Ear: Some Key Filmmakers of the Sixties* (New York, 1964).

Weber, E., 'An Escapist Realism', *Film Quarterly*, 13/2 (1959) 9–14.

Germany

Albrecht, G., *Die grossen Filmerfolge* (Ebersberg, 1985).

Bauschinger, S., Cocalls, S. L. and Lea, H. A. (eds), *Film und Literatur. Literarische Texte und der neue deutsche film* (Berne and Munich, 1984).

Bliersbach, G., *So grün war die Heide. Der deutsche Nachkriegsfilm in neur Sicht* (Wenheim, Basel, 1985).

Blum, H. R., *30 Jahre danach. Dokumentation zur Auseinandersetzung mit dem Nationalsozialismus in Film, 1945 bis 1975* (Cologne, 1979).

Blumenberg, H. C., *Kinozeit. Aufsätze und Kritiken über Filmemacher und Filme, 1980–1983* (Frankfurt, 1984).

Bredow, W. von and Zurek, R., *Film und Gesellschaft in Deutschland. Dokumente und Materialien* (Hamburg, 1975).

Bronnen, B. and Brocher, C., *Die Filmemacher. Der neue deutsche Film nach Oberhausen* (Munich, Vienna, 1973).

Bucher, F., *Germany. An Illustrated Guide* (London, New York, 1970).

Buchkor, P., *Augen kann man nicht kaufen. Wim Wenders und seine Filme* (Munich, 1983).

Cehak, M., *Das Bild der Familie im deutschen Film* (Hamburg, 1958).

Collins, R. and Porter, V., *WDR and the Arbeiterfilm. Fassbinder, Ziewer and Others* (London, 1981).

Corrigan, T., *New German Film: The Displaced Image* (Austin, 1983).

Der Krieg im Kino, Film April–May 1964; June–July 1964.

Dost, M., Hopf, F. and Kluge, A., *Filmwirtschaft in der B.R.D. und in Europa. Götterdämmerung in Raten* (Munich, 1973).

Elsaesser, T., *New German Cinema* (London, 1986).

Endres, E., *Die Literatur der Adenauerzeit* (Munich, 1980).

Filmstatistische Taschenbücher (since 1952).

Fischer, R. and Hembus, J., *Der neue deutsche Film, 1960–1980* (Munich, 1981).

Franklin, J., *New German Cinema. From Oberhausen through the 1970s* (London, 1986).

Furstenau, T., *Wandlungen in Film: Junge deutsche Produktion* (Berlin, 1970).

Glaser, H., *Kulturgeschichte der Bundesrepublik Deutschland: Zwischen Kapitulation und Währungsreform, 1945–1948*, vol. I (Munich, 1985).

Gmur, L., *Der junge deutsche Film* (Munich, 1968).

Gregor, U., *Geschichte des Films ab 1960* (Munich, 1978).

Grob, N., *Die Formen des filmischen Blicks. Wenders. Die frühen Filme* (Munich, 1984).

Guback, T., 'Shaping the Film Business in Postwar Germany: The Role of the US Industry and the US State', in P. Kerr (ed.), *The Hollywood Film Industry* (London, New York, 1986).

Hembus, J., *Der deutsche Film kann gar nicht besser sein. Ein Pamphlet von gestern. Eine Abrechnung von heute* (Munich, 1981).

Hembus, J. and Bandmann, C., *Klassiker des deutschen Tonfilms, 1930–1960* (Munich, 1980).

Höfig, W., *Der deutsche Heimatfilm, 1947–1960* (Stuttgart, 1973).

Iden, P. and Jansen, P. W. (eds), *Rainer Werner Fassbinder* (Munich, 1985)

Jahrbuch Film (Munich, since 1977).

Kahlenberg, F. P., 'Film' in W. Benz, (ed.), *Die Bundesrepublik Deutschland*, vol. III, *Kultur* (Frankfurt, 1983).

Kluge, A. (ed.), *Bestandaufnahme: Utopie Film. 20 Jahre neuer deutscher Film* (Frankfurt, 1983).

Kreimeier, K., *Kino und Filmindustrie in der Bundesrepublik Deutschland. Ideologieproduktion und Klassenwirklichkeit nach 1945* (Kronberg, 1978).

Kroner, M., *Film Spiegel der Gesellschaft? Versuch einer Antwort. Inhaltsanalyse des jungen deutschen Films von 1962 bis 1969* (Heidelberg, 1975).

Künzel, U., *Wim Wenders. Ein Filmbuch* (Freiburg, 1985).

Kutter, A., *Die wirtschaftliche Entwicklung der deutschen Filmtheater nach 1945* (Biberach am Riss, 1972).

Limmer, W., *Rainer Werner Fassbinder, Filmemacher* (Reinbeck, 1982).

Loiperdinger, M., 'Amerikanisierung im Kino? Hollywood und das westdeutsche Publikum der fünfziger Jahre', *Theater Zeitschrift* 28 (1989) 50–60.

McCormick, R. (ed.), *Fassbinder* (New York, 1981).

Manvell, R. and Fraenkel, H., *The German Cinema* (London, 1971).

Meyn, H., *Massenmedien in der Bundesrepublik Deutschland* (Berlin, 1974).

Möhrmann, R., *Die Frau mit dem Kamera. Filmemacherinnen in der Bundesrepublik Deutschland* (Munich, 1980).

Montgomery, G., ' "Realistic" War Films in Weimar Germany: Entertainment as Education', *Historical Journal of Film, Radio and Television*, 9/2 (1989) 115–34.

New German Cinema, New German Critique, 24–5 (1981–2).

Neumann, H. J., *Der deutsche Film heute. Die Macher, das Geld; die Erfolge, das Publikum* (Berlin, 1986).

Osterland, M., *Gesellschaftbilder in Filmen. Eine soziologische Untersuchung des Filmangebots der Jahre 1949 bis zum 1964* (Stuttgart, 1970).

Ott, F., *The Great German Films* (London, 1987).

Pflaum, H. G., and Prinzler, H. H., *Cinema in the Federal Republic of Germany. The New German Film. Origins and Present Situation* (Bonn, 1983).

Philips, K. (ed.), *New German Filmmakers: The First Generation* (New York, 1984).

Pleyer, P., *Deutscher Nachkriegsfilm, 1946–1948. Studien fur Publizistik* (Münster, 1965).

—— *Nationale und soziale Stereotypen im gegenwärtigen deutschen Spielfilm* (Münster, 1968).

Prokop, D., *Soziologie des Films* (Frankfurt, 1982).

Pütz, K. H., 'Business or Propaganda? American Films and Germany, 1942–1946', in E. Krippendorf (ed.), *The Role of the United States in the Reconstruction of Italy and West Germany, 1943–1949* (Berlin, 1981).

Rayns, T. (ed.), *Fassbinder* (London, 1980).

Rentschler, E., *West German Film in the Course of Time: Reflections on the Twenty Years since Oberhausen* (New York, 1984).

—— *German Film and Literature: Adaptations and Transformations* (London, New York, 1986).

—— *West German Filmmakers on Film* (New York, 1988).

Riess, C., *Das gibts nur einmal. Das Buch des deutschen Films nach 1945* (Hamburg, 1958).

Sandford, J., *The Mass Media of the German Speaking Countries* (London, 1986).

—— *The New German Cinema* (London, 1983).

Schmidt, M., 'Solange du da bist. Restauration und Regression im bundesdeutschen Spielfilm der Nachkriegszeit und der fünfziger Jahre', *Theater Zeitschrift* 28 (1989) 6–73.

Schmieding, W., *Kunst oder Kasse. Der Ärger mit dem deutschen Film* (Hamburg, 1961).

Sigl, K., Schneider, W. and Tornow, I., *Jede Menge Kohle? Kunst und Kommerz auf dem deutschen Filmmarkt der Nachkriegszeit* (Munich, 1986).

Spagnoletti, G. (ed.), *Junger deutscher Film, 1960–1970* (Milan, 1985).

Voester, C. E., 'Stempel auf der Brotkarte. Filmindustrie und Filmpolitik 1945 bis 1949', *Theater Zeitschrift* 28 (1989) 34–43.

Italy

Aiello, G., *Il cinema italiano negli ultimi vent'anni* (Cremona, 1965).

Apra, A. and Carabba, C., *Neorealismo d'appendice. Per un dibattito sul cinema popolare: Il caso Matarazzo* (Florence, 1976).

Apra, A. and Pistagnesi, P., *Comedy Italian Style, 1950–1980* (Rome, 1986).

Argentieri, M., *La censura nel cinema italiano* (Rome, 1974).

Argentieri, M. and Turchino, A., *Cinema e vita contadina* (Bari, 1984).

Aristarco, G., *Neorealismo e nuova critica cinematografica* (Florence, 1980).

Armes, R., *Patterns of Realism* (South Brunswick, 1971).

Arosio, M., Cereda, G. and Iseppi, F., *Cinema e cattolici in Italia* (Milan, 1974).

Baldelli, P., *Cinema dell'ambiguità* (Rome, 1969).

Bertieri, C., Giannarelli, A. and Rossi, U., *L'ultimo schermo: Cinema di guerra, cinema di pace* (Bari, 1984).

Bondanella, P., *Italian Cinema: From Neorealism to the Present* (New York, 1983).

Brunetta, G. P., *Storia del cinema italiano*, 2 vols (Rome, 1979, 1981).

Brunette, P., *Roberto Rossellini* (New York, 1987).

Bruno, G. and Nadotti, M. (eds), *Off Screen. Women and Film in Italy* (London, New York, 1988).

Cadioli, A., *L'industria del romanzo. L'editoria letteraria in Italia dal 1945 agli anni ottanta* (Rome, 1981).

Canella, M. 'Ideology and Aesthetic. Hypothesis in the Criticism of Neorealism', *Screen* 14/4 (1972) 5–13.

Canziani, A., *Gli anni del neorealismo* (Florence, 1977).

Carrano, P., *Malafemmina. La donna nel cinema italiano* (Florence, 1977).

Chamoux, E. (ed.), *Cinema, storia, resistenza* (Milan, 1987).

D'Amico, M., *La commedia italiana. Il cinema comico in Italia dal 1945 al 1975* (Milan, 1985).

Falaschi, G., *La resistanza armata nella narrativa italiana* (Turin, 1976).

Faldini, F. and Foffi, G., *L'avventurosa storia del cinema italiano racontata dai i suoi protagonisti* (Milan, 1976).

Ferrero, A., Grignaffini, G. and Quaresima, L., *Il cinema italiano degli anni 50* (Florence, 1977).

Foffi, G., *Il cinema italiano: Servi e padroni* (Milan, 1977).

Gori, G. (ed.), *Cinema e parrocchia* (Rimini, 1980).

Lawton, B. R., 'Italian Neorealism: A Mirror Construction of Reality', *Film Criticism* 3 (1979) 8–12.

—— (ed.), *Literary and Socio-Political Trends in Italian Cinema* (Los Angeles, 1975).

Liehm, M., *Passion and Defiance: Films in Italy from 1942 to the Present* (Berkeley, Los Angeles, London, 1984).

Livolsi, M. (ed.), *Schermi e ombre. Gli Italiani e il cinema nel dopoguerra* (Rome, 1988).

Lizzani, C., *Il cinema italiano dalle origini agli anni ottanta* (Rome, 1982).

Magrelli, F. (ed.), *Sull'industria cinematografica italiana* (Venice, 1986).

Malerba, L., *Italian Cinema, 1945–1951* (Rome, 1951).

Marcus, M., *Italian Film in the Light of Neorealism* (Princeton, 1986).

Miccichè, L., *Il cinema italiano degli anni 60* (Venice, 1965).

—— (ed.), *Il neorealismo cinematografico italiano* (Venice, 1975).

Monteleone, F., *Storia della R.A.I. dagli alleati alla D.C., 1944–1956* (Rome, Bari, 1979).

Murialdi, P., *La stampa italiana del dopoguerra, 1943–1972* (Bari, 1973).

Overby, D. (ed.), *Springtime in Italy: A Reader on Neorealism* (London, 1978).

Pintus, P., *Storia e film* (Rome, 1980).

Quaglietti, L., *Storia economico-politica del cinema italiano, 1945–1960* (Rome, 1980).

Rifkin, N., *Antonioni's Visual Language* (Ann Arbor, 1977).

Rondi, B., *Il neorealismo italiano* (Parma, 1956).

Rondi, G. L., *Cinema italiano oggi, 1952–1965* (Cremona, 1965).

Schlappner, M., *Von Rossellini zu Fellini* (Zurich, 1957).

Silverman, M., 'Italian Film and American Capital, 1947–1951', in P. Mellencamp and P. Rosen (eds), *Cinema Histories, Cinema Practices* (Los Angeles, 1984).

Spinazzola, V., *Cinema e pubblico* (Milan, 1975).

Vento, G. and Mida, M., *Cinema e Resistenza* (Florence, 1954).

Willemen, P. (ed.), *Pier Paolo Pasolini* (London, 1977).

Witcombe, R. T., *The New Italian Cinema. Studies in Dance and Despair* (London, 1982).

Zagarrio, V. (ed.), *Dietro lo schermo. Ragionamenti sui modi di produzione cinematografici in Italia* (Venice, 1988).

INDEX

The titles of films are in English when there was an English distribution. Otherwise they are given in the original language with a translation.

241